water

A Comprehensive Guide for Brewers

T0002867

John Palmer and Colin Kaminski

brewers publications

Brewers Publications®
A Division of the Brewers Association
PO Box 1679, Boulder, Colorado 80306-1679
BrewersAssociation.org
BrewersPublications.com

Printed in the United States of America.

10 9 8 7 6 5 4 3

ISBN-13: 978-0-937381-99-1
ISBN-10: 0-937381-99-3

Library of Congress Cataloging-in-Publication Data

Palmer, John J., 1963-
  Water : a comprehensive guide for brewers / by John Palmer and Colin Kaminski.
    p. cm.
  Includes bibliographical references and index.
  ISBN 978-0-937381-99-1 (pbk.)
  1. Brewing. 2. Water use. 3. Water chemistry. 4. Water--Purification. I. Kaminski, Colin, 1965- II. Title.

TP583.P35 2013
546'.22--dc23

                                2013019177

Publisher: Kristi Switzer
Technical Editors: A. J. deLange, Martin Brungard
Copy Editing: Amahl Turczyn Scheppach
Indexing: Doug Easton
Production and Design Management: Stephanie Johnson Martin
Cover and Interior Design: Julie White
Cover Illustration: Alicia Buelow

To all those who have so generously shared their knowledge and passion for brewing with me, thank you for letting me return the favor.
-John

I would like to thank all those people who believed in me to make my life possible. I would also like to thank all those people who did not believe in me for giving me the drive to achieve my accomplishments.
-Colin

Table of Contents

List of Key Figures, Tables, Sidebars and Illustrations

Acknowledgments

No book can be written without managing time. We eagerly volunteered to spend this time but we must thank our families for the time we missed with them. We embarked on this voyage several years ago hoping to collect all of the world's knowledge of brewing water together in one place, and in so doing, unlock brewing's last frontier. We found instead that water was much deeper and broader than we had imagined. That water puns surfaced wherever we turned. We feared we were out of our depth. But with lots of friends to turn to for help, we believe we have compiled a useful book for all brewers.

Both of us started brewing about twenty years ago in the early nineties, and both of us were inspired to learn more about brewing water from the writing of one particular man, A. J. deLange. He was the first person we knew of that took water chemistry beyond 2+2=4 and introduced us to the carbo system, to solubility constants, and milliequivalents. He was the first to warn us that we were missing the point trying to replicate famous brewing waters, that the compositions were not realistic, that they did not add up. His work has enabled us to pursue water science in our brewing careers and brought us to where we are today. Throughout this project, as we would get stuck on a topic, or realize there was an unknown elephant in the room, A. J. was the one we could turn to for help. In fact, just a week before this manuscript was due, we realized that we didn't know how to calculate the effect of phosphoric acid additions on dissolved calcium in brewing water, and A. J. was able to program a spreadsheet to generate curves that could describe it for us; and that appears in Appendix B. It is our conviction that A. J. deLange has done more to help brewers understand water than anyone since Paul Kolbach introduced the concept of residual alkalinity in 1953.

We must also greatly thank Martin Brungard for his expertise and wisdom. Martin is a Diplomate of Water Resources Engineering, and has been guiding brewers in water use since 1999. Martin was instrumental in the technical review of the content, always bringing us back to what was practical, applicable, and verifiable in any brewery setting.

John needs to personally thank Bob Hansen and Dan Bies at Briess Malting and Ingredients for all of their hard work testing the distilled water pH and acidity of various malts. This project consumed nearly four years as we puzzled over the data, and planned and conducted new trials. Likewise, Kai Troester, a self-made brewing scientist, has generously shared his work and ideas on testing malt acidity and predicting mash pH. Most of Chapter 5 would not have been possible without their help.

Colin needs to personally thank Gil Sanchez, Ian Ward, Brian Hunt, Dr. Michael Lewis and Dr. Charles Bamforth for always offering advice in brewing chemistry while he negotiated difficult waters. (Pun intended.) He also needs to thank the Northern California chapter of the Master Brewers Association for providing endless contacts and technical lectures that made his brewing career possible.

We absolutely need to thank the workers and brewers of Stone Brewing Co., New Belgium Brewing Co., Coors Brewing Co., Golden, The Bruery, Eagle Rock Brewery, Golden Road Brewery, Firestone Walker Brewing Co., Moonlight Brewery, Bell's Brewery, Founders Brewery, Anheuser-Busch–Fairfield, and last but not least Sierra Nevada Brewing Co., for their generosity in answering questions, phone calls, and personal tours as we tried to sort out all of the options and practices of water usage today. We must also thank the many brewers who helped us over the years by asking questions and inviting us to speak at conferences. Every question and discussion has helped us keep our oars in the water.

Lastly, we would like to recommend the *NALCO Water Handbook* for anyone tasked with managing water treatment at any brewery. This 1,000+ page book is an encyclopedia of everything in water treatment. It may not cover breweries specifically, but it covers everything else.

Foreword

I have been involved with brewing for perhaps 40 years and in that time I have acquired many books. Some of them include Briggs' *Malts and Malting*, Neve's *Hops*, White and Zainasheff's *Yeast, the Practical Guide to Beer Fermentation* (also included in the Brewing Elements Series) and Jackson's *Applied Water and Spentwater Chemistry*. These books all contain valuable information about the major raw materials used to make beer, but the first three are plainly written for brewers. The fourth is not. The word "brewing" does not even appear in its index. The same is true for several other water titles and several on yeast (though brewing does get mentioned in most of the yeast books). I have lots of books on water, but I don't have one on *brewing* water. You do. You are holding it in your hands, and as soon as my copy comes from the printer, I will too. Mine will go in the space I'm reserving for it, next to the yeast, hops and malt books.

Why has it taken so long to get a brewing water book on the shelf? Simple: it is hard to write one! I speak from experience. I have from time to time tried to write a book on this subject and found it so intricate that at times I felt I was fighting the Hydra. Every time one head got cut off two more grew back. I'm pretty sure that if you ran into John or Colin at a conference or anywhere else and asked either of them if the task turned out to be more daunting than they originally thought, they would answer, 'Yes!'

Then there is the question of readership. I am not sure that many people would have been interested in this book 40 years ago. The demand is strong now. I've had lots of, "When's the water book coming out?" queries. I believe the reason for this is that the sophistication of hobby and craft brewers has advanced dramatically, and this I attribute to advances in technology. The four technologies I have in mind are computers, reverse osmosis systems, pH meters and the Internet. All but the last were well established 40 years ago. While the first three are not new technologies, they have enjoyed huge increases in performance accompanied by dramatic decreases in price. Let's defer discussion of the influence of RO and pH meters for the time being and comment on the influence of the Internet and, necessarily, the computers with which we access the Internet.

Forty years ago, state-of-the-art knowledge of brewing water was to be found in a few all-too-brief chapters in a couple of brewing texts; but this was enough to stimulate the interest of brewers who started thinking about the problem, doing analyses and experiments and communicating with one another over the Internet. (I knew these authors via the net years before I met them in person.) Because the discussions were held using a public medium, other people saw them, got interested and started experimenting and calculating too. Had it not been for the Internet I do not believe the level of activity would have been nearly as high as it was and still is. As the 'traffic' built up, even more people noticed and articles began to appear in journals like *Brewing Techniques, The New Brewer*, and *Cerevesia* as well as on various websites. It eventually occurred to some engineering types that while the relevant chemistry and associated math were intricate (more on that later), they could be hidden from the average user in a cleverly designed spreadsheet or calculator program which, if the user interface were properly done, should be fairly simple to use. These began to proliferate. I've probably encountered a dozen, of which three remain in frequent use today. There is a fair amount of water-related discussion on some of the brewing bulletin board systems and the number of participants seems to be fairly large. The hall was full for the Water Panel at the Home Brewers Conference in Bellevue in 2012. In other words, awareness of what water can potentially do for beer, and interest in that potential, appears to be broader than it was in past. Even so, not everyone is on board. This book should help to bring many into the fold. If you are one of the holdouts, stay with me a bit longer as we explore some aspects of the relationship between brewers and water and see how this book might strengthen yours.

As brewers progress in their careers, they learn quite a bit about malt, hops and yeast before acquiring a similar level of knowledge about water. There are several possible reasons for this. Consider the perspective of a new brewer, who now has a wide variety of malts, hops and yeasts to choose from, each of which may come from anywhere in the world. For example, it is not uncommon to brew classic Bohemian Pilsner with hops and malted barley grown in the Czech Republic. The yeast will probably be obtained from a local source, but that source grew the supplied cells from a strain imported originally from the Czech Republic. It is, conversely, obvious that one cannot import water from Plzeň or České Budějovice. Practical considerations force most brewers to use the water that is available at their breweries (though home brewers sometimes obtain brewing water from nearby health food stores or supermarkets and I did meet one commercial operator who had his water trucked in). Given that the brewer is forced to choose among dozens of hop, malt and yeast varieties, but has practically no choice about the water supply, it is not surprising that our new brewer focuses attention primarily on the first three and begins making beer without giving water much thought. Municipal water supplies in developed countries are such that while they may not be ideal for brewing, one can make many passable beers with them. Many brewers do exactly that for their entire brewing career.

Because potable water doesn't appear to directly contribute tastes or aromas as potent as those from hops, malt and fermentation products, it is understandable that beginning brewers might conclude that water is nothing more than a carrier for flavors from the other beer components. Chlorine and chloramine in appreciable concentration are exceptions to this, and even unsophisticated brewers are generally aware that these chemicals must be dealt with—though a surprising number of beginning brewers make passable beer without any regard for either. This book has a great deal to teach these brewers.

Other brewers, including some very good ones, think of their available water in the same terms that vintners think of terroir. They make a conscious decision to accept their water as it is, and to only brew beers that work with it. It's obvious that this is much easier to do if you are only brewing one type of beer than if your portfolio is extensive. The sections of this book that describe water sources and a breakdown of its components as found in a typical water report will be of value to these brewers, as will the parts which describe the effects of water on mash pH and those that discuss non-brewing (cleaning, cooling, dilution, steam generation, etc.) uses of water in the brewery.

Before leaving terroir we should note that, rightly or wrongly, it is often given as the main reason that, for example, Irish Stout is a very different beer than Bohemian Pilsner. While it is clear that the local hops, malt and available yeast had something to do with this, common sense says that the water had a lot to do with it too. We should also point out that adherence to the terroir philosophy doesn't mean that nothing at all is done to the water. Munich *dunkles* and Munich *helles* are both brewed with Munich water and both have characteristics attributable to this water. In the former case the water is used as-is, but in the latter it is decarbonated.

As a brewer's experience, knowledge and contact with other brewers grows and his desire to make very good or excellent beer rather than just good beer emerges, his attention will eventually turn to water, as it must; because very good and excellent beers cannot be made without considerable attention to water. And here we find the first major obstacle in the path to better knowledge of brewing water. We began this essay with an implication that sources of information on water as applied to brewing are hard to come by. It is not so much that the necessary information is not out there as that it is thinly dispersed and not always in obvious places. The brewer will have a source for everything he needs to know about water if he collects a set of general texts on inorganic chemistry, physical chemistry, qualitative analysis and perhaps biochemistry; some more-specific texts on aquatic chemistry, water analysis and water treatment; those all-too-brief chapters on water in brewing texts; a handful of papers from technical journals, some conference proceedings and a few URLs. None of these sources, except some of the papers and some of the websites, are exclusively about brewing water and some of them are pretty hard to read. Finding the brewing-relevant parts is like finding needles in haystacks. Writing this book required that the authors find those needles, and they have done that well; but in addition to extracting nuggets from the literature, the authors have drawn on the knowledge of experienced brewers—people with special interest in or knowledge of the subject—and those who have developed software for doing some of the complex calculations and experiments. With such a breadth of sources, this book will either answer your brewing water questions or have you well on the way to those answers. I've seen many Internet queries that read something like: "I'm making good beer but something just seems to be lacking. I think it may be my water. Where can I go to learn something about how to improve my brewing through water adjustment?" This book is the obvious reply.

It is not enough to simply collect all the relevant information and put it before the brewer, as many will be completely intimidated by it and will consequently not derive any benefit from it. A comparison with malt, hops and yeast may again lend some insight. If a brewer finds a particular malt to have too much protein, or a yeast strain to throw too much diacetyl, or a hop variety to be too low in geraniol, there isn't much he can do about it other than select different materials, or dilute or augment with materials that have more or less of the desired properties. Water is quite different. While the brewer cannot easily obtain water from a different source, what's available can be modified. In fact, he must do exactly that if he wants to make excellent beers free from the limitations imposed by the terroir school. If there is too much of some ion, that ion must be removed. If there is deficiency in some other ion, that ion must be augmented. To do this requires application of chemistry. It is somewhat paradoxical that brewers are intimidated by the relatively simple chemistry of water as opposed to the much more complex chemistry and biochemistry of the other three ingredients. The discomfort stems, in my opinion, from the fact that the while the chemistry of the living ingredients is extremely complex, only limited *qualitative* understanding is sufficient because the typical brewer cannot practically apply chemistry to improve malt, hops or yeast. To master water, conversely, he must apply what he knows about its chemistry and he must do so *quantitatively,* which means he must do calculations. It is much easier to explain and understand (qualitatively) that the bicarbonate ions in brewing liquor absorb hydrogen ions from an acidic mash component than it is to explain and understand how to calculate (quantitatively) the amount of sodium bicarbonate necessary to eliminate the effect of that acid.

Calculations concerning the carbonic/bicarbonate/carbonate system in water are at the heart of brewing water chemistry. They require the use of things like the Davies extension to the Debye-Hückel theory. If you are unfamiliar with that, as the large majority of readers will be, it is hardly surprising that you might feel a bit intimidated. Don't be! You do not need to understand the Debye-Hückel theory (let alone the Davies extension) to use this book. The intimidating (math) parts of the science have been done for you and the results placed in easy-to-use tables and graphs. This is, in my opinion, one of the places where this book really shines. It makes the most difficult, but very essential, part of the subject matter accessible to those without a science or engineering background. The few who do want to know about the Davies-Debye-Hückel equation and other arcana will find them in an Internet search.

A brewer who seeks to improve his beer by modifying his available water strives to meet two goals: one technical and one aesthetic. The technical goal is establishment of proper mash pH. One could argue that reaching this goal is what this book is really about and that the rest of the material is supporting. That's a bit of a stretch, but proper mash pH is terribly important. The aesthetic goal is a matter of flavor.

Proper mash pH is necessary for the best flavor profile but there are other flavor-related effects that derive more directly from minerals in the liquor. Best known of these are the sweetness and roundness imparted by the chloride ion, and the synergism of the sulfate ion with hop bittering principles. Proper mash pH and good flavor effects both require that certain things be in the liquor at the proper concentration. RO water, one of the two technologies remaining to be discussed, contains practically nothing, so use of it as a liquor source makes it easy to get the ion concentrations we need. We simply add whatever we require, subject to the limitation that the two ions into which an added salt separates are in fixed relative proportion. There is no need to analyze the water or perform any tests upon it other than to verify that the RO system is performing properly. RO water is, in a popular analogy, a 'blank sheet of paper'.

Ready availability of RO water is revolutionizing hobby and commercial brewing, as no matter how difficult the available water may be, it can now be transformed into that blank piece of paper. Not only does RO make it possible to brew good beer in places where this was formerly not possible, it makes the brewer's relationship with his water much simpler. The advice, "Just dissolve 1 gram of calcium chloride in each gallon of RO water and brew" is very simple advice indeed, but it will get you a good beer in a surprisingly large number of cases. To get excellent beer you will, naturally, have to do more than just adding some calcium chloride, and this book will show you how to do that.

The last of our breakthrough technologies is the inexpensive pH meter. You will find pH discussed a lot in this book. The balance of carbonate and phosphate ions depends on pH and each of the many complex chemical reactions of malting, mashing and fermentation are mediated by the biochemical catalysis of enzymes. Enzyme performance depends on temperature, as most brewers know, but it also depends on pH. That is why it is so important to set mash pH properly (if you do that, pH in other parts of the process will tend to be in the right range too). Mash pH prediction is complicated and a natural variation in malt properties makes exact predictions difficult. This is where the pH meter comes in. It gives direct feedback to the brewer just as his thermometer does, and the information from it is as important as temperature information. If temperature is off, the brewer adds or takes away heat. If pH is off the brewer adds or takes away acid. When we say proper water treatment is a major factor in determining whether a beer is good or excellent, we are really saying that pH is a major (though not the only) factor in determining the quality of what comes out of the fermentor.

In summary: You have, essentially, three options in approaching your brewing water. You can brew with it as it is; you can modify it by adding deficient ions and removing ones that are present in excess; or you can start with RO water and build the brewing liquor you need from scratch. I hope that this Foreword has given you some perspective that will help you, as you read on, make that decision, as well as to appreciate the breadth of information found in this book and to understand the major contribution it makes to brewing literature. Dive in and I hope you will enjoy reading it as much as I enjoyed helping John and Colin get it written.

A. J. deLange
McLean, Virginia
May 2013

A Whole Book on Brewing Water

This book is part of the Brewers Publications' Brewing Elements series and is intended for all levels of brewers—from homebrewers to professionals. However, it should be understood that this is a technical book that is *not* intended for the novice. Brewers should have a working knowledge of grain brewing techniques, including mashing, lautering, and expected yields to fully appreciate the discussions in this book. Brewers should also have a basic knowledge of high school level chemistry in order to understand the concepts discussed here. For those who are a bit rusty in chemistry, a glossary and primer is provided in Appendix A. Likewise there are many Internet resources that can explain chemistry concepts if needed.

Before 1990, there was a fairly wide gulf in the level of technical knowledge between brewers at the home level and brewers at the commercial level. But since that time, the gulf has narrowed considerably. Currently we have more small, independent breweries in the United States than ever before in our history, and most of these brewmasters first learned their craft by homebrewing. This statement holds true worldwide as well—new small breweries are opening everywhere as people rediscover beer in all its variety. There is renewed interest in different beer styles and a greater variety of ingredients. New yeast strains are becoming widely available, maltsters have new markets for their specialty malts, and hop growers are constantly being asked for new varieties, all to satisfy the creative needs of new brewers. But water? Well, water comes from a hole in the ground.

In the last century it seems water was often overlooked or over-simplified when it was considered at all. The common theme was that water should be clean, potable, low in alkalinity and hardness, come from pure mountain streams, etc. Here in the United States, the brewing of light Pilsner-type lagers for the every-man seemed to be the only real goal of any brewing operation, especially as breweries consolidated in the 1950s, 60s, and 70s. For the last half of the twentieth century, the general recommendations for water in brewing textbooks have been:

- The water should be clean.
- Pre-boil the water to get rid of temporary hardness.
- The alkalinity of the water should be less than 50 ppm.
- The water should contain 50 to 100 ppm of calcium.

The problem with these generalities is that they were primarily constructed for one style of beer—Pilsener-style lagers—and they don't necessarily meet the requirements of other styles. Beer is the most complex beverage known to man, and the role of water in brewing is equally intricate. Water chemistry textbooks typically run to 500 pages, yet water rarely receives more than a single chapter in modern brewing textbooks. Is it because brewing water is simple? No. Is it because water chemistry has only recently been understood? No, not really.

The influence and importance of water composition on beer has been known for a long time. In 1830, the composition of the water from Burton-upon-Trent was disclosed as the result of a libel lawsuit filed by the city's local brewers against the Society for Diffusing Useful Knowledge, who had claimed that Burton brewers adulterated their beers. The term "Burtonization" was coined in 1882 by Egbert Hooper in *The Manual of Brewing*, and attributed to a process developed by the chemist Charles Vincent in 1878. In 1901, Wahl and Henius published the *American Handy Book of the Brewing, Malting, and Auxiliary Trades*. In the section on water (12 pages) in Brewing Materials, they make note of treatments to improve water, such as aeration to remove odors and precipitate iron, and the addition of salts for Burtonizing, stating, "An addition of plaster of Paris, sulphate of magnesia, or common salt, preferably in a powder in the hot water tank, will make soft water more suitable, particularly for very pale beers." They go on to describe "Making Injurious Constituents Indifferent" such as the reduction of excess alkaline carbonates by additions of a suitable amount of calcium chloride, the softening of boiler feedwater, and discuss different brewing waters for different types of ale and lager. The only real differences in this book from modern texts are the terminology for some the salts (e.g., lime, magnesia) and the units (i.e., grains per gallon vs. ppm).

Much of the same information and more is presented in *Principles and Practice of Brewing* 3rd Ed., by W.J. Sykes in 1907. He provides considerable review of different brewing waters and water treatments to "modify them for better purpose," including the pertinent chemical reactions. This book was published just a few short years before the concept of pH was introduced by Søren P.L. Sørensen of the Carlsberg Laboratory in 1909, and pH was not included in the discussions. The concept of pH had gained better acceptance by 1924 when its definition was refined to agree with contemporary work in electrochemical cells.

Further proof that the business of water treatment is not new is given in the summary from Wallerstein Laboratories' 1935 publication, *The Treatment of Brewing Water in Light of Modern Chemistry*:

"Every brewing water must be carefully studied and treated according to its specific needs. For over 30 years we have made the treatment of brewing water our special study, supplying the brewer with the particular Wallerstein Burton Salts necessary to improve and correct his brewing water."

This book also includes discussion on the value of pH measurement, but notes that the pH of the water is not the goal.

While pH is one of the most important factors in connection with the suitability of a water for brewing purposes, we must keep in mind that it is the pH of the mash and not the pH of the water that will influence the results in brewing. Therefore, our objective in correcting the brewing water is not to achieve any particular pH value in the water but to make it most suitable for brewing and to provide the conditions under which brewing operations may be conducted to the best advantage.

In 1953, Paul Kolbach determined that increased water alkalinity causes wort pH to rise above its distilled-water or "normal" pH. He also determined that calcium and magnesium in water (hardness) reacts with malt phosphates to neutralize water alkalinity and reduce the wort pH. He called the alkalinity remaining after this reaction "residual alkalinity" and this concept has become a cornerstone for understanding and manipulating pH throughout the brewing process.

The mash pH drives the kettle pH, and the kettle pH is a primary factor in determining the way the flavors of the beer are expressed on the palate. In an alkaline water region, a brewer may typically need to use acid or incorporate more acidic malts in the grain bill to bring the mash pH down into the desired range. Conversely, the need for acids or acidic malts is reduced in a region with low alkalinity water.

In general, the American taste for beer in the past century has gotten lighter and lighter. Obviously there are exceptions, but the years of Light, Dry, and Ice beer marketing campaigns tell a consistent story. In fact recently, some very large brewing corporations have spent more ad time talking about the packaging of a new beer than its flavor. The point is that low gravity pale lager beers are the vast majority of the market, and the characteristics for that style's brewing water has been accepted as the norm, without much understanding of why. Hopefully, this book can be a bridge between the past and the future of water use in the brewery.

Water quality requirements in the brewery can vary. The best water for brewing may not always be the best water for other uses in the brewery. Water that is used for cleaning, steam generation, chilling, or dilution may need starkly different parameters from mashing or sparging water. What we hope to do with this book is give you the knowledge to change water from an obstacle into a tool. The first goal of this book is to educate the brewer on water as a beer ingredient. The second is to explain in plain language how water interacts with the malts to create the chemistry of the mash, and how to manipulate that chemistry to improve the beer. The third section of the book gets out of the mash tun and focuses on the needs of other brewery process water and wastewater treatment. Brewing beer should be all about making water work for you, and not the other way around.

Overview of Water as an Ingredient

In his seminal book *"On Food and Cooking,"* author Harold Magee— states that cooking is chemistry. And so is brewing—beer is a complex mixture of sugars, proteins, alcohols, and myriad other organic compounds. A brewer needs to think of water and water sources in the same way as hop varieties and growing regions, or malts and maltsters. Different water sources have different chemical profiles and therefore different benefits for different beer styles. Crystal pure mountain spring water is a great idea in theory, but the reality of brewing is that significant water hardness is actually recommended for better brewing performance and other ions can be beneficial to beer flavor.

Brewing good beer is about more than just having the right water; and conversely, having the right water is about more than just making good beer. In the first part of this book (Chapters 1 to 3), we want you to gain an appreciation of where your water comes from, and what's in it. We will discuss water reports and primary drinking water standards, the various minerals and contaminants and how these can affect your beer. The first requirement for brewing source water is that it be *clean*. A water source may be fit to drink, but it may not be fit for brewing. The water may contain chlorine, or chloramines, dissolved gases, or organic compounds that can adversely affect beer flavor. Although it may initially sound facile, tasting the water before and after every process step, and prior to each key application is highly recommended.

For example, at Sierra Nevada brewery in Chico, California, they taste- and smell-test the water daily, using a minimum of four people, at six different points in the brewing process. They taste the incoming water for anything unexpected; they taste and smell the water after dechlorination, and after carbon filtering for any off-aroma. They test the cold liquor tank, the hot liquor tank, and the deaerated water tank for any off-aroma. Other non-product process waters, such as the bottling jetter and rinse, are tested weekly. The off-flavors and aromas might be musty or earthy, sulfur, ester, or metallic. Some of these test points may not be applicable to your brewery, and different water sources will have different needs, but thorough and consistent sensory analysis of your water's quality is a powerful tool.

Overview of Water and Mash Chemistry

In the second part of the book (Chapters 4 to 7), we are going to explain how water chemistry interacts with mash chemistry. Generally, water for brewing should have a minimum of 50 ppm of calcium to improve mashing performance, good fermentation, and beer clarification. Alkalinity in brewing water has traditionally been viewed as only as a barrier, something to be eliminated. But, the recommended level of alkalinity in brewing water will vary based on the acidity of the mash malt composition and the brewer's desired beer character. In general, low alkalinity is desirable for lighter colored beers and the need for alkalinity increases for darker and more acidic mash grists. Ultimately, the taste of the beer must be the brewer's guide to proper water composition.

For years, there has been talk of developing a model for predicting and controlling mash pH by understanding the interaction of water composition and malts in the grist. We will explore recent research in this area in order to illustrate the big picture and hopefully encourage future research. Chapter 4 discusses the residual alkalinity concept in detail, and Chapter 5 focuses on malt chemistry. Malt chemistry may seem beyond the scope of this book, but it truly is the other half of the equation if you are going to discuss mash pH; and there is really little point in discussing water chemistry if you are not going to discuss mash pH and beer properties.

Chapter 6 looks at methods for controlling alkalinity in more detail —both reducing and increasing alkalinity as needed. Lime softening, decarbonation by heat, and acidification of brewing and sparge water are addressed, as well as the latest research in the effect on mash pH of chalk and slaked lime additions.

We will explain how to manipulate the water chemistry to improve your beer. Although calcium and alkalinity are very important aspects of brewing water, several other ions can have substantial effects on beer flavor and perception. For example, the sulfate-to-chloride ratio in the water can significantly affect the malty to bitter flavor balance and perception of fullness and dryness in the beer. Sodium, magnesium, copper and zinc can be very beneficial in small amounts, but produce off-flavors if used in excess. The effects of these ions on the beer are discussed in Chapter 7.

A frequent question is, what type of water is appropriate for a particular style? How much of this salt should I add to my water? We are also going to teach you how to do the simple chemistry calculations for salt and acid additions. In Chapter 7 we present our recommendations for general water compositions for the different styles, salt recipes for building these waters from distilled or RO water, and a couple of specific examples for adjusting a source water to better brew a particular style. These suggestions are intended to be stepping stones or launch points, not a final destination. The flavor qualities of the beer must be your guide as you navigate these waters. Together these chapters and the appendices should give you the tools to tailor your water for almost any style you wish to brew.

Overview of Brewing Water Processing

The last section of the book, Chapters 8 through 10, focuses on water usage in the brewery for processes other than brewing: what treatment technologies are available, requirements for different process waters, and brewery wastewater treatment. Water treatment is an old science, with processes such as boiling, sand filtration and carbon filtration going back to the time of the Egyptian pharaohs. Lime softening was developed in 1841 and is discussed as a standard practice in both *Principles and Practice of Brewing* and *American Handy Book of Brewing*. Modern technology has moved water treatment forward from there. The purpose of this section of the book is to acquaint the new brewer(y) with the current state of the art, with processes that are more adaptable to small and mid-size breweries, and not to rehash older technologies that may be more suited to large-scale brewing.

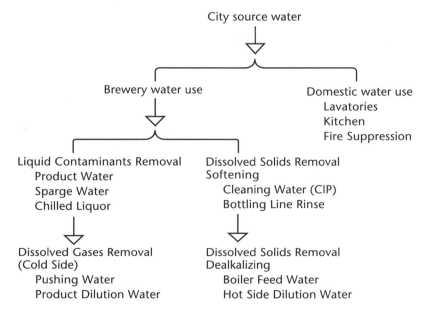

Figure 2—Water Distribution and Processing in the Brewery.

Brewing is a very water-intensive activity, using anywhere from 5–10 volumes of water for each volume of beer produced. Most of this water is used for cleaning, some is lost to evaporation, and almost all of it ends up going down the drain unless it is reclaimed. Water used for cleaning often needs to be softened for best results. The colloquial terms "hard water" and "soft water" actually came from the cleaning industry. The term "hard" means that it is hard to raise a lather due to the chemical binding of the soil-binding sites in soaps by calcium and magnesium ions.

Figure 3—A typical brew day at The Bruery in Placentia, CA.

Once the calcium and magnesium ions in the water have been bound, more soap is needed for the actual cleaning. Detergents and surfactants are less sensitive to hard water and make up the majority of cleaning chemicals in use today. Water hardness is also responsible for carbonate scale on equipment, which inhibits thorough cleaning. Therefore it is common to soften hard water before use in cleaning.

But there is more to brewery water treatment than softening. There are several technologies that water supply utilities use to remove suspended solids, dissolved solids, and liquid contaminants and gases from the water, and these same methods can be put to use in the brewery. Once we understand the technologies available to us, we can look at brewery process water requirements with a better eye toward options and feasibility.

Figure 4—Glycol chilled fermentation tanks at Dama Bier, Piracicaba, SP, Brazil.

Water is used for chilling wort in heat exchangers, it is used in polypropylene glycol solutions around jacketed fermentors, and it is used as steam and feedwater in boiler systems. Boiler water treatment is essential for maintaining energy efficiency and the integrity of steam generating systems. Poor management of equipment and water use can have major effects on system performance, energy costs, water and gas emissions, and equipment life. Each of these thermal exchange applications has potentially different requirements.

Figure 5—The Boiler at Stone Brewing Co, Escondido, CA.

While much of the craft beer produced today is sold in-house, straight from the bright tanks, a lot of it needs to be bottled and kegged as well. Current labeling laws require strict adherence to the declared alcohol content. Thus, many breweries practice high gravity brewing to some degree to enable them to dilute the wort or beer to more consistently hit their numbers. Dilution water needs to be highly deaerated to prevent premature staling, as it is often added right before packaging. Water is also used for rinsing and fobbing/jetting on the bottling line, and for washing and rinsing stainless steel kegs, though usually without the need for deaeration.

Dilution water may be used at many different points in the brewing process: pre-boil, post-boil, and/or post-fermentation. Pre-boil and post-boil dilution water can be used to adjust original gravity or batch volume.

The popularity of high-gravity boiling and fermentation in production breweries often requires a dilution water supply. The requirements for post-boil dilution water are the highest in the brewery. The water must be both disinfected and deaerated before use because it is being used for finished beer. Water that is not disinfected has a greater risk of spoiling the beer in the package, even if pasteurized. Lastly, the calcium content of the dilution water must be less than the calcium content of the concentrated beer in order to prevent calcium oxalate precipitation in the package. These oxalate crystals act as bubble nucleation sites and can cause gushing when the beer is opened.

Figure 6—A look into the water treatment room at Sierra Nevada Brewing Co, showing the bottom half of the deaeration column.

Figure 7—This is the aerobic digestion tank at Sierra Nevada Brewing Co, in Chico, CA.

The treatment and disposal of wastewater is the proverbial thorn in the side of many growing breweries. As brewery production grows, the load and character of the wastewater sent to the wastewater treatment facility comes under increasing scrutiny. What was previously a minor inconvenience, or a wink and a nod to the treatment provider, becomes a daily problem—how to dispose of wastewater, spent yeast and cleaning chemicals while avoiding fines and surcharges for the brewery's wastewater discharges?

To reduce the load and improve the character of brewery wastewater, pretreatment at the brewery may be required. The goal of wastewater pretreatment is to remove the dissolved and suspended solids from the water, keep wastewater pH within allowable limits, and reduce the strength of the discharge. In many areas, allowing untreated wastewater to enter the sewer can lead to high fees and fines from the local wastewater treatment facility. Brewery wastewater strength can be reduced chemically, aerobically, or anaerobically. Each type of system has its pros and cons, and these will be discussed in more detail in Chapter 10.

Hopefully this overview gives you a better understanding of water as a brewing ingredient and as a production resource. Refining your water for its many brewery uses is an important part of improving the taste of your beers and improving brewery operations. The environmental requirements on a brewery have never been more stringent than they are today and we hope that by bringing these aspects together in one book, we can give you the knowledge and tools to make water really work for you and your beer.

2

Where Does Your Water Come From?

Understanding where our water comes from and how the environment can alter its character and constituents are important factors for brewing water. This chapter illustrates how water changes as it progresses through the water (hydrologic) cycle and ultimately influences our brewing.

The Water Cycle

We can consider the water cycle to start as a gas or vapor in clouds. It starts the cycle as pure H_2O (a.k.a. dihydrogen monoxide, or oxidane), but not for long. As it condenses to form water droplets, it absorbs carbon dioxide and other gases from the air. The atmosphere is also full of dust particles and tiny mineral crystals, such as sand and sodium chloride. All of these substances help water droplets to condense, but they also contaminate the water during formation. The droplets agglomerate and fall to the earth as precipitation (rain or snow).

When rain and snow fall to earth and collect, it becomes surface water. The longer the surface water remains in contact with the earth (days or years), the more substances from the environment will be dissolved or suspended into it. These substances can be organic matter from plants or animals, other compounds such as herbicides and pesticides, and minerals such as sodium chloride and calcium sulfate to name but a few.

Figure 8—The water cycle from gas to liquid and back. Image © Shutterstock.com.

As surface water seeps into the ground, most of the organic matter is filtered out and the water is exposed to more minerals. This water is termed groundwater and it may reside in these aquifers for hundreds if not thousands of years. The long exposure allows plenty of time for minerals to dissolve into the groundwater. In areas with carbonate soil and rock formations, those dissolved minerals often lead to higher hardness and alkalinity concentrations than can be achieved at the surface.

Wells, springs, and seepage into rivers and streams bring groundwater back to surface waters. At any time, both groundwater and surface water may evaporate back into the atmosphere to restart this water cycle.

Water Sources and Mineralization

The point of this introduction is to illustrate that there are three principal sources of fresh water (precipitation, surface water, and groundwater) and each has its pros and cons for use in the brewery. Precipitation from recent rainfall or snowpack will tend to have a lower pH than surface water and contain very little organic matter or dissolved minerals. Surface water from rivers or lakes may have more organic matter and a moderate concentration of dissolved minerals and alkalinity. Surface water is more likely to be contaminated with organics, including plankton and debris. The quality of surface water varies greatly with location because of environmental conditions and human activity. Groundwater tends to have low organics but may have higher dissolved mineral content and is susceptible to contamination from industry, agriculture, and other man-made sources.

Brewers have obtained their brewing water from surface and groundwater sources for centuries. The majority of water drawn from these sources is for drinking water or uses other than brewing. The water may be softened or hardened, the pH adjusted, and problem ions or organics removed to make the water more appealing to customers and protect the water utility's infrastructure. In the United States and other countries, laws often require that public utilities disinfect water to remove microbial contamination prior to distributing it to water users. The fact that the water has been treated prior to distribution does not mean that it is suitable for brewing use, even though it is suitable for drinking. Disinfection is traditionally not as important for brewers because the brewing process typically involves boiling. In fact, brewing has been used for thousands of years as a means of rendering questionable water safe to drink. Public water disinfection can be a problem for brewers because some common disinfectants can be difficult to remove, can cause residual byproducts, and can have negative flavor effects on the beer. (This will be discussed further in Chapter 3.)

This is the first take-home message: Know your water source and what to expect from it. A more detailed description of common water sources follows.

A Quick Note About pH and Buffers

pH will be defined in more detail later in the book, but the key point to understand for now is that pH is the measure of hydrogen ion concentration, or the acidity of a solution. pH is measured on a scale from 0 to 14, with 7 considered neutral. Values less than 7 are increasingly acidic and those with a pH greater than 7 are more basic. By itself, the pH of water is not very useful to brewers. For the brewer, the alkalinity of brewing water is more important than its pH.

In order to understand your brewing water, you not only need to understand the pH but also the buffer systems in the water. A buffer is a chemical compound in a solution that reacts (dissociates/associates) to the addition of another chemical (salt, sugar, acids, bases) to effectively resist changes in pH of the solution. The primary buffer in drinking water is usually alkalinity. Measuring the pH of water without knowing the type and quantity of the buffer system is like measuring voltage on an unknown battery. Voltage does not tell us the size or capacity of the battery. Likewise, you have to know the type and quantities of the buffers in solution to have some context for the pH.

So that being said, water pH *will* be mentioned throughout the next few chapters as we discuss water sources and composition because it is a useful point of reference. pH becomes critically important later when it comes to understanding and controlling mash chemistry. For more information on buffers, see Appendix A.

Precipitation

Rainwater or snow can be very pure, typically containing less than 20 ppm of total dissolved solids. As the water condenses from a gas into a liquid in the atmosphere, other gases will dissolve into the liquid water, although inert gases like nitrogen, argon, and helium are not very soluble in water.

A review of the gaseous composition of standard dry air shows that it is roughly 78.1% nitrogen, 20.95% oxygen, and 0.9% argon. Moisture accounts for 1% to 4% of the typical atmosphere, which displaces some dry air—in other words, 3% moisture would mean 97% dry air. Looking at the dry air alone, these proportions leave only about 0.04% of the volume for the rest of the gases, including carbon dioxide. The current concentration of CO_2 in the atmosphere is about 390 ppm (0.039%). Therefore, CO_2 comprises most of the remaining gas total. The rest of the gases like helium, ozone, krypton, etc. are typically at 5 ppm or less and do not significantly affect atmospheric water quality. Although all of these gases may dissolve into the atmospheric water (i.e., clouds) to some degree, carbon dioxide is by far the most soluble and it plays the most important role in determining the eventual composition and chemistry of our brewing water. This will be explored further in later chapters.

Rainwater typically has very low levels of inorganic molecules, but air pollution can contribute significant amounts of sulfates, nitrates, aldehydes, chlorides, lead, cadmium, iron and copper. In high pollution areas, nitrogenous and sulfurous oxides can create acid rain with destructive effects ranging from acidification of natural waters to eroding the monuments of Greece. The pH of acid rain has been measured as low as 2.6 due to these causes.

For example, one study[1] of 90 samples of rainwater at Avignon, France from the period of October 1997 to March 1999, found the following average ion concentrations:

Chloride	2.1 mg/L
Sulfate	4.6 mg/L
Nitrate	2.8 mg/L
Bicarbonate	2.5 mg/L
Sodium	1.1 mg/L
Potassium	0.5 mg/L
Calcium	2.4 mg/L
Magnesium	0.2 mg/L
Ammonium	0.9 mg/L
pH	4.92

Total Dissolved Solids: 17.1 mg/L

Thus, the water in fog, clouds, and precipitation is not always pure. Although the example above illustrates that contaminants can depress water pH, carbon dioxide is usually the major determinant of water acidity and

---

[1] Hélène Celle-Jeanton, Yves Travi, Marie-Dominique Loÿe-Pilot, Frédéric Huneau and Guillaume Bertrand, "Rainwater Chemistry at a Mediterranean Inland Station (Avignon, France): Local Contribution Versus Long-Range Supply," Atmospheric Research 91 (2009): 118–126. www.elsevier.com/locate/atmos.

its resulting pH. The dissolution of carbon dioxide into rainwater forms aqueous carbon dioxide and carbonic acid that lowers pH from 7 (distilled water) to somewhere in the range of 5 to 6, with a typical mean value of 5.0 to 5.5. The pH of pure water in contact with carbon dioxide can be directly calculated. For example, at 0.03% carbon dioxide in the atmosphere, the resulting pH of pure water would be 5.65 (at 68°F/ 20°C).

To summarize, water from precipitation will typically have very low ionic content and very low alkalinity. However, the very low ionic content may be elevated in industrialized areas, and winds can easily cause contamination far from the contaminant source.

Surface Water

Surface water can be any body of water above ground, including lakes, ponds, rivers, or puddles. The pH of surface water is usually between 6.0 and 8.0 due to dissolution of minerals and some organic matter. The quality and character of surface water can vary greatly depending on many factors such as rate of flow, depth, surface area and geography. The water quality in rocky, fast-moving mountain streams can be very similar in character to fresh precipitation. There is little opportunity for the water to pick up or erode sediments in that setting and the waters tend to be clear. However, even that water may still require treatment before potable use. For example, the introduction of sheep to the Sierra Nevada Mountains of California caused a sharp increase in microorganisms and human pathogens in the streams and rivers of the coastal range.

On the other hand, large slow-moving rivers, like the Mississippi, tend to pick up more soil, organic matter, and agricultural runoff and become turbid as they flow through wide flood plains composed of soils and erodible rock. There can be a lot of variation in the water quality of rivers due to the differing land uses and geology in the watershed. River chemistry can vary greatly with geography, vary seasonally from precipitation, or change rapidly due to local environmental stresses. To illustrate this point, the Mississippi River cuts through a drainage basin that was once an inland sea. The river water picks up alkalinity from the limestone that was formerly the seabed. The pH of the Mississippi varies a bit with location, but tends to be around 8. By contrast, the Amazon River flows through siliceous rock (flint, quartz, and sandstone) and does not pick up much alkalinity. The dead leaves and loam in the Amazon basin form humic and other organic acids in the water. The water can be stained quite brown, like tea. The organic acids and low alkalinity of the Amazon's water prevents its pH from ever rising much above 6.

Surface water sourced from lakes in colder temperate regions can change seasonally due to thermal stratification. The densest water is at the bottom of the lake in both winter and summer at a temperature of 39°F (4°C). The surface water is less dense, either being warmed by the sun or frozen. When the temperatures become more uniform in spring and fall, the stratification disappears and mixing can occur by wind action, bringing nutrients up from the bottom of the lake and taking oxygen-rich surface water into the lake depths. Lakes in warm regions may also suffer from algal blooms and organic matter. Seasonal biological cycles such as algae blooms or autumn leaf introduction can also affect surface water quality; they can cause concentrated flavors or odors that need stronger treatment and may result in higher residual treatment byproducts. For example, the chlorination of decaying plant material creates TCA (2,4,6-Trichloroanisole). This off-flavor, described as earthy, mildew, wet dog, or dank basement, is detectable at very low thresholds. Other off-flavors in surface water can be a result of MIB (methylisoborneol) and geosmin (i.e., earthy smell) that are produced by microbes living in the water. Filtration through activated carbon can be effective for removal of these taste- and odor-causing chemicals.

Groundwater

As noted above, surface water that seeps into the ground and permeates rock and soil layers is called groundwater. The semi-permeable layer that the groundwater flows through is called an aquifer. The age of groundwater (time since it entered the ground) does vary. Some aquifers hold water that is less than a year old and some hold water that is thousands of years old. The average age of groundwater worldwide is about 250 years.

In those aquifers, groundwater may be exposed to high heat and pressure that may result in higher dissolved mineral concentrations than can be achieved in surface water. Reproducing those highly mineralized water chemistries in the lab by adding salts and acids to distilled water can be difficult as well. However, not all groundwater is highly mineralized. In aquifers composed of non-carbonate or siliceous rock and soil, those minerals may not be very soluble and the water may not become as mineralized. The typical pH of groundwater ranges from 6.5 to 8.5. Groundwater with pH lower than this range can be more prone to dissolving metals such as iron, manganese, etc. These metals are typically undesirable in brewing water, even at very low concentrations.

From a brewer's point of view, it would be nice if groundwater sources were classified according to brewing character. Unfortunately, that is not the case; aquifer classifications were devised by soil scientists and hydrogeologists, not brewers. These scientists are more concerned with water sources—how easily the water flows and how far you have to dig to get it. According to hydrogeologists, there are two main types of aquifers: confined and unconfined. A confined aquifer has a relatively impermeable layer (such as clay) overlaying the more permeable zone. The underlying aquifer is somewhat shielded, or confined, from surface contamination by the impermeable layer. If permeable soil or rock extends all the way to ground surface, then the aquifer is unconfined. In addition, hydrogeologists typically name water sources by location, so if you happen to live in northern Arkansas, you will be gratified to know that your water comes from the Ozark Plateaus aquifer system (or not.)

Geologists on the other hand, are mainly concerned with rocks and strata. The United States Geological Survey (USGS) identifies five principal types of aquifers in North America: sand and gravel, sandstone, carbonate rock, interbedded sandstone and carbonate rock, and igneous and metamorphic rock. Information on the geologic units (i.e., the type of rock) of specific aquifers in North America is generally available through usgs.gov. There are probably similar resources for other countries.

Geologic classifications are not useful descriptors for brewing water character either. But they are a step in the right direction, if you know the types of minerals and ions you can expect to find there. So how does geology affect water? To clarify, a mineral is a specific chemical compound, such as calcium carbonate, gypsum, cinnabar, garnet, or quartz. Rock is a naturally occurring combination of minerals or non-minerals. A specific kind of rock, such as granite, is a specific combination of minerals. Water that contacts those rocks has the opportunity to erode or dissolve the components in them. While identification of rocks and strata is not specifically what we want, it does give us a good starting point for understanding the groundwater they provide.

Sand and gravel aquifers are typically composed of silica-type rocks such as granite that are relatively insoluble. The groundwater tends to be low in dissolved minerals, but their typically high hydraulic permeability may make them more susceptible to contamination from surface sources. This type of aquifer can be found throughout the Missouri and Mississippi River drainage basin, North Texas to Arkansas, Nevada, South Carolina, Georgia, and Florida.

Sandstone aquifers are composed primarily of sand-sized grains that are cemented together. Sandstone may include various sedimentary rocks including gypsum, which forms under high evaporation conditions in shallow marine basins and coastal tidal flats. Gypsum is found in many forms, but the most common is a white rock that is mined for plasters and wallboard. The hydraulic conductivity of sandstone aquifers tends to be low and the water can have a long residence time, possibly producing highly mineralized water. This type of aquifer is prevalent through the Rocky Mountains to the Northern Plains in the US.

Carbonate rock aquifers are very common all over the world, and they consist mostly of limestone (calcium carbonate) and dolomite (calcium magnesium carbonate). The limestone is the result of sedimentation of billions of shells and corals from ancient seas. Groundwater can have significant acidity from dissolved CO_2 produced by soil bacteria or atmospheric contact. The acidic groundwater can dissolve limestone, creating caves and underground rivers. Carbonate rock aquifers that emerge from the ground develop what is known as a karst topography, which is characterized by springs, sinkholes, disappearing streams, blind valleys caused by subsidence, and mogotes (isolated limestone hills, as in China and South America). This karst topography is common in Appalachia and Florida in the US. A classic example of a carbonate aquifer outside North America is the London Basin and the Koom Valley in the UK. The London Basin has a layer of clay over a sand aquifer that is underlain by a floor of chalk (a soft limestone). The chalk contributes alkalinity to the groundwater and therefore shallow wells in the sand aquifer have lower alkalinity than the deep bore wells because the deeper wells draw groundwater that is in closer proximity to the chalk layer.

The fourth aquifer type is the sandstone and carbonate rock aquifer, which is composed of carbonate rocks interbedded with nearly equal amounts of sandstone. These aquifers occur in south Texas, from

Appalachia into the Adirondacks and Ohio. These aquifers can contain gypsum as well, and tend to produce highly mineralized water. Burton-Upon-Trent in the UK is the most famous hard water region of the brewing world, having both high hardness from gypsum and high alkalinity from the carbonate rock.

The fifth and final type of aquifer is composed of igneous and metamorphic rocks (i.e., basalt and granite, or marble and quartzite, to name but a few). These rocks are not porous and hydraulic flow is typically achieved through fissures and fractures in the rock. These aquifers are common in northern Appalachia, eastern Washington, Oregon, and Idaho. These rocks are relatively insoluble and typically contribute very little hardness or alkalinity to the water. An example of an igneous aquifer would be in the Sierra Nevada Mountains of California. Water falls in the winter as snow and is released slowly throughout the summer as it melts. The water quality in this aquifer remains very similar to the initial precipitation.

From Source to Faucet

Not all communities are supplied from a large and consistent water source. A water supply may be mixed from several sources in order to supply a large population with consistently high quality water year-round. While some large breweries may have their own wells or long-term water rights, homebrewers and many small brewers receive their water from the municipal water supplier. Varying sources may affect the water supply's ionic composition. All municipal water suppliers in first-world countries

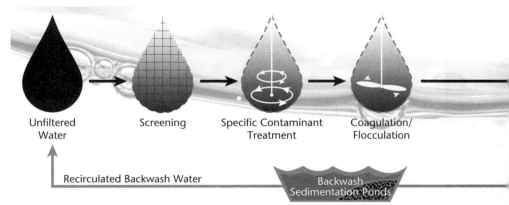

Unfiltered Water → Screening → Specific Contaminant Treatment → Coagulation/Flocculation

Recirculated Backwash Water

Backwash Sedimentation Ponds

Figure 9—Common Water Purification Process.

are typically held to strict laws for water purity and sanitation. The specific purification steps required will vary with the source water, but an overview of the most likely processes is shown in Figure 9.

The first treatment step for surface water sources is filtration through screens to remove environmental debris such as sticks and leaves. The next steps vary depending on the types of contaminants. The order of these treatment processes may vary between treatment facilities. If organic taste and odor compounds are present in the water, treatment with activated carbon may be performed. If the water contains objectionable concentrations of iron or manganese, the water is aerated or ozonated to oxidize soluble forms of these metals into their insoluble forms. Once in an insoluble form, the metals can be filtered from the water. Another treatment to remove dissolved iron and manganese is filtration through 'greensand,' which oxidizes and traps those ions. If the water is excessively hard, it may be softened with lime to precipitate calcium carbonate and magnesium hydroxide. Fine particulates in water may be coagulated with alum (aluminum sulfate), ferric chloride, or polymer additions. These coagulants help flocculate the fine particles by agglomeration so that the particles clump together to speed their settling or aid their filtering. Larger particles such as fine sand and silt will settle out within minutes. However, smaller particles such as bacteria could take days to settle without the aid of coagulants.

The clarified water is then fine-filtered through sand or media filters to remove micro-particles and microbes. After filtration, the water is ready

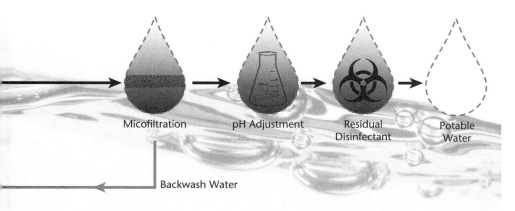

Micofiltration   pH Adjustment   Residual
                                           Disinfectant   Potable
                                                               Water

Backwash Water

Chlorine or Chloramines?

There are inexpensive ways to determine if you have chlorine or chloramine in your water. Test kits for free chlorine and total chlorine are available from aquarium stores or laboratory supplies. These kits can indicate the presence of these disinfectants in water. Free chlorine tests will only respond to the free chlorine in the water. A total chlorine test can test for the bound chlorine that is present in chloramines. If the free chlorine test measures lower than the total chlorine test, you have chloramine. If the two tests measure the same value, then you have chlorine. These tests are also useful to check for the completeness of disinfectant removal from activated carbon filters. Perform frequent checks of the filtered water when the carbon media has been in use for a long time.

There are also some DIY lab methods to check for the presence of disinfectants in the water supply. A simple method is to leave a glass of water out overnight and in the morning pour it between two glasses and smell. If it smells and tastes like chlorine then it is more likely that it has chloramine because most of the chlorine should have evaporated. You may want to compare the smell with a fresh glass of water to compare the intensity. Regardless, it is always good to smell and taste a chilled sample of your strike water before brewing with it.

for the final steps: pH adjustment and disinfection. The pH adjustment may be performed with lime, caustic, or acid additions to move the finished water pH into an acceptable range to avoid either corroding or scaling the utility's pipelines and the customer's plumbing. A residual disinfection chemical is required in the utility's pipelines to prevent bacterial contamination and growth after the water leaves the treatment plant. Disinfection usually includes the addition of chlorine, or chlorine and ammonia (to create chloramine) to the finished water.

Chlorine is very volatile and is easily removed by exposure to air or heating. Therefore, a large amount needs to be added to the water in the summer to ensure that enough is retained in the pipelines to do the job. Chlorine is a very effective water disinfectant, but the large quantities create objectionable odor and flavor, and are responsible for the formation of so-called "disinfection byproducts" (DBP) when they react with natural organic matter (NOM). NOM is often found in surface water sources and infrequently found in groundwater sources. Several DBPs are considered to be carcinogens. Chloramines are often used instead of chlorine for disinfection to reduce the formation of DBPs. Chloramines are a family of chlorine and ammonia compounds that are relatively stable in water supplies and they stay effective longer than chlorine. Chloramines are significantly less volatile than chlorine and most water customers notice less chlorine character in the water. However, chloramines are less effective at destroying microbes and a larger dose of the compound is typically required to achieve the same disinfection. Their low volatility and higher dosing makes them more difficult for the brewer to remove. Disinfectant removal will be discussed more in a later chapter.

In the next chapter, we describe a typical (US) water report and discuss most of the items that you need to be concerned with in brewing.

3

How to Read
a Water Report

The best way to use something effectively is to understand it, know what it is made of, and know how it works. Without going into too much detail, it is sufficient to say that water is unique and it derives its unique properties from its molecular shape.

Water is a polar solvent, which means that each water molecule has poles, or negatively and positively charged ends. The hydrogen side of the molecule is more positively charged than the oxygen side, due to the electron distribution. The polarity of the molecule allows it to attract other polar molecules, such as sodium chloride, calcium sulfate, and calcium carbonate. Polar molecules often dissociate (split) into positive and negative ions under the influence of a polar solvent. See the sidebar for the standard solubility rules of common ionic substances in water.

The water molecule is composed of two hydrogen atoms and one oxygen. The shape of the molecule is affected by the sharing of the electrons between the atoms. The two hydrogens each share an electron with the oxygen giving its outer shell a total of 4 complete pairs. These get distributed as far apart as possible around the oxygen nucleus as the corners of a tetrahedron. The presence of the hydrogens distorts the shape a little and the two hydrogens end up being 104.45° apart rather than the normal tetrahedral angle of 109°.

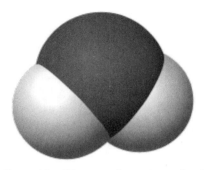

Non-polar molecules do not have poles because the negative and positive charges are well-distributed within the molecule. Water has been called the universal solvent because it dissolves so many substances, both polar and non-polar. As a general rule, non-polar molecules do not dissolve very well in water, but some

Figure 10—Diagram of a water molecule. dissolve slightly. Water can dissolve some non-polar molecules by the process of hydration, which means the water molecules are able to fully surround, or 'wet' these molecules. Carbon dioxide is an example of a non-polar molecule that becomes hydrated by water. Other examples of non-polar molecules with limited solubility are hop alpha acids, benzene, and iodine. Thermal or chemical reactions with other substances can increase the solubility of non-polar molecules, changing the substance from a suspended solid into a dissolved solid.

Table 1—General Solubility Rules for Ionic Compounds in Water

Ion	Rule
Nitrate NO_3^-	All nitrate compounds are soluble.
Chloride Cl^{-1}	All chloride compounds are soluble.
Sulfate SO_4^{-2}	All sulfate compounds are soluble except barium and lead. Calcium, silver, and mercury have limited solubility.
Carbonate CO_3^{-2}	Carbonate compounds are generally insoluble, except sodium, potassium, and ammonium. (For calcium see Chapter 4)
Phosphate PO_4^{-3}	Phosphate compounds are generally insoluble, except sodium, potassium, and ammonium.
Silicate SiO_4^{-4}	Silicate compounds are generally insoluble, except sodium, potassium, and ammonium.

Hydroxide OH^{-1}	Most hydroxide compounds are insoluble, except lithium, sodium, potassium, and ammonium. Barium is moderately soluble. Calcium and strontium have limited solubility.
Sulfide S^{-2}	All sulfide compounds are insoluble, except alkali metal sulfides such as sodium, potassium, ammonium, magnesium, calcium, and barium.
Sodium, Potassium, Ammonium	All sodium, potassium, and ammonium compounds are soluble, except a few compounds which include the addition of a heavy metal, such as K_2PtCl_6.

What is an Ion?

An ion is an atom or group of atoms that has a net positive or negative charge, due to the loss or gain of electron(s). An ionic compound is a polar molecule composed of 2 or more ions that are held together by ionic bonds (i.e., electrostatic attraction). The electrical charge of an ion is indicated as a superscript after the chemical symbol for the ion. Positively charged ions are called cations (pronounced "cat-ions"), and negatively charged ions are called anions (pronounced "an-ions"). For example, the mineral sodium chloride (NaCl) dissolves into the cation Na^{+1} and the anion Cl^{-1}. The hydrated mineral calcium chloride ($CaCl_2 \bullet 2H_2O$) dissociates into 1 Ca^{+2}, 2 Cl^{-1}, and 2 water molecules. Note that the sum of the positive and negative charges for any ionization products from a single compound is always zero. For example, the +2 charge of the calcium and the two -1 charges of the chloride ions sum to zero.

Throughout this text, we will refer to either dissolved minerals and/or ions and mean essentially the same thing—if we refer to a mineral such as calcium sulfate or calcium carbonate being in the water, we are assuming that it is dissolved and dissociated, in accordance with any natural limits such as its solubility constant.

This is also a good point to state that the sum of the dissolved cations and anions in a natural water supply must sum to zero as well. If they do not, it may be that the stated composition is a list of averages, or that it's the result of different tests for different ions taken throughout the year. The point is that the concentrations of charges of dissolved ions in water must sum to zero at any given moment in time. This is addressed more fully in Chapter 6 and Appendix D.

Water Quality Report Parameters

Many minerals and compounds occur naturally in water, dissolving into solution from various environmental sources. Some manmade compounds can also be found in water, but these are usually unwanted and referred to as contaminants. Contaminants can be natural as well: molds, bacteria, nitrates, etc., are all naturally-occurring water contaminants. As we have discussed in the previous chapter, the main purpose of water treatment is to remove these contaminants and the purpose of a water quality report is to inform the public about the types and levels of these substances in the water supply.

We will start our review of a water report by identifying the key constituents—the main ions, chemicals and compounds in typical water supplies. Next, we will show you where to find them on an example of a typical (USA) water report. Actually, there really is no such thing as a typical report. In the USA, the Environmental Protection Agency and the Clean Water Act mandate the testing and disclosure of a specific list of harmful contaminants, which does not include the ions that brewers are most concerned with—calcium, etc. Often these ions are included in a water report, but that decision is up to the water supplier.

Typical water quality reports focus on how the water complies with safe drinking water laws for contaminants like pesticides, micro-organisms, and toxic metals. These items are regulated by maximum contaminant levels (MCL) and referred to as the Primary Drinking Water Standards in the United States. MCLs are legally enforceable standards for water quality that protect public health. While the primary standards are important for assuring water quality, as brewers, we are usually more interested in the Secondary or Aesthetic drinking water standards. Secondary Standards are guidelines for parameters that affect taste, pH, and carbonate scale and are often specified by secondary maximum contaminant levels (SMCL) that are not legally enforceable in the United States.

In many areas, the source of the public water supply can change seasonally, and can often make a big difference in brewing character. Brewers should contact the water department at least monthly to get current information. The water department is usually happy to supply information on the Secondary Standards for brewers. However, not all utilities test for all the parameters brewers are interested in. In that case, the brewer may have to test the water at an external laboratory or perform in-house testing of the parameters. The cost of equipment and reagents for such in-house testing can, however, be prohibitive.

Of the parameters of interest to brewers, the principal ions affecting brewing water performance in mashing and fermentation are calcium (Ca^{+2}), magnesium (Mg^{+2}), and total alkalinity as $CaCO_3$, which is sometimes simply, though inadequately, listed as bicarbonate (HCO_3^{-1}). Their interaction in the mash tun, boil kettle and fermentor influence the pH and other factors throughout the brewing process. Sodium (Na^{+1}), chloride (Cl^{-1}) and sulfate (SO_4^{-2}) can influence the taste of both water and beer, but generally do not affect pH or fermentation performance like the first three ions mentioned above. Ion concentrations in water are typically presented as parts per million (ppm), or milligrams per liter (mg/l), which are generally equivalent in dilute solutions like drinking water, one liter of which weighs about one kilogram.

Table 2—Key Brewing Parameters in Water Quality Report for the Source Water

Primary standards have maximum contaminant levels (MCL) that are legally enforceable requirements in the USA. Secondary Standards are official guidelines and typically have (unenforceable) secondary maximum contaminant levels (SMCL). Unregulated Standards are industry guidelines.

Brewing source water recommendations are indicated in italics. These recommendations are for the source water only. Source water treatment techniques are discussed in more detail in Chapter 8.

Constituent	Category	Parameter (ppm)	Why
Alkalinity (as $CaCO_3$)	Unregulated	*0–100 brewing*	High alkalinity is problematic for mashing and promotes carbonate scale when combined with calcium and magnesium.
Bromate	Primary	<0.01 MCL *<0.01 brewing*	Disinfection byproduct, Industrial contaminant. Possible carcinogen.
Calcium	Unregulated	*50–150 brewing*	Fermentation, Clarity, Mash pH
Chlorine	Primary	<4 MCLG *0 brewing*	Residual disinfectant that can cause off-flavors in beer.

Chloride	Secondary	<250 SMCL *0–100 brewing*	Beer flavor—emphasizes malt character.
Copper	Secondary	<1 SMCL *<1 brewing*	Copper is a toxin at high doses but is otherwise a nutrient. Oxidation catalyst in beer.
Haloacetic Acids (HAA5)	Primary	<0.060 MCL *<0.060 brewing*	Disinfection byproducts and probable carcinogens.
Iron	Secondary	<0.3 SMCL *0 brewing*	Off-flavor, scale, corrosion risk.
Magnesium	Unregulated	*0–40 brewing*	Fermentation, Clarity, Mash pH, but also supplied by malt.
Manganese	Secondary	<0.05 SMCL *0 brewing*	Off-flavor, scale, precipitation causes gushing.
Nitrate as N Nitrate	Primary	<10 MCL(as N) <44 MCL(NO_3) *<44 brewing*	Excessive nitrates can indicate agricultural runoff. Nitrates can be reduced to Nitrites.
Nitrite as N Nitrite	Primary	<1 MCL (as N) <3 MCL (NO_2) *<3 brewing*	Nitrites are a food preservative and as such are poisonous to yeast cells.
Silicate	Secondary	<25 SMCL *<25 brewing*	Scale former and damaging in boiler systems and membrane systems.
Sodium	Unregulated	*0–50 brewing*	Beer flavor—less is generally better.
Sulfate	Secondary	<250 SMCL *0-250 brewing*	Beer flavor—emphasizes hop character and dryness.
Total Dissolved Solids	Secondary	<500 SMCL *<500 brewing*	Increase indicates high mineralization and greater scaling potential
Trihalomethanes (THM)	Primary	<0.1 MCL *<0.1 brewing*	Disinfection byproducts and probable carcinogens.
Turbidity	Secondary	<0.5 ntu SMCL *<0.5 ntu brewing*	Increase indicates contamination and higher scaling potential

Primary Standards

In the following section, many of the substances from the US EPA/Clean Water Act for drinking water are listed with the maximum contaminant level (MCL) requirement. If the level requirement for a particular substance has not been ratified yet, the maximum contaminant level goal (MCLG) is listed. An MCLG is a non-enforceable health goal. Brewing Source Water Guidelines, based on notable brewing texts (see References), are listed for all substances for consistency, even though a specific guideline may not be determined. In those cases, the guideline will be given as "undetermined." In some cases, such as with residual chlorine, the guideline is simply 'as low as possible' and will be listed as "zero goal."

This is not a complete list due to space considerations. Typically rare contaminants like antimony and thallium are left out, as are a multitude of organic contaminants such as Dalapon (herbicide). A complete list can be found at the US EPA website (www.epa.gov).

Arsenic

MCL = 0.01 ppm
Brewing Source Water Guideline = zero goal

The solubility of arsenic in water is so low that its presence usually indicates contamination from mining operations or from soil/rock deposits. In its particulate form, arsenic can be eliminated by conventional filtration through a filter with a rating of 0.45 micron or less. Dissolved arsenic occurs in both organic and inorganic forms. Generally, the inorganic form is more toxic. If it's in an organic form, such as a polymer chain, it can be eliminated by coagulation and filtration or by adsorption in a resin-activated carbon media. If it's in an inorganic form, a number of treatment options exist. These treatment options typically incorporate sorbents (ion exchange, alumina, iron), oxidizers (greensand, chlorination, ozonation), or filtration/precipitation (lime softening, reverse osmosis).

Barium

MCL = 2 ppm
Brewing Source Water Guideline = <2 ppm

The typical solubility limit in most waters for barium is less than 0.1 ppm and it is seldom found at concentrations over 0.05 ppm. It is a primary standard because its soluble compounds are poisonous as a neurotoxin, but it primarily occurs as barium sulfate and barium carbonate, which are very insoluble and non-toxic. In fact, barium sulfate is commonly ingested for x-ray imaging. Barium can be removed from water using ion exchange, reverse osmosis, or lime softening processes.

Bromate/Bromide
MCL = 0.01 ppm
Brewing Source Water Guideline = zero goal

Bromine is typically found in seawater at a concentration of about 65 ppm. It is a common industrial chemical and can be found in industrial waste, pesticides and biocide residue. It is typically only found at very low levels in fresh water, and its presence at concentrations greater than 0.05 ppm may indicate contamination by industrial waste or pesticides. Bromate and bromide are disinfection byproducts. Bromide is oxidized to bromate through disinfection with ozone. Bromide and bromate can be removed from water with ion exchange, activated carbon, and reverse osmosis processes.

Cadmium
MCL = 0.005 ppm
Brewing Source Water Guideline = zero goal

Cadmium is a toxic heavy metal and can occur naturally, but is more likely to occur due to corrosion of galvanized steel, in which it is a trace element. Cadmium is often an industrial pollutant and is used in batteries, paints, and corrosion protection coatings. It can be removed with ion exchange, iron adsorption, or reverse osmosis processes.

Chlorine, Residual
MCL = 4 ppm
Brewing Source Water Guideline = zero goal

This parameter includes chlorine from chloramine additions as well as straight chlorine. Chlorine and chloramines are very effective disinfectants that act by oxidizing the cellular membranes of microorganisms and rupturing the cell. Excess residual chlorine can lead to higher levels of disinfection byproducts that can be hazardous to health and generate off-flavors in beer. Medicinal chlorophenol compounds are one example of an off-flavor. Residual chlorine and chloramine should be removed before use in brewing. Although the maximum residual disinfection limit is 4 ppm, water utilities will occasionally super-chlorinate the supply (ex. late summer) to assure residual disinfection in the distribution piping. Brewers should be aware that additional removal steps may be occasionally required, such as activated carbon filtration or chemical neutralization. Chlorine will oxidize and destroy membrane filtration equipment.

Chromium

MCL = 0.1 ppm
Brewing Source Water Guideline = undetermined

Chromium comes in several forms, but only one form (Cr^{+6}) is known to be a potential carcinogen. This form is only found as a result of industrial contamination, and does not occur naturally. Chromium, like many other trace metals such as zinc, is a human nutritional supplement. Chromium can be removed with ion exchange, iron adsorption, or reverse osmosis processes.

Cyanide

MCL = 0.2 ppm
Brewing Source Water Guideline = zero goal

Industrial pollutant and toxin. Often used in pigments, plastics, and metal plating baths. It can be removed by ion exchange and activated carbon filtration.

Fluoride

MCL = 4 ppm
Brewing Source Water Guideline = zero goal

Fluoride, a halogen like chlorine and iodine, can be found in many minerals. It is commonly added at 1.5–2.5 ppm to potable water to help provide protection against tooth cavities. Concentrations above 5 ppm can cause tooth brittleness and spots. Wastewater from glass, steel, and foundry operations can have much higher concentrations. Lime precipitation can drop high concentrations to 10–20 ppm. Other useful removal processes are reverse osmosis, granular activated carbon, and activated alumina.

Lead

MCLG = 0 ppm

Brewing Source Water Guideline = zero goal

The limit on lead in drinking water is 0.015 ppm, which is easily achievable by modern water treatment plants. The most likely source of lead contamination these days is metallurgical waste or from lead-containing industrial waste. But lead can also appear due to corrosion of lead-containing alloys such as brass or structural solder. Modern plumbing solder is a tin-silver alloy and does not contain lead. The lead levels in brass are typically low, less than 5% by weight. All brass plumbing fittings in the US after 2014 will be required to be lead-free, and will be stamped NL. Lead is most readily dissolved by caustics. Lead can also dissolve and bind with organics, which necessitates oxidation for complete removal. Lead can be removed by lime softening, ion exchange, or reverse osmosis processes.

Mercury

MCL = 0.002 ppm

Brewing Source Water Guideline = zero goal

Mercury is typically an industrial pollutant, but can occur naturally. It can be reduced by lime softening, ion exchange, reverse osmosis or activated carbon processes.

Nitrate

MCL = 44 ppm

Brewing Source Water Guideline = <44 ppm

Nitrates come into water from the nitrogen cycle (plants) or from agricultural runoff as fertilizer. Nitrates can be converted to nitrites under anaerobic conditions (i.e., fermentation), poisoning the yeast cells and disrupting the fermentation cycle. Nitrates are also injurious to human health via a similar mechanism. Nitrates are particularly hazardous to infants, but are tolerated at higher concentrations by children and adults. Some laboratories report nitrate as nitrogen and that is typically denoted (NO_3–N). 1 ppm (NO_3–N) is equal to 4.43 ppm (NO_3^{-1}). Nitrates can be removed by ion-exchange, or reverse osmosis processes. Carbon filtration is not effective.

Nitrite

MCL = 3 ppm

Brewing Source Water Guideline = <3 ppm

Nitrites are used in curing meats and can reduce the iron in hemoglobin from ferrous to ferric, which decreases the ability to transport oxygen throughout the human body. Nitrites are particularly hazardous to infants, but are tolerated at higher concentrations by children and adults. Nitrites can be removed by ion exchange, or reverse osmosis processes. Carbon filtration is not effective.

PCE

MCL = 0.005 ppm

Brewing Source Water Guideline = zero goal

Tetrochloroethylene, otherwise known as PCE, or PERC, is a colorless industrial solvent predominantly used by dry-cleaners and metal finishers. The major source of PCE in drinking water is discharge from factories and dry-cleaners. Long-term exposure to higher levels can lead to liver damage and an increased risk of cancer. Actually there are 21 volatile organic compounds like PCE that also have MCL. PCE is one of the more common and cited here for example. PCE can be removed with an activated carbon process.

TCE

MCL = 0.005 ppm

Brewing Source Water Guideline = zero goal

Trichloroethylene (TCE) is an industrial solvent and was commonly used as a metal degreaser for the last 50 years, although its use is now highly restricted due to its high vaporization and solubility in groundwater. TCE exposure has similar effects to PCE carrying increased risk of cancer and liver/kidney damage. TCE can be removed with an activated carbon process.

Total Coliform Bacteria

MCL = <5% Detection in Samples Tested

Brewing Source Water Guideline = zero goal

The presence of coliform bacteria indicates contamination of the water supply by human waste, sewage, or stormwater. Not a health threat in and of itself, but it is tested for as indicator for the presence of other potentially harmful bacteria such as cholera. Heating or disinfectant use are typically effective in coliform destruction.

Total Haloacetic Acids (HAA5)

MCL = 0.06 ppm

Brewing Source Water Guideline = zero goal

Haloacetic acids are a disinfection byproduct and have been linked to an increased risk of cancer. Haloacetic acids are formed when hydrogen atoms in acetic acid, CH_3COOH, are replaced by atoms from the halogen group. The five most common in water are referred to as HAA5, which are monochloroacetic acid (MCA) $ClCH_2COOH$, dichloroacetic acid (DCA) $Cl_2CHCOOH$, trichloroacetic acid (TCA) Cl_3CCOOH, monobromoacetic acid (MBA) $BrCH_2COOH$ and dibromoacetic acid (DBA) $Br_2CHCOOH$. Reverse osmosis or activated carbon filtration are effective removal methods.

Total Trihalomethanes (TTHM)

MCL = 0.08 ppm

Brewing Source Water Guideline = zero goal

Trihalomethanes are chlorinated organic compounds principally found in water as disinfection byproducts. Specifically, these substances are chloroform, dibromochloromethane, bromodichloromethane and bromoform. Formation is encouraged by water containing organic precursors, pre-chlorination treatment, and (residual) free chlorine. Animal studies (at much higher levels than requirement) have linked long term exposure to effects on the central nervous system, liver, kidneys, and heart. Aeration, oxidation, or activated carbon filtration are effective removal methods.

Turbidity

Brewing Source Water Guideline = 0–0.5 Nephelometric Turbidity Unit (NTU)

Turbidity is a measure of water clarity as a function of suspended solids in water. These solids include fine sand, silt, clay, decomposed vegetation, algae, bacteria, etc. Turbidity is an indicator of how well the water was filtered prior to distribution. Elevated turbidity increases the opportunity for unsafe water quality. Turbidity can be reduced by standard filtration processes.

Turbidity can be measured several ways. The preferred method is the nephelometric turbidity unit or NTU, which shines a focused incandescent light source at a sample and measures the intensity of the light scattered at right angles to the sample. A previous method, the Jackson turbidity unit, utilized a candle and measured transmittance of the light through the sample.

Secondary Standards

Aluminum
SMCL = 0.2 ppm
Brewing Source Water Guideline = <0.2 ppm
Aluminum metal is relatively insoluble in drinking water so the presence of aluminum ions is most likely due to coagulation and flocculation treatments using aluminum salts. Aluminum phosphates, silicates, and oxide deposits can be problematic in cooling water systems. Aluminum is most soluble at both low (<4) and high pH (>10).

Chloride (ion)
SMCL = 250 ppm
Brewing Source Water Guideline = 0–100 ppm.
Chloride is common in most water supplies. The chloride ion helps accentuate the malt sweetness and fullness of beer, but levels greater than 250 ppm in most beers tastes pasty or salty. Levels greater than 300 ppm are said to affect yeast health. Elevated chloride levels may lead to a minerally or salty flavor when combined with sulfate or sodium. Chloride is not related to residual chlorine and does not have the same disinfection effect.

Copper
SMCL = 1 ppm
Brewing Source Water Guideline = <1 ppm
The most common source of copper in water is from corrosion of brass and copper plumbing, or it may be residual from copper sulfate additions to control algae in the reservoir. Copper is toxic at high concentrations, but 200 milligrams per kilogram of bodyweight is the lowest lethal dose. Small amounts of copper are beneficial in brewing wort to reduce sulfides and other sulfur compounds like H_2S in the beer. Yeast are very good

scavengers of copper because it is an essential nutrient, and residual copper is typically not found in beer. Excess copper can be reduced by lime softening, ion exchange, or reverse osmosis processes.

Iron
SMCL = 0.3 ppm
Brewing Source Water Guideline = zero goal

The most soluble form of iron is ferrous (Fe^{+2}). Iron in water tastes metallic or bloodlike. High iron levels can lead to corrosion of stainless steel piping, particularly in combination with chlorides and sulfides. Iron can be removed by filtration after aeration and oxidation. It can also be removed with ion exchange or reverse osmosis processes.

Manganese
SMCL = 0.05 ppm
Brewing Source Water Guideline = <0.1 ppm

Manganese is present in many soils and is readily dissolved in water that is free of oxygen. Manganese will accumulate in sediments and can be found in higher concentrations in deep water wells. It is a difficult metal to deal with because it readily complexes with organic materials, and can later precipitate with changes in pH, carbonate species equilibrium, or oxygen levels. Water sources that pull from deeper parts of lakes may have significantly higher levels of manganese where oxygen levels are lower. These levels can vary seasonally due to thermal inversion in the spring and fall, diminishing when oxygenated water from the surface mixes with the water at the bottom. At relatively high levels (>2 ppm), manganese has been linked to gushing due to precipitation, but is a necessary yeast nutrient at low levels (<0.2 ppm) and is usually adequately supplied by the malt. Manganese causes a very metallic taste in water, even at low concentrations (0.1 ppm). Manganese can be removed by filtration after oxidation, ion exchange, greensand, or reverse osmosis processes.

pH (Water)
SCML = 6.5–8.5
Brewing Source Water Guideline = 5–9.5

The US EPA recommends a water pH of 6.5–8.5 for potable water suppliers and recommends 5.5–11 for wastewater discharge prior to treatment. Discharge beyond these limits requires pretreatment. pH is discussed further below. In general, the pH of the water supply has little effect on brewing. The pH of the water supply can give clues about the origin and treatment of the water before it arrives at the brewery. The guideline here provides caution against extreme pH conditions in the water supply.

Sulfate

SMCL = 250 ppm
Brewing Source Water Guideline = 0–250 ppm

The sulfate ion accentuates hop bitterness, making the bitterness seem drier and more crisp. At concentrations over 400 ppm however, the resulting bitterness can become astringent and unpleasant. Sulfate is only weakly alkaline and does not contribute to the overall alkalinity of water. It is recommended that the source water be lower rather than higher in sulfate because it can always be added, and is not readily removed. Sulfate salts are generally very soluble, but can be removed by ion exchange or reverse osmosis processes.

Total Dissolved Solids (TDS)

SMCL = 500 ppm
Brewing Source Water Guideline = <500 ppm

The total dissolved solids (TDS) are what is left behind when water is evaporated. Some are salts, some are organics, and some are chemical residues. The TDS of the water is useful for industrial purposes, but it is not terribly useful for describing the suitability of brewing water. The TDS value is just a quick indicator of how mineralized a potential water source is. In general, a water with high TDS tends to produce more carbonate scale than a water with low TDS. Water with high TDS tends to be more corrosive than water with low TDS, although corrosivity greatly depends on the specific materials involved. Monitoring the TDS of the source water with a conductance test is a good way to be alerted to a sudden change in the water supply source.

Total Dissolved Solids (TDS) Testing

TDS is determined in the laboratory. A water sample is filtered to remove any suspended materials that could skew the test. A measured volume of the filtered water is then heated to evaporate all the water, leaving behind the dissolved content. The mass of the dissolved content is measured and divided by the initial volume of the sample to determine a result, typically expressed as milligrams per liter (mg/L). In the dilute solutions typical for drinking water, mg/L is generally equivalent to parts per million (ppm).

TDS can also be estimated via the conductivity characteristics of the water. A specialized meter is used to measure the solution's conductivity. That conductivity value can then be correlated to an estimate of the solution's TDS with the following equation:

TDS (ppm) = Conductivity (μS/cm) x F

Where: F is a conversion factor that typically varies between 0.54 and 0.96, with a typical value of 0.67. Conductivity is measured in micro-Siemens (μS) per centimeter or micro-mhos per cm.

TDS meters that provide a direct reading of TDS are conductivity meters that include the conversion equation above. TDS meters can provide valuable quality assurance checks on incoming tap water or on treatment effectiveness of demineralization processes (RO, nanofiltration, etc.).

Zinc

SMCL = 5 ppm
Brewing Source Water Guideline = 0.1–0.5 ppm

Zinc metal is generally less soluble in water than calcium but dissolves readily in acids. Natural zinc levels in drinking water are normally less than 1 ppm, typically near 0.05 ppm. The SMCL for zinc of 5 ppm is based on its taste threshold. An astringent taste can be noted at that level. However, zinc is a vital yeast nutrient and recommended levels in wort for optimum fermentation are 0.1–0.5 ppm. Concentrations greater than 0.5 ppm can cause over-activity and off-flavors in beer. Zinc is commonly used in proprietary corrosion inhibitor products. Zinc can be removed from water with ion exchange, lime softening, or reverse osmosis processes.

Unregulated/Aesthetic Standards

Boron

Brewing Source Water Guideline = undetermined

Boron behaves like silicon in most aqueous systems and is not known to be hazardous. It is used for pH adjustment and buffering in closed-loop cooling systems.

Calcium

Brewing Source Water Guideline = 50–150 ppm.

Calcium is typically the principal ion that determines hardness in drinking water. Calcium is instrumental to many yeast, enzyme, and protein reactions, both in the mash and in the boil. It reacts with malt phosphate in the mash to precipitate calcium phosphates and release hydrogen ions, which in turn lower the mash pH. Calcium promotes clarity, flavor, and stability in the finished beer. It promotes protein coagulation and yeast flocculation. Calcium additions may be necessary to assure sufficient enzyme activity for mashes in water that is low in calcium. On the other hand, too high a concentration of calcium in wort (ex. >250 ppm, due to gypsum additions) can inhibit magnesium uptake by the yeast and may impair fermentation performance.

Calcium concentration may be reported in a variety of units. These include: as $CaCO_3$, degrees Clark, German degrees, French degrees, Grains per US gallon, milliequivalents per liter, or millivals. In these cases, the reported concentration would require conversion to an actual calcium concentration in ppm. Conversions are given in Chapter 4.

Calcium is essentially flavor neutral but it can reduce the somewhat sour flavor perception of magnesium. The recommended calcium concentration in brewing water is 50–150 ppm. However, beer can be successfully brewed with more or less calcium than this suggested range.

Oxalate is present in barley malt and reacts with calcium to form beerstone. Calcium oxalate can precipitate at any point in the brewing process, but it is a particular problem if it precipitates in the beer package because the calcium oxalate crystals act as gas nucleation sites and cause foaming and gushing. It is recommended that the water have sufficient calcium (i.e., 3 times more than oxalate in the malt) to initiate precipitation earlier in the process, such as in the mash tun and kettle, instead of during fermentation or packaging.

Calcium and magnesium concentrations are often referred to as being temporary or permanent hardness. Temporary hardness can be removed by boiling or lime softening, where it combines with bicarbonate to precipitate as calcium carbonate ($CaCO_3$). This is the origin of the unit "as $CaCO_3$." If the alkalinity as $CaCO_3$ is greater than the hardness as $CaCO_3$, then all of the hardness is temporary. If the hardness as $CaCO_3$ is greater than the alkalinity as $CaCO_3$, then some of the hardness will remain after boiling, and that is permanent hardness. Other calcium removal processes include ion exchange and reverse osmosis.

Magnesium

Brewing Source Water Guideline = 0–40 ppm.

This ion behaves similarly to calcium in water, but is less effective at reducing mash pH by reacting with phosphate. Magnesium is an important yeast nutrient for yeast pyruvate decarboxylase metabolism and should be present in the wort at a minimum level of 5 ppm. A 10° Plato (1.040) all-malt wort made with distilled water was measured as having 70 ppm Mg, so it is reasonable to assume that an all-malt wort will supply all of the magnesium the yeast could want. It is possible that a wort with high amounts of refined sugars or adjuncts may need a minor magnesium addition to provide the 5 ppm minimum. Levels higher than 125 ppm have a laxative and diuretic affect on the drinker. Although magnesium is generally unneeded in brewing water, it may be added to enhance the beer's character with its sour, astringent flavor. Magnesium can be removed from water with lime softening, ion exchange, or reverse osmosis processes.

As indicated above for calcium, magnesium concentration may be reported in a variety of units. If the concentration is not reported as the actual magnesium ion concentration in ppm, it will require conversion to this more useful unit.

Phosphate

Brewing Source Water Guideline = undetermined (but should be low)

Phosphates are not part of the standard guidelines in source water but they can be both a contaminant and a common additive in water treatment. Contamination typically comes from agricultural runoff and industrial waste and can be treated with aluminum or iron salts to render it insoluble for removal by filtration.

Phosphate compounds are prevalent in malt and wort. High residual phosphate levels are common in brewery wastewater and those can be treated both aerobically and anaerobically. Phosphate can also be removed by ion exchange or reverse osmosis processes.

Potassium

Brewing Source Water Guideline = <10 ppm

Potassium salt's solubility is very similar to sodium, but it is much less prevalent in natural water supplies. High potassium levels in source water may be due to excess silt, i.e., water with high turbidity. Potassium ions can taste salty at concentrations greater than 500 ppm. Wort and beer have a relatively high natural concentration of potassium (300–500 ppm), contributed by the malt. Therefore potassium-softened water is potentially just as bad for brewing as sodium-softened. However it may be preferred to sodium salts as a means of increasing the anion content of beers if initial malt contribution levels permit. Potassium can be removed by reverse osmosis.

Silica

Brewing Source Water Guideline = <25 ppm

Silica is ubiquitous in water supplies and many minerals but it can also be extracted as silicate from grain husks. High levels can cause slow runoff during lauter and haze in beer. Most silica in water exists as colloidal silica, meaning that it exists as small polymeric chains of varying sizes. The very small chains tend to be dissolved in solution, and the large as suspensions. These colloids can be concentrated by evaporation in boilers. Treatment processes that remove silica include adsorption on magnesium precipitates in lime softening, adsorption on ferric hydroxide in coagulation processes using iron salts, anion exchange in the demineralization process, and reverse osmosis. Silica can combine with calcium and magnesium to produce heavy scale in pipes and can foul reverse osmosis membranes. If reverse osmosis is used to reduce high levels (>30 ppm), then the recovery should be limited to less than 50% to avoid premature fouling.

Sodium

Brewing Source Water Guideline = 0–50 ppm.

Sodium can occur in very high levels in drinking water, particularly if the water is softened with a salt-based (i.e. ion exchange) water softener. In general, softened water is not suitable for brewing, although there may be the rare case where controlled softening is useful for iron and manganese removal despite an increase in sodium. For sodium levels of 70–150 ppm, it rounds out the beer flavors and accentuates the sweetness of the malt, especially in association with chloride ions. Sodium ions can contribute a salty taste at concentrations of 150 to 200 ppm and may taste harsh and sour in excess, especially when greater than 250 ppm. Brewing with lower sodium concentrations will generally produce a cleaner flavor in beer. The combination of high sodium and a high concentration of sulfate ions will generate a very harsh, sour/bitter minerally flavor.

Specific Conductance

Brewing Source Water Guideline = undetermined

Specific conductance or conductivity is a general measurement of the ability of a solution to conduct an electric current, and is dependent on both the type and quantity of dissolved substances. It does not work well for comparing different water sources, but is useful for gauging variation from a single water source, because it can be correlated to TDS. Pure water would theoretically have a conductivity of zero, but it is slightly dissociated at pH 7 and tends to be about 1 micro-mho/cm. Seawater has a typical conductivity of about 37,200 micro-mhos/cm. (A mho is the inverse of an ohm—the unit for electrical resistance.)

Total Alkalinity

Brewing Source Water Guideline = <100 ppm

The alkalinity is arguably the most important parameter to the brewer, because it has the biggest effect on mash performance. Total alkalinity is defined as the amount of strong acid, in milliequivalents per liter, required to convert the carbonate and bicarbonate in the sample to carbon dioxide, at 4.3 pH.

Depending on the initial pH of the water sample, both the carbonate alkalinity and bicarbonate portions of the alkalinity can be part of the titration and the sum defines the total alkalinity. If the initial water pH is higher than 8.3, the carbonate alkalinity is defined as the amount of acid required to titrate to pH 8.3. This is referred to as the P Alkalinity and is typically measured using phenolphthalein indicator solution. If the initial water pH is less than 8.3, the carbonate contribution is not significant and the sample is typically titrated using methyl orange indicator, which has a color range of 3.2–4.4 pH. This bicarbonate-dominated portion of the titration is referred to the M Alkalinity. The Total Alkalinity is the sum of P Alkalinity and M Alkalinity. The total volume of acid required to reach the 4.3 pH endpoint is converted to mEq/liter and multiplied by the equivalent weight of 50 to obtain the typical unit of "total alkalinity, ppm as $CaCO_3$."

However, the methyl orange color change that determines the 4.3 pH endpoint is said to be subtle and difficult to observe accurately. The current ISO standard specifies the use of bromocresol green–methyl red indicator solution with the endpoint defined as 4.5 pH. The decision for which pH endpoint to use is up to the lab, but the ISO standard is 4.5. The difference in the calculated Total Alkalinity for these endpoints is not large; it's about 5%. That accuracy is probably better than the resolution of most of the aquarium or swimming pool dropper-style test kits, and is comparable to the error potentially introduced in the lab by volume measurement of the sample and reagents. Contacting the laboratory is recommended if the endpoint or indicator is not specified in the alkalinity result. See Chapter 4 for further explanation of alkalinity.

Total Hardness

Brewing Source Water Guideline = 150–500 ppm as $CaCO_3$

Total hardness as $CaCO_3$ is generally equal to the sum of the two primary constituents, calcium and magnesium, measured as $CaCO_3$, according to the equation:

$$Total\ Hardness = 50*([Ca]/20 + [Mg]/12.1)$$

where the brackets [ ] indicate the concentration of the ion species in ppm.

This equation converts the individual concentrations to their as-$CaCO_3$ equivalent. Other divalent metal ions such as iron, manganese, chromium, zinc, etc., also contribute to hardness if present in significant amounts, and would be added to the total in a like manner. Calcium and magnesium are the most prevalent hardness constituents in typical drinking water.

An example of a typical water report from a utility is presented below:

Table 3—Los Angeles Metropolitan Water District Quality Report from LA Aqueduct Filtration Plant (2010 data)

Parameter	Maximum Contaminant Level (mg/L)*	Delivered Average (mg/L)
Primary Standards		
Total Coliform (detection)	5% of samples	0.9%
Polychlorinated Biphenyls (PCB)	0.0005	ND
Tetrachloroethylene (PCE)	0.005	<0.0005
Trichloroethylene (TCE)	0.005	<0.0005
Total Haloacetic Acids (HAA)	0.06	0.027
Total Trihalomethanes (THM)	0.08	0.056
Aluminum	1	<0.05
Arsenic	0.05	0.004
Barium	1	<0.1
Bromate	0.01	<0.005
Cadmium	0.005	ND
Copper	(zero)	ND
Fluoride	2	0.8
Lead	(zero)	ND
Mercury	0.002	ND
Nitrate (as NO_3)	45	<2
Nitrate + Nitrite (as N)	1	<0.4
Uranium (picocuries/liter)	20	3

Parameter	Maximum Contaminant Level (mg/L)*	Delivered Average (mg/L)
Secondary Standards—Aesthetic		
Chloride	(250)	42
Color	(15)	3.5
Foaming Agents	(0.5)	ND
Iron	(0.3)	ND
Manganese	(0.05)	<0.02
pH	(6.5–8.5)	7.4
Silver	(0.1)	ND
Sulfate	(250)	33
Total Dissolved Solids	(500)	226
Turbidity (NTU)	(5)	<0.1
Zinc	(5)	<0.05
Unregulated Parameters		
Calcium	undetermined	25
Magnesium	undetermined	8
Phosphate	undetermined	0.051
Potassium	undetermined	4
Silica	undetermined	17
Sodium	undetermined	45
Total Alkalinity as $CaCO_3$	undetermined	106
Total Hardness as $CaCO_3$	undetermined	93
Total Organic Carbon		1.5

* ( ) = Recommended Level, ND = Not Detected

What is a Mole?

The term "mole" is derived from "gram molecule" and is used to describe an equal quantity of chemical "things," be they atoms or molecules (or ions or electron charges). It is useful to chemists for describing the quantities of things involved in a chemical reaction. Therefore, we can say that 2 moles of hydrogen react with 1 mole of oxygen to produce 1 mole of water.

Interestingly, the mole was developed with the advent of atomic theory as scientists were quantifying atomic mass, and there were at least three candidates for the standard, namely hydrogen, oxygen, and carbon. Eventually, the isotope carbon 12 was chosen, and a mole was defined as the number of atoms in 12 grams of carbon 12. Therefore Avogadro's number is defined as being the number of atoms in 1 mole of carbon 12, and that number has been experimentally determined to be $6.02214078 \times 10^{23}$ +/- 1.8×10^{17}.

An isotope of an element has the same number of protons in its nucleus as the parent element, but a different number of neutrons. Isotopes are identified by the total number of protons and neutrons in the nucleus. For example, the nomenclature Carbon 12 means that the atom contains 6 neutrons in addition to the 6 protons, signified by its atomic number, 6.

Water Hardness, Alkalinity, and Milliequivalents

Hardness and alkalinity of water are often expressed "as $CaCO_3$" because when 100 mg of calcium carbonate is dissolved in one liter of water using carbonic acid (imitating the way nature dissolves limestone), the calcium hardness and alkalinity (as measured by standard methods) will each be 100 ppm. Water Hardness is often listed on water quality reports as "Hardness as $CaCO_3$" or "Total Hardness" and is defined as the sum of the calcium and magnesium ion concentrations in milliequivalents per liter (mEq/l) multiplied by 50 (the "equivalent weight" of $CaCO_3$). Water hardness is often measured with a chelating-type test, where a chemical agent such as EDTA is used to bind and precipitate all of the cations out of the solution. This mass is weighed and that weight per volume is the total hardness for the solution. Iron, manganese, and other metals can also be counted in the chelating test, such that the total hardness number on a water report is often greater than the sum of the calcium and magnesium as $CaCO_3$.

An "equivalent" is defined as the amount of a substance that will either supply or react with one mole of hydrogen atoms in an acid-base reaction or with one mole of electrons in an oxidation-reduction reaction. If the ion has a greater charge (ex. 2), then a mole of that substance is defined as containing (2) equivalents. Therefore the equivalent weight of a substance is equal to the mole weight divided by the number of equivalents it supplies. Usually the number of equivalents of a substance is equal to its valence charge, as in the case of calcium, although some substances change with pH and this will be discussed in Chapter 6. The equivalent weight of Ca^{+2} is half of its atomic weight of 40, i.e. 20. Therefore if you divide the calcium concentration in ppm or mg/l of Ca^{+2} by 20, you have the number of milliequivalents per liter of Ca^{+2}.

The Total Alkalinity is defined as the total volume of acid required titrate a water sample to reach the (typical) endpoint of pH 4.5, converted to mEq/liter and multiplied by the equivalent weight of 50 to obtain the typical unit of "ppm as $CaCO_3$." In most public water supplies in the US, with a water pH of about 8.3, the total alkalinity is equal to the M Alkalinity, i.e., the amount of alkalinity solely due to bicarbonate $[HCO_3^{-1}]$, converted by the ratio of equivalent weights. In other words, you can convert from bicarbonate concentration in ppm to Total Alkalinity as $CaCO_3$ by multiplying the bicarbonate by 50/61. See Table 4 below. If your local water analysis does not list the bicarbonate ion concentration (ppm), or "Alkalinity as $CaCO_3$", then you will need to call the water department and ask to speak to one of the engineers, or someone in the lab. They should have that information.

Equivalent weights are the key to understanding how the calcium ion concentration in ppm relates to the "Total Hardness as $CaCO_3$" number. The conversion factor is the equivalent weight of the substance. The concept of equivalents and equivalent weight gets more complicated with other substances like copper and iron—elements that have several different oxidation states (ex. Cu^{+1}, Cu^{+2}, and Fe^{+2}, Fe^{+3}). These elements each have two equivalent weights, depending on the other substances in the reaction. But that is beside the point.

As an example, to calculate the total hardness as $CaCO_3$ of a water sample from the cation concentrations, you would first convert those

Table 4—Conversion Factors for Ion Concentrations

To Get	From	Do This
Ca^{+2} (mEq/l)	Ca^{+2} (ppm)	Divide by 20
Mg^{+2} (mEq/l)	Mg^{+2} (ppm)	Divide by 12.1
HCO_3^{-1} (mEq/l)	HCO_3^{-1} (ppm)	Divide by 61
$CaCO_3$ (mEq/l)	$CaCO_3$ (ppm)	Divide by 50
Ca^{+2} (ppm)	Ca^{+2} (mEq/l)	Multiply by 20
Ca^{+2} (ppm)	Ca Hardness as $CaCO_3$	Divide by 50 and multiply by 20
Mg^{+2} (ppm)	Mg^{+2} (mEq/l)	Multiply by 12.1
Mg^{+2} (ppm)	Mg Hardness as $CaCO_3$	Divide by 50 and multiply by 12.1
HCO_3^{-1} (ppm) (@ pH 8-8.6)	Alkalinity as $CaCO_3$	Divide by 50 and multiply by 61
Ca Hardness as $CaCO_3$	Ca^{+2} (ppm)	Divide by 20 and multiply by 50
Mg Hardness as $CaCO_3$	Mg^{+2} (ppm)	Divide by 12.1 and multiply by 50
Total Hardness as $CaCO_3$	Ca as $CaCO_3$ and Mg as $CaCO_3$	Add them
Alkalinity as $CaCO_3$	$HCO3^{-1}$ (ppm) (@ pH 8-8.6)	Divide by 61 and multiply by 50

ppm quantities to equivalents. (Actually milliequivalents, since an equivalent is generally measured in moles (i.e., grams) per liter and parts-per-million are milligrams per liter.) So, the first step is to divide both the calcium and magnesium ion concentrations in ppm by their equivalent weight, yielding their concentrations in milliequivalents per liter. The conversion factor between calcium hardness and calcium carbonate hardness is the inverse ratio of their equivalent weights, i.e., 50/20. Since the total hardness as calcium carbonate is defined as being the sum of the calcium and magnesium hardness, the milliequivalents of calcium and magnesium are added together, and multiplied by 50 (the equivalent weight of $CaCO_3$) to yield the total hardness as milliequivalents per liter of $CaCO_3$.

$$(Ca^{+2} \, (ppm)/20 + Mg^{+2} \, (ppm)/12.1) \times 50 = \text{Total Hardness as } CaCO_3$$
Similar conversion factors are summarized in Table 4.

To summarize, there may be hundreds of substances in the water supply, but only a couple dozen that really matter to the brewer. The water hardness and alkalinity affect the mash pH and mash pH will be discussed further in Chapters 4 and 5. Optimizing water chemistry for each of the brewing processes and other uses will be addressed in Chapters 6, 7, 8, and 9.

References

1. ISO standard 9963-1: *Water Quality – Determination of Alkalinity, Part 1 – Determination of Total and Composite Alkalinity* (1994).

2. *Standard Methods for Water and Waste Water Treatment* – Alkalinity, American Water Works Association, 1999.

3. Faust, S.D., Osman, M.A., *Chemistry of Water Treatment*, 2nd Ed., CRC Press, 1998.

4. Benjamin, M.M., *Water Chemistry*, Waveland Press, 2010.

5. Flynn, D.J., Ed., *The Nalco Water Handbook*, 3rd Ed., McGraw Hill, 2009.

6. Eumann, M., *Brewing – New Technologies, C. Bamforth, Ed.*, Ch. 9 – Water in Brewing, CRC Press, 2006.

7. Taylor, D., *Handbook of Brewing*, 2nd Ed., F. Priest, G. Stewart, Ed., Ch. 4 – Water, CRC Press, 2006.

4

Residual Alkalinity
and the Mash

In the previous chapters, we have discussed water sources, water composition, and water treatment methods. We also pointed out that water pH is only one piece of the puzzle, because in order to understand your brewing water, you need to know the pH *and* the composition of the water. The minerals in the water have a more significant effect on the mashing process than the water pH does because they include a buffer system. A buffer is a substance in the solution that resists changes in pH. The stronger the buffer, the more it will resist a pH change (meaning more H^{+1} or OH^{-1} ions will be needed to cause the pH to change). Measuring the pH of water without knowing the quantity of the buffer system is like measuring voltage on an unknown battery. Voltage alone does not tell us how long the battery will last. Likewise, knowing the water pH without knowing the quantity of buffer in the water will not help us predict the pH response of the mash. The only buffer in potable brewing water is alkalinity via the carbonic, bicarbonate, and carbonate equilibrium. The other buffer, phosphate, comes from the malt. It is the interaction of these two buffer systems with calcium and magnesium that determines how hard you have to work to change the mash pH. (There is another group of buffers, malt melanoidins, which also have significant effects on mash pH—that effect will be discussed in Chapter 5.)

Why is mash pH more important than water pH? Because the best beers are produced when a mash is controlled within fairly narrow ranges of temperature and pH. pH is the result of a chemical equilibrium—it is a test output. Water pH is the result of the equilibrium of the chemical reactions that occurred in the water. The mash pH is the result of equilibrium in the mash, which is what we want to control. The water and the malts are the new reaction components and the mash pH is a measurement of the reaction product. Although it is confusing, the mash pH is both a factor for mash performance *and* the result of that performance. To help understand this, take a step back and consider that the hydrogen ion concentration (the pH) at any given time is a result of the chemical equilibrium of that system. Therefore, the performance of the mash i.e., optimum enzyme activity and conditions that are favorable for it, are also the result of that same chemistry. Therefore we can discuss enzyme activity and mash performance as a function of mash pH, because we have a good understanding of the chemistry that drives it. The water pH, by itself, is *not* a factor for mash performance, because it is the measurement of different and unrelated reactions. Ok? Ok.

In this chapter, we introduce the concept of residual alkalinity and how it affects mash pH. The pH of the mash is important because it is a significant factor for enzyme activity and it influences the final pH of the beer. Perhaps David Taylor said it best in *The Importance of pH Control During Brewing*[1]: "The key point for control of pH throughout the brewing process is during mashing. This is due to the major influence that can be exerted at this stage on the content and format of the buffer systems that will operate subsequently in the wort and beer." So, what is the ideal pH for the mash? That is a very good question. In a *Textbook of Brewing*,[2] Jean De Clerck notes that the pH of a base-malt mash made with distilled water is "normally about 5.8." This value refers to the cooled wort. De Clerck notes that the measured wort pH decreases with increasing temperature, citing the work of Hopkins and Krause. The decrease in pH is roughly linear with temperature and the difference is 0.34 between 18 and 65°C with distilled water, and 0.33 with "medium hard water" for the same temperatures. This means that there is a consistent offset between the pH of wort at mashing and room temperatures. Since most technical studies have used the room-temperature standard for measuring wort pH and room-temperature measurements are gentler on analytical equipment, the room-temperature standard for measurement and reporting is used throughout this book.

De Clerck does not state what the optimum mash pH is. He only states that, "The majority of enzymes exhibit their greatest activity at a pH lower than that of wort, which is normally about 5.8. On this account, the mash is often acidified to reduce the pH to 5.0–5.2, which is more suitable for proteolysis and the breakdown of organic phosphates." This statement must be qualified by noting that De Clerck was speaking in reference to the Continental Pilsner and Munich malts of the day (c. 1950) which had a soluble-to-total protein ratio of 29.8% and 38.8% respectively, compared to British Pale malt which he considered to be highly or over-modified. No number was given for the British Pale malt, but it probably was about 40%. In other words, less-modified malts benefitted from lower mash pH to optimize proteolysis, and thereby improve total extract and free amino nitrogen (FAN).

Wolfgang Kunze in *Technology Brewing and Malting*,[3] states that the optimum pH range for the amylases and starch degradation is 5.5–5.6 because the total extract and attenuation limit is higher compared to the "normal" mash pH range of 5.6–5.9. He indicates that "normal" is dependent upon the malt and brewing water composition. Later in the text, he states that the benefits of lowering the mash pH include shortening and optimization of the mashing process, more rapid lautering, better yield, better color stability, better fermentation, and better foam. In summary, he states that brewers should control the pH so that the mash has a pH range of 5.4–5.6 and the final wort pH after boiling should be 5.1–5.2.

In *pH in Brewing: An Overview*,[4] Charles Bamforth notes that the optimum pH for the various proteolytic and saccharification enzymes seems to vary substantially with the substrate chosen by the researchers for the experiment, and suggests that the heat stability of the enzymes is more important to their efficacy than pH. However, Bamforth also notes that pH seems to have a strong effect on the extraction of enzymes from the malt, as demonstrated by the work of Stenholm and Home,[5] who showed that dropping the mash pH from 5.7 to 5.4 increased the extraction of limit dextrinase. Additionally, the method of pH reduction seems to be a significant factor: that calcium additions seem to have a more synergistic affect on mash performance as a whole versus mineral or organic acid additions. To illustrate these effects, the mash lautering or filtration performance optimum pH was 5.5–5.7 in one experiment using calcium salts versus 4.4–4.6 in another using acid additions.

In summary, these resources indicate an "optimum" room-temperature mash pH target range of anywhere from 5.0 to 5.6. The low end of this range is probably not as applicable as it once was since today's highly modified malts reduce the need for proteolysis. Therefore, the target mash pH range should probably be 5.2–5.6. However, the brewer can pick a value within that range that seems to best suit their beer. The brewer should also try to control mash pH to a tighter tolerance of +/-0.1 pH to assure consistency.

There are many factors that affect mash pH, and several of them are based on the barley variety and the malting process—factors that are typically out of the brewer's control. The best the brewer can do is find a consistent, high-quality source for the malt and focus on the factors he can control, namely the brewing water composition, salt and/or acid additions, and consistency of sampling and measurement methods. The key factor to understanding the effect of brewing water composition and adjustment is residual alkalinity. Residual alkalinity (RA) is the interplay of water hardness and alkalinity in the mash, and that concept will be presented below.

Water Alkalinity

The first step to understanding residual alkalinity is understanding how alkalinity gets into water in the first place. It is a two-part system that is controlled by the pressure of available carbon dioxide gas in the air. The alkalinity of water is determined by the carbonate content, which is formed when acidic groundwater (i.e., water with dissolved CO_2) reacts with chalk ($CaCO_3$) or dolomite ($CaMg(CO_3)_2$). The amount of carbonate that can be dissolved into the water depends on the partial pressure of carbon dioxide that in turn determines the amount of carbon dioxide dissolved into the water—in other words, dissolved carbonate and dissolved carbon dioxide are always in equilibrium. Or they try to be; carbonate concentrations in water are always chasing changes in dissolved carbon dioxide levels.

In nature, this restoration of equilibrium occurs slowly and calcium carbonate (chalk) dissolves very slowly. In fact, this is why carbonate scale is so common on faucets and shower heads—the rapid decrease in pressure, and subsequent aeration as the water discharges, releases the dissolved CO_2 and leaves the water in essentially a super-saturated condition for carbonate. The super-saturated carbonate gradually builds up on the nearby surfaces. Conversely, a super-saturated solution of CO_2 will dissolve calcium carbonate into water more quickly. Carbonating water with pure CO_2 under higher pressure will speed the process of dissolving calcium carbonate into water.

Approximate Relationship between CO_2
and Total Alkalinity in Pure Water

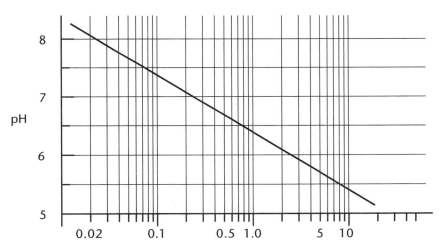

Ratio of CO_2 (aq) to Total Alkalinity both expressed as ppm as $CaCO_3$

Figure 11—Equilibrium solubility diagram for calcium carbonate and CO_2 as a function of pH at standard (i.e., room) temperature and pressure. The ratio of dissolved CO_2 to $CaCO_3$ is a constant for a given pH.

The equilibrium of the carbonates to dissolved carbon dioxide determines the pH in pure water. See Figure 11. In a real world situation, there are more factors that also apply, but partial pressure of CO_2 and the resultant carbon dioxide/carbonate equilibrium are the major pH factors in most potable waters.

There are several chemical equations that govern the equilibrium between the solid, liquid, and gas carbonate species. Carbon dioxide gas dissolves into water according to Henry's Law, where the concentration $[CO_2]$ is determined by the partial pressure of the gas, P_{CO_2}, in atmospheres and the constant $K_H = .032$:

$$[CO_2] = 0.032 P_{CO_2}$$

The dissolved CO_2 is a hydrated oxide molecule with two associated water molecules, like calcium sulfate ($CaSO_4 \cdot 2H_2O$). It is often written as CO_2 (aq) to distinguish it from gaseous CO_2. And, dissolved CO_2 is not the same thing as carbonic acid—only a small proportion of carbonic acid (H_2CO_3) actually forms, typically 0.17% of the total dissolved carbon dioxide. The combination of these two forms i.e., $[H_2CO_3] + [CO_2$ (aq)]$, is usually written as, "H_2CO_3*". It's important to understand that discussions of carbonic acid and the low-pH-end of the equilibrium are in fact mostly discussions of aqueous CO_2, which is subject to Henry's Law and the partial pressure of carbon dioxide.

Equilibrium Constants

Not all chemical reactions go to completion. An equilibrium constant describes the continual forward and reverse reactions of a chemical equilibrium equation. In the reaction $A + B \leftrightarrow C + D$, the double headed arrow means that the reaction does not go to completion, and that some amount of A and B reacts to form C and D, and some C and D reacts to form A and B. The equilibrium between the two sides, at a given temperature and pressure, is defined by the equation $[A][B]/[C][D] = K$, which is the equilibrium constant.

The two most important reactions in water chemistry are:

$H_2CO_3 \leftrightarrow H^{+1} + HCO_3^-$ and $HCO_3^- \leftrightarrow H^{+1} + CO_3^{-2}$

Using the first as an example, $[H^{+1}][HCO_3^-]/[H_2CO_3] = K_1$

When hydrogen ions are involved and the numbers are very small, we like to take the negative logarithm of the number to make it more manageable, as in the case of pH, such that:

$-\log[H^{+1}] = pH$ and $-\log K_1 = pK_1$

In the cases of chalk and water, where the parent material dominates the equilibrium, (meaning very little of the substance dissolves or reacts) the denominator (parent) is considered to be a constant and is incorporated into the K, such that for:

$$CaCO_3 \leftrightarrow Ca^{+2} + CO_3^{-2} \quad pK_S = 8.38 = [Ca^{+2}][CO_3^{-2}]$$

$$H_2O \leftrightarrow H^{+1} + OH^{-1} \quad pK_W = 14.17 = [H^{+1}][OH^{-1}]$$

In each case the constant allows you to calculate the concentration of an unknown, assuming you have measured the others. See Appendix A for more information.

The dissolution of chalk in water with aqueous CO_2 is described by the following equations. These chemical equations at 20°C (68°F) are each governed by equilibrium or dissociation constants:

$$[CO_2] + H_2O \leftrightarrow H_2CO_3^* \quad pK_H = 1.41$$

$$H_2CO_3^* \leftrightarrow HCO_3^{-1} + H^{+1} \quad pK_1 = 6.38$$

$$HCO_3^{-1} \leftrightarrow CO_3^{-2} + H^{+1} \quad pK_2 = 10.38$$

$$CaCO_3 \leftrightarrow Ca^{+2} + CO_3^{-2} \quad pK_S = 8.38 = [Ca^{+2}][CO_3^{-2}]$$

$$H_2O \leftrightarrow H^{+1} + OH^{-1} \quad pK_W = 14.17 = [H^{+1}][OH^{-1}]$$

Where the overall reaction is $aCO_2 + bH_2O + cCaCO_3 \leftrightarrow dH2CO_3$ and the equilibrium between $H_2CO_3^* \leftrightarrow HCO_3^{-1} \leftrightarrow CO_3^{-2}$ is governed by pK_1 and pK_2.

In other words, once dissolved, the carbonate can exist in any of three equilibrium forms (species) depending on pH: aqueous carbon dioxide/carbonic acid ($H_2CO_3^*$), bicarbonate (HCO_3^{-1}), and carbonate (CO_3^{-2}). The dissolution reactions are depicted in Figure 12. The proportions of the equilibrium forms as a function of pH are shown in Figure 13. Please remember that "equilibrium" means that the species have been allowed sufficient time to reach a steady, balanced state. Also note that "sufficient time" is usually many hours, and that changes to one species will indeed initiate changes to the other species, but that the change indicated in the diagram will often take many hours to complete.

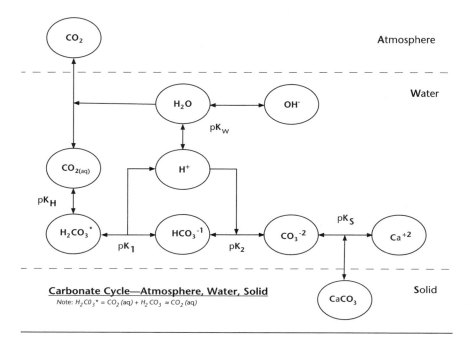

Carbonate Cycle—Atmosphere, Water, Solid
Note: $H_2CO_3{}^* = CO_2 (aq) + H_2CO_3 \approx CO_2 (aq)$

Figure 12—This diagram illustrates the two most common sources of carbonate species in water—CO_2 from the air, and dissolved chalk from limestone. The aqueous carbon dioxide-carbonic acid form dominates at low pH, the bicarbonate form at 6–10 pH, and the carbonate form at high pH. Only a small fraction of aqueous CO_2 actually forms carbonic acid—the equilibrium ratio is typically 1/650, depending on partial pressure and pH.

The relative proportions of the carbonate forms vary with pH. The aqueous CO_2/carbonic and bicarbonate molar concentrations are equal at pK_1, and the carbonate and bicarbonate molar concentrations are equal at pK_2. The bicarbonate form is dominant at $(pK_1 + pK_2)/2 = 8.3$. Below pH 4.3, the carbonate has entirely converted to aqueous CO_2 and carbonic acid, and this region (<4.3) is said to consist of free mineral acidity. In the mash pH range, under equilibrium conditions, the proportion becomes mostly aqueous CO_2, with a lesser proportion of bicarbonate. Figure 13 provides a visual representation of the variation of these carbonate species with pH. As mentioned above, the transition between the carbonate species may occur slowly, over many hours, even in the mash.

The solubility of the carbonate system decreases with temperature, and this is due to both the decreased solubility of gases (i.e., CO_2) in water (due to the decrease in Henry coefficient), and to a decrease in the solubility product itself. The solubility of calcium carbonate in pure water (no dissolved CO_2) at room temperature is only about 14 ppm, although its solubility increases to about 50 ppm (i.e., 1 mEq/L) when in contact with air, i.e., normal pressure, and can increase to 75 ppm with higher dissolved carbon dioxide. The solubility of calcium carbonate will increase slightly in the presence of other salts that don't contain calcium or carbonate, such as sodium chloride, or magnesium sulfate. These salts increase the solubility slightly because their ions tend to shield the calcium and carbonate ions from one another so that they are less likely to associate and precipitate out as calcium carbonate. Calcium sulfate also decreases in solubility with rising temperature, but its solubility is orders of magnitude higher at 3 to 8 grams per liter. The addition of calcium sulfate to water with dissolved calcium carbonate will cause precipitation of calcium carbonate in time because the additional calcium ion will raise the solubility product $[Ca^{+2}][CO_3^{-2}]$ past its limit.

How does high alkalinity water form in nature then? The key is the partial pressure of carbon dioxide underground. The CO_2 partial pressure underground can reach 0.03 to 0.05 atmospheres (atm) compared to normal atmospheric partial pressure of 0.0003 to 0.0005 atm, mainly due to bacterial respiration. When the groundwater is brought to the surface, the excess CO_2 is released to the atmosphere. However, the restoration of equilibrium by precipitation of the extra calcium carbonate occurs slowly, as evidenced by the gradual buildup of scale on household plumbing.

You would assume by looking at the low pH of the mash, that any alkaline salt (sodium bicarbonate, calcium carbonate, calcium hydroxide, etc.) would readily dissolve and all of its alkaline potential would be available to affect mash pH if quantified in terms of Total Alkalinity as $CaCO_3$. However, practical experience has shown that it does not. The reasons for this will be discussed more thoroughly in the following chapters (5 and 6).

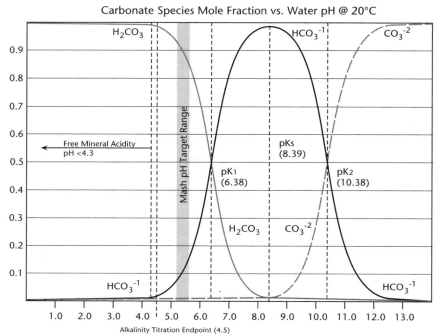

Figure 13—The carbonate system exists in three forms, depending on the pH. The predominant form in potable water is bicarbonate, being greater than 50% of the species between pH 6.3 and 10.3, and peaking at about pH 8.3. The mash pH region is shaded gray for convenience.

Precipitation of Calcium Phosphates in the Mash

Malted barley contains about 1% by weight of phosphate and this is one of the keys to reducing the mash pH to the range favored by the enzymes. The phosphate is primarily bound up as malt phytin and is hydrolyzed during the mash. Phytin is a mixed potassium and magnesium salt of phytic acid. This hydrolysis is (or would be) catalyzed by the enzyme phytase, but phytase is readily denatured by kilning in all but the lightest malts. Fortunately, the hydrolysis occurs anyway and the various phosphate ions (mostly $H_2PO_4^{-1}$, but also including H_3PO_4, HPO_4^{-2}, and PO_4^{-3}) are available for reaction with calcium.

The chemical reactions in the mash are fairly simple, but there are at least ten separate but co-dependent reactions that combine to lower the pH. These reactions precipitate calcium phosphates, releasing hydrogen protons that react with dissolved carbonate (alkalinity) to form water and CO_2 gas, thereby reducing the alkalinity of the system. The precipitate is mainly hydroxyl apatite, $Ca_{10}(PO_4)_6(OH)_2$, but can also consist of such species as $CaH(PO_4)$, $Ca_4H(PO_4)_3$, etc. The amount of CO_2 produced in this reaction is equivalent to the reduction in the alkalinity of the water because alkalinity is defined as the amount of acid (i.e., mEq/l of hydrogen ion) to convert carbonate and bicarbonate to carbonic ($H_2CO_3{}^*$). A summarized version of the reaction is:

$$10Ca^{+2} + 12HCO_3{}^- + 6H_2PO_4{}^{-1} + 2H_2O \rightarrow$$
$$Ca_{10}(PO_4)_6(OH)_2 + 12CO_2 + 12H_2O + 2H^{+1}$$

The bottom line is that malt phosphate reacts with dissolved calcium to precipitate calcium phosphate, releasing protons that react with dissolved carbonates to create water and carbon dioxide, which reduces the alkalinity and lowers the pH. The reduction of alkalinity is usually limited by the amount of calcium available in the water/mash. There is plenty of phosphate in the mash—at nearly 1% of the malt by weight and assuming a grist ratio of 4 liters/kg, this works out to nearly 2 grams per liter or 2,000 ppm, versus the typical calcium content of less than 100 ppm in most natural water sources.

Residual Alkalinity

And now to bring it all together—carbonate solubility, alkalinity, and water hardness. How do these factors combine to affect the mash pH? The answer is a quantity called, "Residual Alkalinity".

In 1953, German brewing scientist Paul Kolbach[6] conducted a series of experiments on base malt worts in which he determined that 3.5 equivalents (Eq) of calcium react with malt phosphate to "neutralize" 1 equivalent of water alkalinity. Further, he determined that magnesium worked in a similar manner, but to a lesser extent due to higher solubility of magnesium hydroxide, needing 7 equivalents to neutralize 1 equivalent of alkalinity. Alkalinity that remained in the water after this reaction was termed "residual alkalinity" (abbreviated RA). This residual alkalinity raises the mash pH away from the distilled water mash pH (considered to be "normal"). In other words, Kolbach determined that brewers could manipulate wort pH to a value equal to or lower than that of distilled water by adding calcium and magnesium salt additions.

On a per volume basis, this can be expressed as:

$$mEq/L \; RA = mEq/L \; Alkalinity - [(mEq/L \; Ca)/3.5 + (mEq/L \; Mg)/7]$$

where mEq/L is defined as milliequivalents per liter. Another equivalent unit may be used, like "as $CaCO_3$," but not simply concentration as ppm—the chemical equivalence must be taken into account. This equation can be restated in more familiar units as:

$$RA \; (ppm \; as \; CaCO_3) = Alkalinity \; (ppm \; as \; CaCO_3) - \\ [(Ca \; (ppm)/1.4) + (Mg \; (ppm)/1.7)]$$

Any positive value of residual alkalinity will cause the mash pH to be higher than it would be using distilled water. Likewise, a negative RA will cause the mash pH to be lower than it would be using distilled water. To counteract positive RA from alkaline waters, brewers can add calcium or magnesium brewing salts, add acid, or make use of the natural acidity of dark malts to reduce RA and bring the mash pH back into the right range.

Historically, darker beer styles have originated in regions with higher residual alkalinity water because the natural acidity of the dark malts helped neutralize the alkalinity of the water, improving the yield and flavor of the beer. Brewing a dark beer with a low RA water can result in a mash pH of 5 or less, causing a more one-dimensional grainy or roast flavor, and even impairing beta amylase activity. Beta amylase is reported to have a relatively narrow preferred activity range of 5.0–6.0 pH. The fermentability of the wort may be increased and the body of the resulting beer may be decreased.

Low mash pH can ultimately contribute to low wort pH in the kettle. Low wort pH can reduce hop utilization and reduce hop expression and bittering.

Conversely, pale beers brewed in water with high residual alkalinity can result in a mash pH exceeding 6, leading to increased tannin and silicate extraction, harsh hop bitterness, and beta amylase impairment. This condition also results in a more one-dimensional character, with the malt character being described as "dull." This high mash pH can subsequently contribute to high wort pH in the kettle. The high wort pH can alter the hop character as well. While higher wort pH allows better isomerization of the hop alpha acids, the resulting bitterness is different—brewers say that the difference produces a different beer, one that tastes as if it was brewed with a different, higher-alpha variety. The higher wort pH may extract more polyphenols from the hops to create the rougher hop character.

Residual alkalinity has been known and utilized by European brewers for several decades, but the preponderance of pilsner lager brewing has narrowed the utilization of the concept. The most common directives are that 1) water alkalinity should be as low as possible, and that 2) calcium levels should be at least 50 ppm. The resurgence of variety in beer styles in craft brewing has caused brewers to look at how both light and dark classic beer styles originated with regard to local water supplies. In his paper *Brewing Water—Overview*,[7] A. J. deLange plotted the RA of several of the major brewing cities of the world and noted that in general, a higher RA was correlated with darker local beer styles. See Figure 4. John Palmer explored this concept in his book, *How To Brew*,[8] and developed a nomograph that suggested a range of beer color for a range of residual alkalinity. The goal of this work was to enable a brewer to use their local

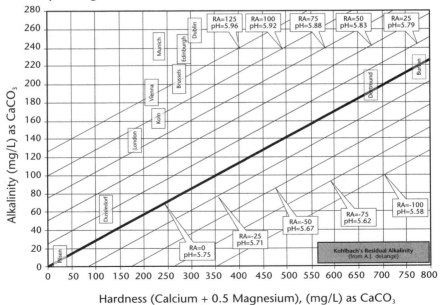

Figure 14—Alkalinity vs. Kolbach's Hardness. Showing lines for constant values of residual alkalinity, and tags for various brewing cities based on the local water report. Original drawn by A. J. deLange, revised by M. Brungard.

water, and salt additions or other treatment, to achieve the target mash pH with any recipe, light or dark, and thereby help achieve an optimum pH in the final beer—where the multitude of flavors are best expressed.

Refinement of RA

More recent work by Troester[9] has validated Kolbach's work, but also pointed out factors that were not taken into account by deLange and Palmer, specifically mash thickness and degree of malt crush at milling. Further review of Kolbach's articles shows that the experiments were conducted on 12°P (1.048 SG) wort after mashing and sparging, as opposed to the mash itself. Kolbach determined that the relationship between a distilled water mash pH shift and 1 mEq of alkalinity was 0.084 pH•L/mEq or 11.9 mEq/(pH•L) or about 595 ppm residual alkalinity as $CaCO_3$/(pH•L). Troester conducted a series of mash experiments using pulverized grist, which demonstrated that the slope or buffering capacity of the mash varied as a function of grist ratio. Test mashes were conducted across three levels of alkalinity (0, 2.7, 5.3 mEq/L) for Weyermann Pilsner malt (1.6–1.8°L spec.) and Malteries Franco-Belges Light Munich malt (6–8°L spec.) across the range of grist ratios of 2–5 liter/kg (~1–2.5 qts/lb). Calculations of the buffering capacity for various grist ratios are listed in Table 5. The results of Troester's work indicate that Kolbach's coefficient would equate to a mash grist ratio of near 5 liter/kg, which would be consistent with a sparged wort of 12°P and a typical initial grist ratio of near 4. The mash pH/residual alkalinity nomograph in Palmer's *How To Brew*, uses Kolbach's value (11.9 mEq/(pH•kg), as does deLange (Figure 14).

Table 5—pH Shift with Grist Ratio

Grist Ratio in liters/kg (qts/lb)	Buffer Capacity of Pilsner base malt mash mEq RA/(pH•L)	Buffer Capacity of Munich base malt mash mEq RA/(pH•L)
2 (0.96)	23.8	28.6
3 (1.44)	17.2	20.4
4 (1.92)	15.2	15.2
5 (2.40)	12.5	13.0

The change in buffer capacity of base malt mashes as a function of grist ratio. Pulverized grist, 10 minute mash. Data from Troester[9].

The degree of crush of the grist was also determined to be a factor by Troester. The previous data was obtained by using pulverized grist. He repeated the experiment using three waters (0, 2.9, 5.7 mEq/L) with various mill gaps corresponding to normal commercial settings for multi-roller mills: (pulverized), 0.5, 0.8, and 1.2 mm. The 0.8 mm setting on a two roller mill is probably most similar to the American Society of Brewing Chemists (ASBC) coarse grind condition, which is not determined by roller spacing but by 75% of a malt sample remaining on a No. 30 sieve (sieve opening of 0.0232 inch). The data showed that the buffering capacity of the mashes decreased with increasing gap size, in much the same magnitude as for grist ratio. However, it is speculated that this effect should diminish with longer mashing time, as the grist becomes fully hydrated and more phosphates are available for reaction. See Table 6.

Table 6—pH Shift with Gap Setting

Mill Gap mm (inches)	Pilsner Malt ppm mEq RA/(pH·L)	Munich Malt (6–8L) mEq RA/(pH·L)
Pulverized (replication)	15.8	17.8
0.5 (0.020)	13.4	14.8
0.8 (0.032)*	12.2	14.8
1.2 (0.047)	10.6	12.0

* Most similar to ASBC Coarse Grind. The change in buffer capacity of base malt mashes as a function of degree of crush. Grist ratio of 4 L/kg, 10 minute mash. Data from Troester[9].

In summary, the key points of this chapter are:
- Mash pH is the best lever for influencing wort pH and flavor quality.
- Calcium, magnesium and malt phosphates react to produce calcium hydroxyl apatite and magnesium hydroxide. This releases hydrogen ions into the mash, and lowers the pH to levels where saccharification enzymes operate more efficiently.
- The concept of residual alkalinity is a very good tool for estimating the effect of water alkalinity on base malt mash pH and predicting the effect of calcium salt and acid additions.

- The caveat to residual alkalinity is that the amount of change of mash pH with a change in residual alkalinity varies with grist ratio and grist size, ranging from about 10 to 30 mEq/(ph•L), decreasing as the ratio of water to malt increases. A typical modern value at 3 L/kg, coarse grind, is probably about 15 mEq/(pH•L), which is not far from Kolbach's value of about 12 mEq/(pH•L).

In the next chapter we will look at how the natural acidity of the different kinds of malts can buffer and change the pH of the mash. Before we do, we want to emphasize that the goal of these chapters is not to definitively calculate the mash pH, nor to calculate precise salt or acid additions to achieve a particular mash pH. This book does not contain all of the answers to the complexities of mash chemistry; it only contains a few. The goal of these two chapters is to give you a better understanding of how the mash pH works and what the principal levers are, so you can have more consistent mashes and thereby achieve better consistency in your beer.

References

1. Taylor, D.G., The Importance of pH Control during Brewing, *MBAA Tech. Quart.* 27:131–136, 1990.

2. DeClerk, J., *A Textbook of Brewing, Vol.* 1, Siebel Institute, Chicago, 1994.

3. Kunze, W., *Technology Brewing and Malting,* Intl Ed., BLB Berlin, 1999.

4. Bamforth, C., pH in Brewing: An Overview, *MBAA Tech. Quart.* 38(1): 2–9, 2001.

5. Stenholm, K., Home, S., A New Approach to Limit Dextrinase and its Role in Mashing, J. Inst. Brew. 105:205–210, 1999.

6. Kolbach, P., *Der Einfluss Des Brauwassers auf das pH von Würze und Bier*, Monatsschrift fur Brauerei, Berlin, 1953. Translated by A. J. deLange.

7. deLange, A. J., Alkalinity, Hardness, Residual Alkalinity and Malt Phosphate: Factors in the Establishment of Mash pH, *Cerevesia* 29(4)2004.

8. Palmer, J., *How To Brew, 3rd Ed.,* Brewers Publications, Boulder, 2006.

9. Troester, K., The Effect of Brewing Water and Grist Composition on the pH of the Mash, Braukaiser.com, 2009.

Residual Alkalinity, Malt Acidity, and Mash pH

The mash is a buffered environment where water chemistry and malt chemistry (hopefully) combine to create highly favorable conditions for saccharification and yield. A detailed explanation of the malt chemistry that produces this environment is beyond the scope of this book. However, we need to describe the basics of malt production and chemistry in order to understand how they affect our decisions about our brewing water.

As was discussed in the previous chapter, residual alkalinity allows us to understand how water hardness and alkalinity interact in the mash, and sets the basis for the eventual mash pH. Residual alkalinity helps quantify the effect of the water composition on mash pH due to the precipitation of hydroxyl apatite and the release of hydrogen ions.

But the changes affecting mash pH do not have to only come from changes in residual alkalinity; they may also come from the malt directly as acidity. Specialty malts also contain weakly acidic buffers that neutralize alkalinity and lower the mash pH. These buffers are thought to be melanoidins and organic acids that are created by Maillard reactions during kilning and roasting. Melanoidins are formed from the reaction of amino acids and sugars, and are responsible for the toasty and roasty flavors we associate with the browning of foods.

Kolbach, Troester, and Bies determined that it can take anywhere from 1 to 2.5 mEq/liter of acid to move the pH of the mash/wort by

0.1 unit, depending on the water-to-grist ratio and other factors. There were some inconsistency issues with the data, however. Replications of experiments with a different sample from the same malt lot showed minor variability, but replications using different lots from the same maltster gave results that varied beyond anticipated experimental error. Experimentation has also shown that the same type of malt (base, caramel xx, chocolate malt, etc.) from different maltsters can have significantly different results. The following section will illustrate the reasons for differences in malt acidity, and why it is difficult to predict.

Malts and Malt Color

To begin our digression into malt chemistry, there are basically four kinds of malts: base malts, highly-kilned malts, caramel malts, and roasted. Base malts have a distilled water or congress mash pH of 5.6–6.0, depending on barley variety, growing conditions, modification, and microflora such as lactic acid bacteria in the husk. The amount and viability of the bacteria is quite variable, depending on the local environment and the particular kilning regimen. Therefore, each lot of malt can have a slightly different base malt mash pH, even within a particular brand from the same maltster.

Base malts such as Pilsner, lager malt, and pale ale malt are produced by germination at 15–17°C (59–63°F) and dried in a cool airflow to about 8% moisture. These malts are kilned at low temperatures of 50–70°C (122–158°F) before curing at a final temperature of 70–85°C (158–185°F). Pale ale malts are typically given kilning temperatures of 60–90°C (140–194°F) and are cured at up to 105°C (221°F) to develop higher color (3–5 SRM) and more flavor. The flavors expressed are lightly grainy with hints of toast and warmth. Note that these temperatures are ranges of typical conditions that maltsters might choose at their discretion—there are no standardized recipes for specific types of malt.

Highly-kilned malts are base malts (or base malts that have not been fully cured) that have been kilned to a higher color, such as pale ale, Vienna, Munich, and aromatic malts. The highly kilned malts are heated dry (3–10% moisture) at low temperatures (120–160°F/50–70°C) to retain their diastatic enzymes. Aromatic and Munich malt are kilned at higher temperatures than base malts (195–220°F/90–105°C) to produce richly malty and bready flavors. Only Maillard reactions are involved; caramelization reactions occur at higher temperatures. The congress mash pH of these malts drops by a couple tenths from that of the base malt.[1] The higher curing temperature reduces or eliminates acid-producing microflora.

Caramel malts are produced by roasting green malt, i.e., malt that was not dried by kilning after germination. These malts are put into a roaster and stewed at the saccharification range of 150–158°F (65–70°C) until starch conversion takes place inside the husk. Afterwards, these malts are roasted at higher temperatures of 220–320°F (105–160°C), depending on the degree of color wanted. Heating at these temperatures causes both caramelization and Maillard reactions. The maximum color achievable is about 150 SRM or 300 EBC.

Malt Color

Historically, the color of beer and malts was rated as degrees Lovibond (°L). J.W. Lovibond was a brewer and brewer's son from Greenwich, UK. He created the Tintometer® in 1883 and it consisted of glass slides of various shades that could be combined to produce a range of colors. Lovibond determined the malt color by conducting a congress mash (a standardized method) of the malt and using his system to measure the wort color. This system was later modified to the Series 52 Lovibond Scale, which consisted of individual slides or solutions for specific Lovibond ratings, but the system suffered from inconsistency due to fading, mislabeling, and human error. In 1950, the American Society of Brewing Chemists (ASBC) adopted the utilization of optical spectrophotometers to measure the absorptance of a specific wavelength of light (430 nanometers) through a standard-sized sample. A darker wort/beer absorbs more light, and returns a higher number. This method allowed for consistent measurement of samples and the Standard Reference Method (°SRM) for determining color was born. The SRM method was originally set up to approximate the Series 52 Lovibond scale and the two scales are considered nearly identical for most of their range. The Series 52 Lovibond scale is still in use today, in the form of precision visual comparators and photometers. The use of Lovibond comparators is most prevalent in the malting industry for determining the rating of dark/roasted malts, and thus the color of malts is discussed as °L, while beer color is typically discussed as °SRM, though the basis (absorption at 430 nanometer) is the same.

Prior to 1990, the European Brewing Convention (EBC) used a different wavelength for measuring absorptance, and conversion between the two methods was an approximation. Today, the EBC scale uses the same wavelength for measurement. The conversion factor for rating beer color is EBC=1.97 x °SRM, or about twice the °SRM rating.

Roasted malts include amber, brown, chocolate, and black malt. These malts start out green like the caramel malts above, but are kilned to a lower percentage of moisture (5–15%) before roasting. Amber malts are produced by roasting fully kilned pale ale malt at temperatures up to 335°F (170°C). These temperatures give the malt its characteristic toasty, biscuity (cookie), and nutty flavors. Brown malts are roasted longer than amber malts, but at lower temperatures, and achieve a very dry, dark toast flavor, with color equal to that of the caramel malts.

Chocolate malt starts out with more moisture before roasting than brown malt, but less than caramel. The roasting process begins at about 165°F (75°C) and is steadily increased to over 420°F (215°C), where the malt develops chocolaty flavors. Some degree of caramelization occurs, but the majority of the flavors are from Maillard reactions and some degree of pyrolysis (controlled charring). Black (Patent) malts are roasted to slightly higher temperatures of 428–437°F (220–225°C) producing coffee-like flavors. Roast barley is produced in a similar manner but the difference is that it is never malted to begin with. Again, the majority of flavors come from Maillard reactions and pyrolysis.

Malt Acidity

The primary mechanism for pH drop (e.g. 8–5.8) in a mash consisting solely of base malts appears to be calcium phosphate type reactions, and the effect from Maillard reaction acidity, if any, is small. However, the melanoidins and organic acids would seem to be a significant factor in mashes incorporating a high percentage of specialty malts. In addition, experiments have demonstrated that there are apparently only two kinds of specialty malts, not three, in terms of Maillard-based acidity: kilned or roasted (or roasted and not-roasted). The difference occurs during roasting, when the color of the Maillard products shifts from red to brown. The transition appears to be in the range of 325–355°F (~165–180°C), corresponding to the highest processing temperatures for highly kilned and caramel malts, and the lowest temperatures for roasted malts. This shift is visually apparent when worts are made from different specialty malts to the same SRM or EBC color value. See Figure 15 for a picture of worts prepared by Briess Malting and Ingredients Co., as presented at the 2008 Craft Brewers Conference in San Diego, CA. The picture shows a dramatic shift in hue from left to right, yellow/red to brown as the malts transition from Munich to caramel to chocolate to black. This transition is supported by the work of Coghe et al.,[2,3,5] who show that the molecular weight (MW) of the Maillard reaction products changes with the amount of heat applied. Specifically, that low molecular weight (<7 kDa) yellow colorants form first, red second (also <7 kDa), and that these are apparently consumed or transformed into higher molecular weight compounds (>100 kDa) at the higher temperatures associated with roast malts.

Note: kDa stands for kilo-Dalton. The Dalton unit is synonymous with atomic mass unit (u) and is defined as being $1/12$ of the mass of the carbon 12 isotope. For more information, see Appendix A.

Table 7—Acetic Acid Content as a Function of Malt Color

Malt Type	Wort Color (EBC units)	Acetic Acid (ppm)
Pilsner	5	25
caramel	19	56
caramel	25	63
color (kilned)	37	69
caramel	79	66
caramel	110	165
caramel	240	75
roasted	610	36

Source: Coghe, S., et. al, Impact of Dark Specialty Malts on Extract Composition and Wort Fermentation, J. Inst. Brew. 111(1):51–60, 2005.

Table 8: Congress Mash pH Changes as a Function of Malt Type

Malt Name	Malt Type	Wort Color –SRM (Converted from EBC)	Congress Wort Composition (with base malt)	Congress Mash pH
Pilsner malt[1]	base malt	2	100%	5.96
Melanoidin malt[1]	kilned	28	50%	5.50
Cara-aroma® malt[1]	caramel	228	50%	5.08
Carafa® malt[1]	roasted	558	50%	5.18
Pilsner malt[2]	base malt	4.5	100%	5.79
Melanoidin malt[2]	kilned	31	50%	5.32
Cara-aroma® malt[2]	caramel	198	50%	4.93
Carafa® malt[2]	roasted	450	50%	5.10

Sources: [1] Coghe, S., et al, Fractionation of Colored Maillard Reaction Products from Dark Specialty Malts, J. Am. Soc. Brew. Chem. 62(2):79–86, 2004.
[2] Coghe, S., et al, Impact of Dark Specialty Malts on Extract Composition and Wort Fermentation, J. Inst. Brew. 111(1):51–60, 2005.

Figure 15—Each column of wort was prepared from a single malt, left to right—Munich 10, caramel 20, caramel 60, caramel 120, chocolate and black, to SRM values of 30, 20, 10, 2 (descending the column). Notice the visual shift in hue and density from left to right as the malts change degree of kilning and roasting. (Briess Malting, 2008. Used by permission.)

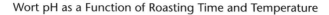

Wort pH as a Function of Roasting Time and Temperature

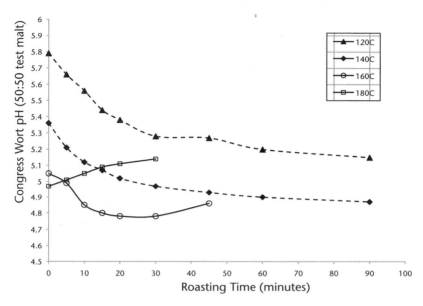

Figure 16—This chart shows the decrease in congress wort pH with roast time at the specified temperature. The malt samples all started as the same lot of base malt, with a congress mash pH of 5.98. Malt samples were heated at a consistent rate to the test temperature from saccharification. These curves start (T=0) when the malt samples reached the specified roasting temperature. Samples of the malt were pulled at the indicated intervals and pH was measured in a congress mash (50% base/50% sample). It is notable that the mash pH decreased with an increase in time and roasting temperature until the point of 30 minutes at 160°C, at which point it subsequently increased. Likewise, the data for roasting at 180°C shows a T=0 mash pH of 4.97, higher than the last 160°C measurement (4.86), which is consistent with the trend of a decrease in acidity as the roasting temperature rises through the range of 165-180°C. Date from Vandecan[8].

In addition, work by Coghe et al.[6] in 2004 demonstrated that acetic acid forms during Maillard reactions, and the amount of acid in the various malts follows the same trend as the molecular weights of the reaction products. In other words, acidity increases with malt color for kilned and caramel malts, but decreases in roasted malts. See Table 7. Whether this decrease is due to evaporation or incorporation in further Maillard reactions at these higher temperatures is not known.

The point is that the Maillard reaction products physically and chemically change as a result of a change from kilning to roasting temperatures.

Interestingly, this transition is seen in pH measurements for the worts as well. Note in Table 8 that the pH rises as the malt color climbs from 198–228 to 450–558 SRM. Other researchers such as Troester[2] and Bies[9] et al. have also observed this change.

A Discussion of Malt Acidity and Alkalinity

A malt that is mashed with distilled water will *generally* stabilize at or near a typical pH for that malt type. This is called the 'de-ionized water pH' (DI pH). The DI pH for base malts is generally in the range of 5.6–6.0, although, depending on a variety of barley and malting factors, it can be lower. The DI pH of the lowest color base malts (i.e., 1–3 SRM, 2–6 EBC) is principally driven by calcium phosphate reactions, including the enzyme phytase. Higher color base malts such as pale ale, Vienna, and Munich 10, often have a lower DI pH (ex. 5.5–5.6) due to a small amount of melanoidin acidity. (Melanoidin acidity will be discussed later in this section.) A base malt that has a DI pH higher than the target mash pH is alkaline. Remember, alkalinity is defined as the amount of acid (in mEq) that is required to change the pH of a substance to a lower pH endpoint. In the case of the carbonate system, the "total" alkalinity is the amount of acid required to reduce 99% of the carbonate and bicarbonate species to carbonic acid, and that pH endpoint is 4.3 (although 4.5 is now the ISO standard).

In the case of a mash, the pH endpoint is the mash pH target, such as 5.4. Therefore, if a base malt has a DI pH of 5.7, it is considered to be alkaline compared to the target (ex. 5.4). The alkalinity of the malt is measured by titrating, i.e., adding measured amounts of acid or base to reach a set endpoint. As the acid or base is added, the pH of the solution will change as a function of the milliequivalents added. If you plot the change in pH as a function of acid or base additions (mEq), the slope of the curve is the substance's buffering capacity.

Therefore, the alkalinity or acidity of a substance is equal to the total change in pH multiplied by the buffering capacity.

$$\text{Acidity/Alkalinity} = (pH_{\text{End pt}} - pH_{\text{Malt DI}})(\text{Buffer Capacity})$$

The units for malt alkalinity and acidity are milliequivalents per kilogram (mEq/kg). The units for buffering capacity are $mEq/(pH \bullet kg)$.

When you multiply the buffering capacity by the change in pH, the pH units cancel, and you are left with mEq/kg. This is very important: the acidity or alkalinity of a substance is defined by the *change in pH* multiplied by the substance's *buffering capacity*, or resistance to pH change. You cannot talk about the acidity or alkalinity of a substance without knowing or stating the pH interval to qualify it. It's like trying to compare commutes between home and the office without knowing the differences in distance; if you only know the speed limits, you really don't know how long each route will take you.

The buffering capacity of water or wort can be quantified similarly to that of malts, the only difference being the use of liters instead of kilograms. You can convert between liters and kilograms of solution once you know the density of the solution. Volume x Density = Weight.

Specialty malts, on the other hand, have a DI pH that is less than the DI pH of base malts, and is generally less than the mash target pH. The DI pHs for specialty malts typically range from 4–5.5, depending on the type. In general, the DI pH of specialty malts decreases with increasing malt color, but that trend is not consistent. The fact that their DI pH is generally below the mash target pH range makes them acidic compared to base malts. Logically, you can see that if you had two malts, a base malt with DI pH of 5.7, and a specialty malt with a DI pH of 5.1, and you mashed equal amounts of them with distilled water; you could expect the alkalinity of the base malt to be balanced by the acidity of the specialty malt. You could expect that the mash pH would settle out in the middle at 5.4, assuming the buffering capacities of the two malts are equal. In general, this is how the mash pH is actually determined, although there are usually more malts and you have to take the buffering capacity of the water into account as well. This takes us back to our analogy about comparing commutes: the buffering capacities of the various malts are not equal and they are not constant. It is probably easier (or faster if you will) for one malt to move through a specific pH range than the other. So, the two malts in our example probably would not meet in the middle at 5.4. In fact, the buffering capacity of specialty malts tends to be higher than that of base malts, so it is more likely that the mash pH would settle at 5.3 or 5.2, than at 5.4.

Specialty malts owe their acidity to Maillard reaction products (i.e., melanoidins, acetic acid, etc.) created during the kilning and roasting process. Acidulated or "sauer" malts are even lower, typically in the 3–4 pH range due to lactic acid and/or soured wort that is added to the malt before drying.

To date, two separate studies have been conducted to characterize the DI mash pH of the different malt types. The first was conducted by Troester.[2] The second was conducted by Bies et. al.[9] Both studies attempted to define both the DI mash pH for the different malt types, the buffering capacity of the malts, and to look for a link between malt color and these properties. The mashing procedure differed between the studies, however. Troester used a single infusion mash with a water-to-grist ratio of 4 to 1, while the Bies study used the ASBC Congress Mash procedure, and this may account for some of the differences in results.

The experimental procedure in the Bies study consisted of mashing 75 grams of each malt, and titrating it using 10 milliliters at a time of a 0.1N sodium hydroxide solution to a pH 7 endpoint. The pH was measured at temperature, generally between 150° and 130°F as the sample cooled during titration. The acidity of the malts in the Bies study were recalculated afterwards using an endpoint of 5.7 pH instead of 7 to better compare with the Troester data. A couple of assumptions were made in the setup and analysis of these experiments. They assumed that:

- The buffering capacity of a malt is linear and constant, i.e., that you would calculate the same slope if you titrated to pH 7 versus 5.7. In fact this is not the case, as you will see.
- The basis for comparison of malt acidity was 5.7 pH.
- The laboratory data for malt DI mash pH, malt buffering capacity, and malt acidity/alkalinity were assumed to be representative for all normal mash conditions. This is a big generalization. For example, the DI mash pH of any particular malt will gradually decrease with time after strike as the strike water takes time to penetrate, solubilize, and release all of the constituents. The DI mash pH "stabilizes" by dramatically slowing the rate of change. Thus, the pH change may not actually stop during the duration of the test. In addition, malt acidity derives from a variety of acids, each of which has one or more acidity constants (pK), which vary with temperature. Thus, the effect of specialty malt acidity and buffering capacity on DI mash pH also depends on mash temperature. A laboratory would have to do multiple measurements at different temperatures (cold, beta glucan rest,

protein rest, saccharification rest) to properly quantify the behavior of a particular malt under most mash conditions.

A fundamental problem with these assumptions is the fact that the acidity or alkalinity of a malt depends on the destination: the pH endpoint. All of the malts in the Troester and Bies studies were titrated with base (upwards) to a pH or 5.7 or 7 to quantify the acidity. A partial summary of both data sets is presented in Table 9 to illustrate the similarities and differences between both malt type and malt samples of the same type. (The significance of the titration endpoint did not become apparent to the authors of this book until only recently.)

Attempts to analyze this data led to several discussions between the authors and A. J. deLange[10], who decided to carefully titrate one base malt in the hopes of discovering the source of the apparent problems. In a normal titration, acid or base is added to the substance being titrated and the change in pH (downward for acid addition and upward for base addition) is recorded. A curve of pH vs. added acid (i.e., considering base as negative acid) is then drawn and analyzed. If the analyst makes several acid additions (and constructs the curve) and then makes base additions to the same solution, again plotting the pH, the base additions should cancel the acid additions and the pH values for base additions should therefore retrace the acid addition curves. Addition of X mEq of acid followed by X mEq of base results only in the production of X mmol of water—the acid neutralizes the base. deLange had done this in earlier experiments with malt, and noted that the titration curves did not retrace themselves. He attributed this to long reaction times (also noted by Troester and Bies) and theorized that it takes so long for the acid to fully react with the malt that pH measurements made by conventional techniques are not the true (equilibrium) pH values. This was consistent with his observations in the brewery, that mash pH can take half an hour or more to stabilize. He therefore modified his titration procedure to account for the time factor. Rather than obtain pH points sequentially on the same sample, i.e., by adding grain to distilled water, measuring pH, adding 10 mEq/kg acid, measuring pH again, adding 10 mEq/kg, measuring pH again, etc., he made separate mashes for each level of acid (or base) addition, and monitored pH over time. Thus, the first measurement for the DI mash pH (no acid additions) was recorded continuously over a 35 minute period. Then a second identical mash was made but with the addition of 10 mEq/kg acid. Again, pH was monitored and recorded for 35 minutes. This process was repeated for each acid or base addition. At the conclusion of the titrations, separate curves were prepared from the 20 minute, 25 minute and 30 minute pH data. These curves are shown in Figures 17–20, and confirm that the titration characteristics of malt depend, to some extent, on the time after strike.

A Note About pH Meters and Automatic Temperature Compensation (ATC)

Temperature affects a pH measurement in two ways: 1) the electrochemical response of the electrode changes with temperature, and 2) the chemical activity of a solution (e.g., the wort) changes with temperature. The electrode probe of the pH meter needs to be calibrated with buffered calibration solutions, typically at values of 4 and 7 pH. Those solutions are buffered to be most accurate to their declared pH at room temperature 20–25°C (60–77°F). However, the companies also publish charts specifying the precise change in the pH of the buffer solution with temperature.

Modern pH meters have a feature called automatic temperature compensation (ATC). This feature compensates for the electrochemical response change of the probe with temperature. In other words, it maintains calibration of the probe away from the calibration temperature. However, it does nothing to account for any actual change in pH of the solution due to temperature.

The pH of the wort at mash temperature (~65°C, 150°F) is known to be about 0.3 lower than the same wort when it is cooled to room temperature (~20°C, 68°F). That is why brewers always refer to pH measurements at room temperature. It is the standard because when the pH scale was first invented and used for beer analysis, before the age of electronics, there was no other option than to measure it at room temperature and that is the basis of comparison.

The change in wort pH as a function of temperature can be approximated by the equation:

$$pH \text{ (room temp)} = pH_{mash} + 0.0055(T_m - T_{room}) \text{ in degrees Celsius.}$$

Table 9—Partial Summary of Malt Titration Data by Troester[2] and Bies[9] et al.

Malt	Malt Source -T Troester -B Bies et al.	Color °L	DI pH	Buffer Capacity mEq/ (pH·kg)	Acidity mEq/ kg (re. 5.7 pH)	Alkalinity / Acidity (re. 5.4 pH)
2-row base	Rahr-T	2	5.56	--	--	--
2-row base	Briess-B	2	5.80	40.3	16.1	16.1
Munich 10	Weyermann-T	10	5.54	35	5.6	4.9
Munich 10	Briess-B	10	5.52	36.9	15.9	4.4
caramel 20	Briess-T	20	5.22	29.6	14.2	⁻5.3
caramel 20	Briess-B	20	4.81	37.6	6.7	⁻22.2
caramel 40	Briess-T	40	5.02	37.6	25.6	⁻14.3
caramel 40	Briess-B	40	4.51	46.5	41.3	⁻41.4
caramel 60	Briess-T	60	4.66	48.5	50.4	⁻35.9
caramel 60	Briess-B	60	4.67	46.3	55.0	⁻33.8
caramel 120	Briess-T	120	4.75	48.4	46.0	⁻31.5
caramel 120	Briess-B	120	4.67	59.3	61.0	⁻43.3
roasted barley	Briess-T	300	4.68	38.8	39.6	⁻27.9
roasted barley	Briess-B	300	4.42	48.5	62.0	⁻47.5
black malt	Briess-T	500	4.62	41.5	44.8	⁻32.4
black malt	Briess-B	500	4.40	43.4	54.6	⁻43.4

-- = data not measured
In the last column, positive numbers indicate that the malt is alkaline in the mash, and negative numbers indicate it is acidic.

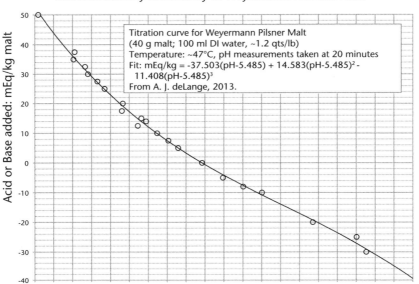

Titrated Alkalinity and Acidity of Weyermann Pils Base Malt

Figure 17—The titration curve for multiple samples of Weyermann Pils malt from deLange[10]. The pH data (circles) has been curve fit using a Taylor Series Expansion centered on the DI pH. The pH at zero acid addition is the DI pH of the malt (5.485), as measured by deLange.

One advantage of a Taylor Series Expansion for curve fitting the data, as in Figure 17, is that the derivative of the curve is easily calculated. (From calculus: the derivative of a point on a curve is, by definition, the slope at that point, just as the integral of a curve is the area beneath the curve.) Plotting the derivative of the curve as a function of pH allows us to see just how much the buffering capacity of the malt changes as the sample is titrated. See Figure 18.

The experiments were replicated at different times and for two additional malts: Briess caramel 80°L malt, and Crisp Malting's chocolate 600°L malt. The results are illuminating. See Figures 19 and 20. The results confirm that time is an important factor for pH change in the mash. In the particular pH range of a typical mash, the acidity or alkalinity of the malts is approximately linear, and any deviation from linearity could be interpreted as scatter or minor data error, but the non-linearity and trend of these curves is repeated over nine data sets. This strongly suggests that malt acidity is non-linear with respect to pH.

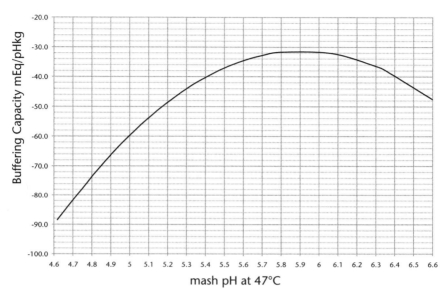

Figure 18—The change in buffering capacity of the Weyermann Pils malt as a function of pH. From deLange[10].

The curves in Figures 18 and 20 clearly show the amount of change in the buffering capacities of the malts as the pH changes during titration. This is probably the largest source for the apparent variability of the recalculated alkalinity and acidity numbers in the last column of Table 9. The recalculation assumes that the slope of the titration curve (buffer capacity) is the same from the DI pH of a malt to 5.7 as it is to 5.4; or in the case of base malt that the slope below the DI pH is the same as the slope above the DI pH, and clearly it is not. Of course, the change of the endpoint from 5.7 to 5.4 also changes the magnitude of the alkalinity or acidity of a malt. These effects are illustrated more clearly in Figure 21.

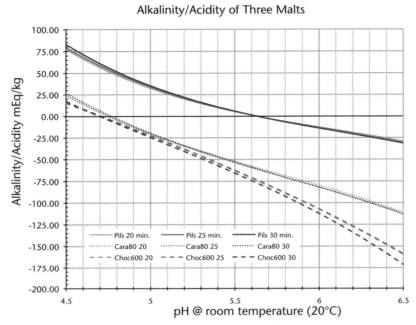

Alkalinity/Acidity of Three Malts

Figure 19—This plot from deLange[10] shows the Taylor Expansion curve fit for the data. In general, the non-linearity of the three curves for each malt type increases with mashing time (20, 25, and 30 minutes). It is interesting to note that the acidity curves for the caramel 80°L malt lay fairly close to the curves for the chocolate 600°L malt in the general range of interest for mash pH (4.5–5.5).

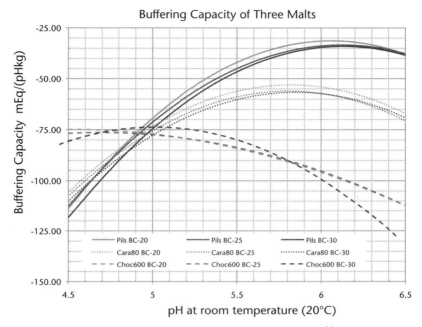

Figure 20—The plots of the buffering capacities from deLange[10] of the three malts in Figure 19. Note how the degree of change of the buffering capacity for each malt type generally increases with mashing time (20, 25, and 30 minutes).

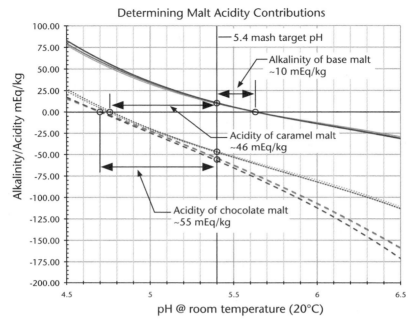

Figure 21—Determining Malt Acidity Contributions to Mash: The alkalinity or acidity contribution of a malt is calculated from its DI mash pH to the target pH. A target of 5.4 is shown here. The target could just as easily be 5.2, and that would change the contributions of the malts. For instance, the alkalinity of the base malt with respect to 5.2 would be about 20 mEq/kg.

At this time, the best conclusions we can draw from all of this data are that:

- The titrated acidity of the different malt types follows the same general trends in all studies.
- Base malts are generally alkaline with respect to the target mash pH range of 5.2–5.6.
- Specialty malts are generally acidic with respect to the target mash pH range of 5.2–5.6.
- The buffering capacity of a malt changes depending on the pH range it is being titrated through.
- The amount of alkalinity or acidity that a malt has (mEq/kg) depends on the malt's DI pH, the magnitude of the pH change, and the buffering capacity of the malt across that pH change.
- For small magnitudes of pH change, the buffering capacity can be approximated by an average value for the range.

- More malt titration data from multiple sources needs to be conducted using a common procedure, replicated, and compiled for better confidence in malt trends and general parameters by type.

Determining the Alkalinity of Water in the Mash

The buffering power of water ($mEq/pH \bullet L$) is primarily dependent on the carbonate species. However, the distribution of carbonate species changes as a function of pH and this changes the number of milliequivalents per mole. Therefore, the 'alkalinity' of water changes as a function of pH and endpoint, just like malt alkalinity and malt acidity do.

The 'total alkalinity as $CaCO_3$' of water is defined as the amount of acid (in mEq/L) required to bring the pH down to 4.3, where (theoretically) all of the bicarbonate and carbonate has converted to carbonic acid, and is no longer alkaline. The definition of Kolbach's 'residual alkalinity' is that RA equals the total alkalinity minus the effective calcium and magnesium hardness divided by the factor of 3.5. The problem with these definitions when it comes to evaluating the alkalinity (mEq/L) of water in the mash is that we are not going to 4.3 pH; we are only going to 5.4 (for example). Our mash pH target could be 5.2, 5.5, or whatever; the point is that it is not 4.3, but as you will see, a mash pH target of 5.4 is convenient for the calculations.

In general, the alkalinity of water can be defined as the total millimoles per liter of carbonate species (C_T) multiplied by the charge ($mEq/mmol$) as a function of pH. In other words:

Water alkalinity (mEq/L) =
$$C_T \ (mmol/L) \bullet Charge \ (mEq/mmol) \ at \ a \ specific \ pH.$$

Note: The term 'charge' is another way expressing the number of equivalents per mole (or $mEq/mmol$) of a substance; e.g., a charge of 1.3 = 1.3 $mEq/mmol$.

To determine the actual alkalinity value that the water exerts in the mash, we will need the total alkalinity as $CaCO_3$ and the water pH from the water report. We also need to choose a mash pH target, such as 5.4. The water alkalinity calculation is similar to the base malt alkalinity calculation shown in Figure 21. The difference is that we use the initial water pH instead of the DI mash pH for the malt, but both are calculated with respect to the mash pH target. For clarity, we are introducing the nomenclature "Z," from the German word "Ziel," meaning goal. It indicates that the alkalinity of a substance, particularly water, is calculated with respect to the target pH. The pH target can be indicated by subscript following the Z, e.g., $Z_{5.4}$, or simply as 'Z pH' in general discussion.

> Note: The Z nomenclature applies to malt alkalinity and acidity as well, where it indicates titration to a target mash pH as opposed to an arbitrary pH such as 7.

The first step in calculating the Z alkalinity is to calculate the total amount of carbonate species in the water (C_T). As noted above, the definition of Total Alkalinity is the milliequivalents of acid per liter necessary to move the water pH from (whatever it was) to 4.3. That number of milliequivalents is multiplied by the equivalent weight of calcium carbonate (50), and you get a number such as 125 ppm as $CaCO_3$. The problem is the charge or number of equivalents per mole of calcium carbonate *changes* with pH. Therefore, we need to calculate exactly how many moles of carbonate species are in solution versus the 50g/mol equivalent weight convention.

The math is not difficult but it is easier to explain with an example. Let's assume we have a brewing water with the following composition:

70 Ca
15 Mg
125 Total Alkalinity, ppm as $CaCO_3$
30 Na
60 Cl
85 SO_4^{-2}
7.5 pH

> Note: The parameters should be measured from the same water sample. Using annual averages will introduce error into the calculations.

1. The first step is to determine C_T—the moles (actually millimoles) of carbonates in the water. The alkalinity is equal to the total mmol of carbonate species multiplied by the change in charge between the initial pH (of the water) and the titration endpoint (assume it is 4.3). See Figure 22—Charge (mEq) per mmol of Carbonate Species.

Using the water data in this example, the charge at pH 7.5 is about $^-0.93$, and the charge at 4.3 is $^-0.01$. (Even if the titration endpoint had been 4.4 or 4.5, the charge value is still about $^-0.01$.) Subtracting: $-0.01 - ^-0.93 = +0.92$ (Alkalinity is considered to be positive for our purposes.)

This is the delta charge (Δc), and for clarity we will refer to the delta charge to 4.3 pH as Δc_0 (i.e., delta 'c-naught'). The total alkalinity as $CaCO_3$, by definition, is the mEq of acid multiplied by 50; therefore, divide the total alkalinity by 50 to get back to mEq/L of acid.

$125/50 = 2.5$ mEq/L

Total Alkalinity $= C_T \times \Delta c_0$ and therefore, $C_T =$ Total Alkalinity$/\Delta c_0$

$C_T = 2.5/0.92 = 2.72$ mmol/L
(a small but significant change from 2.5)

2. The second step is to take C_T and multiply it by the actual change in charge that the water will experience when moving from the initial pH to the target mash pH, Δc_Z. This will determine the Z alkalinity of the water in the mash. Using a Z of 5.4:

    The Δc_Z from the water pH to the mash target pH is:
    $^-0.1 - ^-0.93 = +0.83$ mEq/mmol

    Thus, the $Z_{5.4}$ alkalinity of the water in the mash is
    $2.72 \times 0.83 = 2.26$ mEq/L

Again, this is a small but significant change in the amount of alkalinity compared to the total alkalinity as $CaCO_3$ (2.5 mEq/L). The entire $Z_{5.4}$ alkalinity contribution from the water to the mash is obtained by multiplying 2.26 mEq/L by the mash water volume in liters.

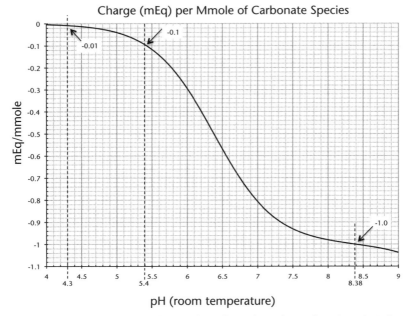

Figure 22—The curve shows the number of mEq/mmol as a function of pH for water. To use the chart, subtract the mEq/mmol values corresponding to the change in pH. For example, the net mEq/mmol contribution for water at pH 7, going to pH 6 would be (about) ⁻0.3 − ⁻0.8 = +0.5 mEq/mmol (positive because it represents alkalinity). The Z alkalinity is equal to the net change in charge (Δc_Z) multiplied by the number of millimoles of total carbonates (C_T).

Introducing Z Residual Alkalinity (Z RA)

Essentially, the Kolbach residual alkalinity needs to be recalculated using the Z alkalinity that we calculated in the previous section. The form of the Kolbach equation for residual alkalinity still applies, but with the substitution of the new Z alkalinity value. The effect of calcium and magnesium is unchanged, although as you will see in the next section, it makes sense to calculate all of the terms as mEq/L, instead of 'as $CaCO_3$'. The equation for Z RA is:

$$Z\ RA = Z\ alkalinity - (Ca/3.5 + Mg/7)$$

Going back to the water composition used in the example so far, the calcium concentration is 70 ppm and the magnesium concentration is 15 ppm. These concentrations convert by their equivalent weights to 3.5

mEq/L Ca and 1.24 mEq/L Mg, respectively. Applying these to the equation gives us:

$Z_{5.4}$ RA = 2.26 mEq/L – (3.5/3.5 + 1.24/7) = 1.08 mEq/L
Z residual alkalinity for a target mash pH of 5.4.

The Hypothesis for Predicting Mash pH

The basis for predicting mash pH is that protons, or total charges, are conserved. In other words, the mash pH will settle where the total positive charge is balanced by the total negative charge. An acid is a proton donor, and a base (i.e., alkalinity) is a proton absorber. Therefore, the mash pH will settle where the total amount of alkalinity in the mash is equalized by the total amount of acidity. Determining the particular mash pH where this occurs for any particular mash can be tedious, but not complex. It is simply a matter of trial and error—choosing an endpoint pH, determining the corresponding delta pH for each component, calculating the alkalinity or acidity of each component from the buffer capacity of each, and summing the mEq/L, positive and negative, to try and reach zero.

The prediction can be approached from the other direction as well, where instead of finding the mash pH that satisfies the zero sum condition, you choose the target mash pH and supply any necessary amount of charge with the addition of a strong acid or base to the mash to zero sum the total.

Here are the components for estimating the mash pH.

The Z malt alkalinities and acidities, consisting of:
- mash pH target (Z pH);
- DI mash pH of each malt;
- buffering capacity of each malt for the pH range of change for each malt, or curves such as Figure 21, that show the change in alkalinity/acidity as a function of pH;
- and weight of each malt in kilograms.

The Z RA of the brewing water, consisting of:
- mash pH target (Z pH);
- initial brewing water pH;
- Z alkalinity of the water;

- calcium and magnesium concentrations in mEq/L;
- and volume of brewing water in the mash.

The basic methodology for predicting mash pH from malts and water is to zero sum the various alkalinities and acidities, much like summing the milliequivalents when determining the validity of a water profile. As noted earlier, alkalinity is considered to be positive and acidity negative. The Z RA factor can also be broken down into its Z alkalinity and calcium, magnesium components for summation if the brewer wishes.

1. Start from the distilled water mash pH of the base malt.
2. Determine your pH target and determine the alkalinity contribution of the base malt as shown in Figure 21.
3. Multiply the weight of the base malt in kilograms by the alkalinity value of the malt. This is your total base malt alkalinity to overcome.
4. Calculate the C_T and Z alkalinity of the brewing water. Calculate the Z RA in mEq/L. Multiply the Z RA by the total volume of mash water in liters. Add this value to the base malt alkalinity. Note that the Z RA may be negative.
6. Determine the acidity contribution (in mEq) from each of the specialty malts (mass x mEq/kg) in the recipe, as demonstrated in Figure 21. Note that Vienna and Munich malt contributions, for example, may be alkaline with respect to the target pH.
7. Determine the sum of the milliequivalents, alkalinity vs. acidity. The sum will either be positive or negative. A positive value means that the pH will settle at a higher value than the target, and vice versa. You have two options at this point: a) you can add the number of mEq necessary to zero sum the mEqs with a strong acid or base to hit the target pH, or b) you can try a different target ph (higher or lower, depending) and run through the method again to try to determine the zero sum pH.

The end result of all this is that it is often more practical to simply put together a scaled-down "test mash," measure the pH, and plan adjustments from there. This may take the fun out of the design process for many people, but it is harder to argue with the results.

References

1. Bamforth, C. "pH in Brewing: An Overview." *MBAA Tech Quart.,* 38(1), 1–9, 2001.

2. Troester, K. "The Effect of Brewing Water and Grist Composition on the pH of the Mash." www.braukaiser.com, 2009.

3. Coghe, S., et al. "Characterization of Dark Specialty Malts: New Insights in Color Evaluation and Pro- and Antioxidative Activity." *J. Am. Soc. Brew. Chem.* 61(3):125–132, 2003.

4. Coghe, S., et al. "Fractionation of Colored Maillard Reaction Products from Dark Specialty Malts." *J. Am. Soc. Brew. Chem.* 62(2):79–86, 2004.

5. Coghe, S., et al. "Sensory and Instrumental Flavour Analysis of Wort Brewed with Dark Specialty Malts." *J. Inst. Brew.* 110(2): 94–103, 2004.

6. Coghe, S., et al. "Impact of Dark Specialty Malts on Extract Composition and Wort Fermentation." *J. Inst. Brew.* 111(1): 51–60, 2005.

7. Coghe, S., et al. "Development of Maillard Reaction Related Characteristics During Malt Roasting." *J. Inst. Brew.* 112(2): 148–156, 2006.

8. Vandecan, S., et al. "Formation of Flavor, Color, and Reducing Power During the Production Process of Dark Specialty Malts." *J. Am. Soc. Brew. Chem.* 69(3):150–157, 2011.

9. Bies, D., Hansen, R., Palmer, J. "Malt Titrations and Mash pH Prediction." Unpublished, Briess Malt and Ingredients Co., 2011–2012.

10. deLange, A. J., wetnewf.org/pdfs/estimating-mash-ph.html, 2013.

Controlling Alkalinity

The Declaration of Non-Adherence

When in the course of brewing events, it becomes necessary for the brewers to dissolve the chemical bonds which have connected them with alkaline water, and to assume among the powers of the earth, the separate and equal station to which the laws of saccharification and fermentation entitle them, a decent respect to the opinions of the Reinheitsgebot requires that they should declare the causes which impel them to the separation.

We hold these truths to be self-evident, that all mashes are not created equal, that they are endowed by their creator with certain unalienable properties, that among these are grist, pH, and the eventual pursuit of hoppiness.

That to secure these rights, brewing practices are instituted among men, deriving their parameters from the consent of the learned,

That whenever any form of ingredient or practice becomes destructive to these ends, it is the right of the brewer to alter or to abolish it, and to institute new practices, laying their foundation on such principles and organizing their powers in such form, as to them shall seem most likely to optimize their pH and yield. Prudence, indeed, will dictate that brewing long established should not be changed for light and transient causes; and accordingly all experience hath shown, that brewers are more disposed to suffer, while yields are sufferable, than to right themselves by abolishing the forms to which they are accustomed. But when a long train of high pH and low yield, pursuing invariably the same beer evinces a recipe of utter mediocrity, it is their right, it is their duty, to throw off such practices, and to provide new guidelines for their future prosperity.

Such has been the patient sufferance of these brewers; and such is now the necessity which constrains them to alter their former adherence to Reinheitsgebot. The history of wholly malt, hops, water, and yeast is a history of repeated misses and transgressions, all the while having in direct object the sustainment of absolute providence within this system. To prove this, let facts be submitted to a candid world.

- *That the preferred mash pH is in the range of 5.2–5.6.*

- *That the de-ionized water pH of base malts typically ranges from 5.6–6.0, depending on many factors such as variety, malting environment, and season.*

- *That alkalinity due to carbonate, bicarbonate, and carbonic acid will act to raise the mash pH away from its (normal) de-ionized water value.*

- *That in the absence of high levels of calcium, magnesium, weakly acidic buffers in colored specialty malts, or the waste products of lactobacillus bacteria, the mash pH will not lower itself to the target value.*

We, variously, the members of the brewing community, appealing to the common sense of the world for the rectitude of our intentions, do solemnly publish and declare, that these brewers are, and of right ought to be, free and independent thinkers; that they are absolved from all allegiance to the Reinheitsgebot, and that all contributions between them and their water supply, are and ought to be totally dissolved; and that as free and independent brewers, they have full power to add acid, reduce alkalinity, change the grain bill, establish the desired pH, and to do all other acts and things which seem like the right thing to do. And for the support of this declaration, with a firm reliance on the protection of divine providence notwithstanding, we mutually pledge to each other our lives, our fortunes and our sacred honor, be they as they may.

In this chapter, we will specifically address methods for controlling alkalinity and the chemistry behind them. Many brewers are a bit averse to learning chemistry, and would rather trust to providence that God loves us and wants us to have beer. But, as attributed to Thomas Jefferson, "I am a great believer in luck, and I find the harder I work, the more I have of it." In other words, you can trust to divine providence that saccharification and great beer flavor will occur naturally, or you can work to improve the chance of that occurrence.

One thing we need to remember as brewers is that we are trying to control or reduce alkalinity, not hardness. Many advertisements for common water treatment processes talk about removing temporary hardness or reducing permanent hardness as the goal. As brewers, we usually don't want to reduce or remove hardness from our brewing water—just alkalinity. (Process water is a different kettle of fish.)

Reducing Alkalinity

The most difficult water to brew with is highly alkaline water. Alkalinity raises the mash pH away from the target range of 5.2–5.6 to the detriment of the reactions we want in the mash tun. It has often been observed that the beer styles we know today emerged from a combination of the water available to the brewers of yore and the methods they took to combat that water's alkalinity. Some brewers relied on the acidity of kilned or roast malts or invented unique mashing and brewing methods to lower the mash pH. Some learned to remove the alkalinity by the methods that we will discuss here. We will examine these methods in turn, from the easiest to the more complicated.

Dilution with RO Water

The simplest method available today for reducing the alkalinity of water is to dilute it with reverse-osmosis (RO) or de-ionized (DI) water. Diluting the source water at a 1:1 ratio effectively cuts the mineral and alkalinity concentrations in half, and is the same as saying that it is diluted by 50%.

To dilute a solution by 70% for instance, means that the concentration of an ion is now 30% of what is was originally, etc. This relationship is only technically true for very dilute solutions where the density of the solution does not change. It is more true for water than for wort, for example.

Boiling

Boiling has been used for hundreds of years to reduce the alkalinity and hardness of water. Broadly, the way it works is that the rise in temperature changes the state of saturation of all the carbonate species in solution. First the carbon dioxide evolves from the water due to the rise in temperature. The removal of CO_2 unbalances the equilibrium between bicarbonate and carbonic which causes conversion of bicarbonate ions to carbonic acid and aqueous CO_2, and in so doing consumes protons. This raises the pH. The increased pH causes some of the remaining bicarbonate ions to convert to carbonate ions. This results in saturation with respect to calcium carbonate, which precipitates. This causes a further imbalance in the equilibrium, in accordance with LeChatelier's Principle, and the conversion of more bicarbonate to carbonate. Thus bicarbonate concentration decreases in favor of carbonic and carbonate until the ion product of calcium and carbonate drops below pKs (which is a little bigger, i.e., actually a lower concentration, 10^{-pKs}, than it would be at room temperature—pKs changes from 8.44 at 20°C or 68°F to 8.67 at 50°C or 122°F).

The carbon dioxide is driven from the water in two ways: first, a reduction in effective partial pressure over the water causes it to coalesce into micro-bubbles; and second, it is scrubbed out by the evolution of steam as the water boils. This evolution and resultant precipitation continues until about 1 millequivalent per liter of either calcium or carbonate remains. This last milliequivalent per liter as $CaCO_3$ does not precipitate; it is still soluble. The calcium carbonate that has precipitated exists as micro-crystals in suspension, which will eventually grow heavy enough to settle out. According to historical brewing texts such as Sykes', the water would typically be boiled for a half hour to allow the CO_2 to be well scrubbed by the steam, and would then be allowed to settle overnight, leaving a white layer of precipitate on the bottom of the kettle. The reduced-alkalinity water would then be decanted off the sediment for use as brewing liquor. This reaction is limited to water with moderate to high alkalinity because the result of the reaction is to reduce the calcium and bicarbonate levels to about one mEq/L of each (20 and 61 ppm respectively). In fact, unless the water contains significantly more than 1 mEq/L of each (ex., 3–5 mEq/L), the driving force for the reaction will be low and boiling to reduce hardness and alkalinity is less effective. The reaction is:

$$Ca^{+2} + 2HCO_3^{-1} \leftrightarrow CaCO_3(ppt) + CO_2(g) + H_2O$$

In other words, one mole of calcium ion (Ca^{2+}) reacts with two moles of bicarbonate ions ($2HCO_3^-$) to yield one mole of calcium carbonate precipitate (ppt), one mole of carbon dioxide gas (g), and one mole of water.

The equation can also be written in terms of the gram molecular weight per mole:

$$40g\ Ca^{+2} + 122g\ HCO_3^{-1} \leftrightarrow 100g\ CaCO_3 + 44g\ CO_2 + 18g\ H_2O$$

This form also shows the proportions that react in solution as mg/L, i.e., 40 mg/L Ca^{+2} + 122 mg/L HCO_3^- etc.

See Appendix A for more information on chemical equations and stoichiometry.

Note: Boiling does not typically affect magnesium levels because magnesium carbonate is much more soluble than calcium carbonate.

The two-headed arrow in this equation says that the reaction is reversible, meaning that not only can bicarbonate react with calcium to form a calcium carbonate, water, and carbon dioxide, but that carbon dioxide can dissolve into water to react with calcium carbonate to form calcium and bicarbonate ions. This is often how the bicarbonate got into the water in the first place. See Chapter 4 for more information on carbonates.

LeChatelier's Principal, which applies to all chemical equilibria, states that if a change or stress is imposed on a system at equilibrium, the position of the equilibrium will shift in a direction to reduce the effect of the change or stress. This means that if we want increase the amount of calcium carbonate precipitate, we can add reactants (left side) and/ or remove product (right side). Thus we can increase the amount of bicarbonate converted, and the amount of precipitate formed, by increasing the concentration of calcium and/or bicarbonate in the water, or by removing the carbon dioxide. (The calcium carbonate removes itself from the system when it precipitates.) Note that while our goal here is to remove bicarbonate (alkalinity), we are simultaneously removing calcium, which is not necessarily desirable. Therefore brewers who decarbonate their water this way often replace the lost calcium by additions of calcium chloride and/or calcium sulfate. It helps if this is done before decarbonation as the extra calcium aids in the decarbonation process, again according to LeChatelier's Principal.

Removal of carbon dioxide can be accomplished by allowing the water to boil so that the CO_2 is scrubbed out by steam, or by spraying the hot water through a nozzle to aerate it. Removal of CO_2 effectively removes acid, removing acid increases pH, and a high pH favors the conversion of bicarbonate to carbonate:

$$Ca^{+2} + 2HCO_3^{-1} \leftrightarrow Ca^{+2} + CO_3^{-2} + CO_2 + H_2O \leftrightarrow$$
$$CaCO_3 + CO_2 + H_2O$$

The higher you can make the pH in this process, the more alkalinity you can remove. This is usually accomplished by bubbling air or steam through the water to agitate it until the pH is 8.5 or more. Water can typically be decarbonated down to 50 ppm alkalinity as $CaCO_3$ without too much trouble, but the amount of calcium in the water is often a limiting factor. The residual calcium after softening by boiling can be calculated with the following equation[1]:

$$[Ca]_f = [Ca]_i - (([HCO_3^-]_i - [HCO_3^-]_f)/3.05)$$

where all of the initial and final concentrations [ ] are in ppm, and the factor 3.05 accounts for the conversion between bicarbonate and calcium equivalents. The quantity, $[HCO_3^{-1}]_f$ is the estimate of the final bicarbonate concentration, 61 ppm of HCO_3, which is equivalent to 50 ppm alkalinity as $CaCO_3$ at a pH of about 8.3. This final concentration of 61 ppm is based on ideal conditions. Using a more conservative value, such as 80 ppm bicarbonate, may be more realistic, allowing for conditions that are not ideal and where the reaction does not proceed to completion. A final bicarbonate concentration between 61 and 80 is more typical when calcium is not the limiting quantity.

For example, if a water had 70 ppm of calcium and 150 ppm of total alkalinity as $CaCO_3$ at a water pH of 8, what would be the final calcium concentration?

First we need to convert the alkalinity to the equivalent bicarbonate concentration, and since the pH is 8, the vast majority of the total alkalinity is bicarbonate, and the conversion factor of total alkalinity x 61/50= $[HCO_3^-]$ is valid (close enough). The equation would look like this:

$$[Ca]_f = 70 - ((183 - 61)/3.05) = 30 \text{ ppm } Ca^{+2} \text{ final}$$

The amount of calcium is often the limiting factor, meaning that the final bicarbonate concentration would be greater than 61 ppm. This precipitation reaction works best when the total hardness as $CaCO_3$ is greater than the total alkalinity as $CaCO_3$. Typically the reaction will stop when the calcium concentration approaches 1 mEq/L or 20 ppm, but it can go lower in some cases, between 12 and 20 ppm. It also works best if the permanent hardness is greater than the temporary hardness, meaning that there is plenty of calcium to fuel the reaction and nearly all of the bicarbonate can be removed, except for that one mEq/L (50 ppm as $CaCO_3$). The best way to increase the permanent hardness-to-temporary hardness ratio is to add calcium sulfate or calcium chloride to the hot water. The salts will also act as nucleation sites and help evolve the CO_2.

Adding calcium carbonate also enhances the precipitation of calcium carbonate. Although it initially seems to be counter to Le Chatelier's Principle, adding some powdered chalk to the water is beneficial because it provides nucleation and growth sites for the calcium carbonate coming out of solution and actually promotes precipitation. The added chalk never dissolves and is therefore never part of the system.

But what if the water is not allowed to cool or the precipitate to settle? A high-alkalinity water can be partially decarbonated by heating it to less than boiling temperature. The saturation point of the calcium carbonate is decreased with a rise in temperature, and calcium carbonate micro-crystals will form as the water is heated to strike temperature. The degree of precipitation will depend on many factors, such as the initial calcium and bicarbonate concentrations, the change in water temperature and how much CO_2 actually comes out of solution. One study[2] on boiling was conducted in London in 1851 using water that had been "artificially prepared...containing 13.5 grains of carbonate of lime per gallon." The results of that experiment are listed in Table 10. The author of the paper concluded, "...that the softening effect does not take place at once, but a prolonged boiling is required in order to produce the greatest degree of softening. In order to get rid of the temporary hardness of water, sharp boiling for not less than 20 minutes is requisite..." So heating of brewing water to strike temperature may result in a small reduction in alkalinity and hardness. Vigorous stirring or aeration can help the CO_2 to evolve and increase the precipitation. The result is that some small proportion of the initial alkalinity would likely precipitate, but still be suspended in the hot liquor when it is added to the mash. What is the effect of the suspended precipitate in the water being added directly to the mash? That is a good question. The effects of this on the residual alkalinity and mash pH will be addressed later in this chapter.

Table 10—Reduction in Hardness and Alkalinity by Heating and Boiling[2]

Time at Boiling Point	Hardness in Grains per Imperial Gallon	Hardness in ppm as $CaCO_3$
(cold)	13.5	192
0	11.2	160
5	6.3	90
15	4.4	63
30	2.6	37
60	2.4	34

From Latham, B., Softening of Water, Journal of the Society of Arts, Vol. 32, London, 1884.

Lime Softening

Reducing alkalinity with slaked lime (calcium hydroxide) is very similar to the boiling method, but slaked lime adds more calcium and raises pH, achieving lower levels of alkalinity than boiling alone. It also has the benefit of reducing iron, manganese, and silica along with natural organic matter compounds such as ammonia. The slaked lime process was first patented in 1841 by Dr. Thomas Clark of Aberdeen, Scotland as a means of softening and purifying Thames River water. In a letter to the Society of the Arts in 1856[3] explaining the process, he noted, "A small residuum of the chalk always remains not separated by the process. Of 17.5 grains, for instance, contained in a gallon of water, only 16 grains would be deposited, and 1.5 grains would remain. In other words, water with 17.5 degrees of hardness arising from chalk, can be reduced to 1.5 degrees, but not lower." These quantities convert to 249 ppm and 21 ppm as $CaCO_3$, respectively. This process is best suited to water with moderate to high alkalinity. The equations for lime treatment are different from the boiling treatment. In cold lime softening (i.e., room temperature), the reactions are:

$$Ca(OH)_2 + CO_2 \leftrightarrow CaCO_3 + H_2O$$

$$Ca(OH)_2 + Ca(HCO_3)_2 \leftrightarrow 2CaCO_3 + 2H_2O$$

$$2Ca(OH)_2 + Mg(HCO_3)_2 \leftrightarrow Mg(OH)_2 + 2CaCO_3 + 2H_2O$$

The common steps of lime softening are:
- Pretreatment with sedimentation and/or aeration to improve feedwater quality.
- Slaking by the addition of calcium oxide (quicklime) to the water to raise the pH to the 10.3 optimum for carbonate precipitation. If magnesium hardness needs to be reduced the pH is increased to 11 with additional quicklime.

$$CaO + H_2O \rightarrow Ca(OH)_2$$

- Mixing, flocculation and clarification with iron or aluminum-based coagulents, added to speed sedimentation of the precipitates. Sodium aluminate is preferred if the raw water is high in sulfates. The necessary contact time is typically 15–30 minutes.
- Recarbonation of the water with CO_2 or aerated to partially reduce the water pH. (Clarified water typically has a pH of 10 to 11.) Sulfuric or hydrochloric acid is often used to further reduce the pH

to a more normal potable water pH of around 8 and an alkalinity of around 32 ppm as $CaCO_3$.

- Filtration with conventional multi-media (sand) filters after lime softening to capture any remaining suspended solids. Membrane technology is becoming more common for filtration at this stage due its better efficiency in removing microorganisms and suspended solids.

The lime softening process can be improved by heating the water and thereby reducing the solubility of each of the reaction products, encouraging each reaction to be more complete. This method can remove more alkalinity than simply boiling and can achieve 25 ppm as $CaCO_3$. Water with elevated sodium, sulfate, or chloride may reduce the effectiveness of the process. High process efficiency requires precise lime dosing and careful monitoring.

In the United States, lime softening is sometimes used for municipal water treatment, but it is not typically used for brewery water. Small-scale lime softening may be conducted as described in the sidebar. Lime softening is considered to be an old-school technology, and is more commonly found in Europe. More modern methods include ion exchange and membrane technologies. The advantage of lime softening over ion exchange is that the former method substantially reduces total dissolved solids. A disadvantage of lime softening is the relatively high volume of solid waste (mineral sludge) produced by the process. The total amount of dry weight solids produced is typically twice the hardness removed. The calcium carbonate precipitate is a fine chalky sediment, but magnesium hydroxide is a fluffy sludge that forms a thick gel in the tank. Both of these minerals are somewhat difficult to dewater for disposal.

A. J. deLange's Method for Using Slaked Lime Decarbonation at Home

1. Add 1 tsp. of chalk for each 5 gallons of water to be treated to the water.

2. Multiply the temporary hardness of the water by 0.74 to get a rough idea of the amount of lime required (in mg) to treat 1 L. Then multiply by the number of liters to be treated and divide by 1000 to get the number of grams required for the entire volume.

3. Increase the result from Step 2 by 20–30% and place this in a small beaker or flask. Add enough water to get this into suspension.

4. Add the slurry from Step 3 to the water in initially large and then smaller increments. Stir thoroughly and check pH after each addition.

5. Continue additions fairly rapidly until a pH between 9.5 and 10 is reached.

6. Monitor pH. As precipitation takes place the pH will fall back.

7. At this point add only small amounts of additional slurry to maintain the pH in the 9.5–10 region.

8. pH will continue to drop as CO_2 from the air is dissolved but the rate of drop will slow. When it does, stop the lime slurry addition and let the water sit while the precipitate settles.

9. Decant the water from the precipitate and measure hardness and alkalinity.

Reducing Alkalinity with Acid

Acids can reduce alkalinity by supplying hydrogen ions to convert all of the carbonates and bicarbonates in solution to carbonic acid, and thereby to carbon dioxide gas. The reaction is the reverse of how alkalinity is created, as presented in Chapter 4.

The reactions are:

$$H^{+1} + CO_3^{-2} \rightarrow HCO_3^{-1}$$

$$H^{+1} + HCO_3^{-1} \rightarrow H_2CO_3$$

$$H_2CO_3 \rightarrow CO_2 + H_2O$$

Note that the gas must be removed from the water for the reaction to be complete. On the home brewing scale where small volumes of water are open to the atmosphere, most of the CO_2 will escape as the water is heated and stirred. On a larger scale with a much smaller surface area-to-volume ratio, this CO_2 should be actively removed by agitation, bubbling with forced air or steam, or spraying, in order to prevent its later release in enclosed piping or tankage where it can be a severe corrosion problem.

Table 11—Preparing 1 Normal Solutions of Common Acids

Acid	w/w %	Density	Molarity	mL of acid to prepare 1L of 1 N Solution
Hydrochloric	10	1.048	2.9	348
Hydrochloric	37	1.18	12.0	83.5
Lactic	88	1.209	11.8	84.7
Sulfuric	10	1.07	1.1	458.3
Sulfuric	98	1.84	18.4	27.2
Phosphoric	10	1.05	1.1	935*
Phosphoric	85	1.69	14.7	68*

*Phosphoric is approximately monoprotic at mash pH.
Note: It is important to understand that the procedure is to dilute the prescribed volume up to a total volume of 1 liter. For example, 348 mL of 10% hydrochloric would be poured into a volumetric flask, add sufficient water added to the flask to make exactly 1 liter. Concentrated acids need to be added to a large volume of water that is already in the flask, before being topped up with additional water to the final volume, to avoid exothermic splashing.

Acid additions to reduce alkalinity are quite simple to calculate if you work in terms of milliequivalents. The total alkalinity as $CaCO_3$ is easily converted to milliequivalents by dividing by the equivalent weight of 50. For example, if the total alkalinity of the water is 125 ppm as $CaCO_3$, that would equal 2.5 milliequivalents per liter. Adding 1 milliequivalent of acid per liter would therefore reduce the total alkalinity to 1.5 milliequivalents per liter, or 75 ppm as $CaCO_3$.

However, there are a couple of questions to consider, specifically:

1. How many milliliters of acid is 1 equivalent?
2. What flavor effect does the acid have?

The first question is fully addressed in Appendices B and C, but the short answer is that the amount of acid required depends on the specific acid, its concentration and density. It helps to have prepared 1 Normal (N) or 0.1 N solutions so that 1 milliliter of the solution supplies either 1 mEq/L or 0.1 mEq/L, respectively. Table 11 lists dilutions for creating 1 N solutions of several common acids. The answer to the second question is that the acid reaction will replace each equivalent of alkalinity with an equivalent of that acid's anion (e.g., chloride, sulfate, lactate, acetate). The flavor effect will depend on the amount of acid used. In the case of hydrochloric or sulfuric acids, this is one way of boosting chloride or sulfate without adding more calcium or magnesium. Choosing the acid and the final alkalinity is a matter of recipe formulation and may take a few trial batches to master. The method presented here reduces the alkalinity without monitoring the pH. The method presented in Appendix B is the opposite, where the pH is reduced to a specific value, and the final alkalinity and amount of acid used are determined from the change in pH. Both methods work, it is simply a matter of preference of pre-measuring the acid and verifying pH, or measuring pH and verifying the amount of acid used.

Acid Safety: Words of Caution for Strong Acids (and Bases)

Always add acid to water and NEVER add water to acid. It sounds silly but "Do what you oughta add acid to water" may help you avoid an acid splash. This warning is most important when handling concentrated sulfuric acid, not only because of its strength, but because of its tremendous affinity for water. If water is poured into concentrated sulfuric acid, the reaction is so violent that the water is likely to flash into steam, splattering acid out of the container and onto the brewer. Do not get concentrated acid (any type) on your skin. Dilute acids vary in hazard, but sulfuric acid is always hazardous, even at 10%.

We discourage anyone from handling concentrated acids without proper training. We remind everyone that they should read and follow the recommendations for personal protective equipment (gloves, goggles, apron, etc.) on the material safety data sheet (MSDS) .

Finally, the acids and bases that you use to treat brewing water should be food grade. While food grade doesn't have a precise definition, it generally means that the substance does not contain hazardous or toxic impurities and is generally recognized as safe and/or suitable for human consumption in accordance with the US Food and Drug Administration. Off-the-shelf acids from the hardware or auto-parts store, for example, *may* contain hazardous amounts of heavy metals or other impurities. Be careful what you buy.

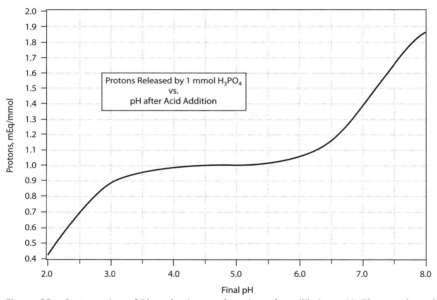

Figure 23—Protonation of Phosphoric as a function of equilibrium pH. The number of protons released depends on the reaction endpoint pH, although in the mash region it is generally 1. From deLange[7].

Mineral Acids

Hydrochloric Acid (HCl)

Hydrochloric acid is a strong monoprotic acid that contributes one equivalent per mole. It contributes 35.4 mg/L of chloride ions per mEq of acid when added to water. The reactions are shown below.

$$HCl + H_2O \leftrightarrow H^{+1} + Cl^{-1} + H_2O$$

$$H^{+1} + Cl^{-1} + HCO_3^{-1} \leftrightarrow H_2CO_3 + Cl^{-1}$$

$$H_2CO_3 \leftrightarrow CO_2 + H_2O$$

Sulfuric Acid (H_2SO_4)

Sulfuric acid is a strong polyprotic acid that contributes two equivalents per mole. It contributes 48 mg/L of sulfate per mEq of acid when added to water. The reactions are shown below.

$$H_2SO_4 + H_2O \leftrightarrow 2H^{+1} + SO_4^{-2} + H_2O$$

$$2H^{+1} + SO_4^{-2} + 2HCO_3^{-1} \leftrightarrow 2H_2CO_3 + SO_4^{-2}$$

$$H_2CO_3 \leftrightarrow CO_2 + H_2O$$

Phosphoric Acid (H_3PO_4)

Phosphoric Acid is technically a weak polyprotic acid, but it acts in the mash like a strong monoprotic acid that contributes about one equivalent per mole. The degree of protonation depends on the final pH of the water it is added to, but generally it is about 1–1.3 equivalents per mole in water between 4 to 7 pH. See Figure 23. It contributes approximately 96 ppm of $H_2PO_4^-$ per mmol of acid when added to water in this range. Only a small percentage (<0.2%) of the phosphoric acid molecules will de-protonate a second time to HPO_4^{-2} if the water is acidified to the mash target range. The primary reactions are shown below.

$$H_3PO_4 + H_2O \leftrightarrow H^{+1} + H_2PO_4^- + H_2O$$

$$H^{+1} + H_2PO_4^- + HCO_3^{-1} \leftrightarrow H_2CO_3 + H_2PO_4^-$$

$$H_2CO_3 \leftrightarrow CO_2 + H_2O$$

Phosphoric is the acid of choice for many home and craft breweries. While it is still dangerous at high concentrations, it is easier to handle than sulfuric acid because it is less reactive. It has minimal flavor impact on the brewing process because the malt also contains large amounts of phosphates. The acidification of water with phosphoric acid runs the risk of precipitating calcium from the water as apatite ($Ca_{10}(PO_4)_6(OH)_2$), which makes the calcium unavailable to the later brewing processes.

From Chapter 4:

$$10Ca^{+2} + 12HCO_3^{-1} + 6H_2PO_4^- + 2H_2O \leftrightarrow$$
$$Ca_{10}(PO_4)_6(OH)_2 + 12CO_2 + 12H_2O + 2H^{+1}$$

Note that the phosphate term ($H_2PO_4^-$) is exactly the same formula as phosphoric acid that has given up one hydrogen ion (i.e., single de-protonation), which in fact is the most common form for phosphoric acid in brewing water because it is a weak acid and doesn't de-protonate beyond one (1) in the mash pH range. Ironically, precipitation of the calcium is most likely to occur when only small amounts of phosphoric acid are used, acidifying to pH 6 for example, versus 5.5 pH. The reason for this is explained more fully in Appendix B, but the short answer is that both calcium carbonate and calcium phosphate (and particularly apatite) are less saturated at lower pH.

Mg will also react with phosphate but it has about twice the solubility of apatite at a pH of 5.2, so most of it stays in solution. That reaction is shown below:

$$2H_3PO_4 + 3Mg(HCO_3)_2 \leftrightarrow Mg_3(PO_4)_2 + 6H_2O + 6CO_2$$

Organic Acids

Lactic Acid ($C_3H_6O_3$)

Lactic acid is a very important part of some beer styles but it can also be used for acidification of water. Both the Reinheitsgebot and Biersteuergesetz German beer laws permit only naturally-occurring acids to be used in the brewing process. In fact, this was the entire reason that Kolbach[8] developed the RA equation in the first place—as a way to illustrate to fellow brewers that alkalinity could be easily controlled and to encourage his fellow brewers to lobby for 'permission' to use mineral acids as the rest of the world did at the time.

Lactic acid can be added in three ways: acidulated malts can be utilized in the mash, lactobacillus can be grown in the mash as part of an acid rest or sour mash, or food-grade lactic acid can be added directly. Lactic acid is a strong monoprotic acid (pK = 3.86) with respect to the mash pH, which contributes one equivalent per mole in the normal mash and potable water pH ranges. It contributes 89 mg/L of lactate ions per mEq of acid when added to water. The reaction of lactic acid in water for dealkalizing is shown below, except that the empirical formula of the acid has been replaced by the structural formula for clarity:

$$CH_3CH(OH)COOH \leftrightarrow CH_3CH(OH)COO^- + H^{+1}$$

$$CH_3CH(OH)COO^- + H^{+1} + HCO3^{-1} \leftrightarrow$$
$$H_2CO_3 + CH_3CH(OH)COO^-$$

$$H_2CO_3 \leftrightarrow CO_2 + H_2O$$

The flavor of lactic acid is typically characterized as a smooth sourness and is the signature flavor of such foods as yogurt, sauerkraut, kimchee, etc. Lactic acid can produce a distinctive "tang" in the beer flavor profile at high concentration. Lactic acid is reported to have a flavor threshold of about 400 ppm in beer[4]. The flavor threshold can vary between tasters. Therefore, the 400 ppm threshold may not hold for all individuals. In addition, many beers typically have a low concentration of lactic acid (typically 50 to 300 ppm) naturally, from fermentation by-products[4]. Therefore, it may not be possible to add more than 400 ppm of lactic acid to water for alkalinity reduction without flavor impact.

Brewers that employ an "acid rest" are making lactic acid in addition to the apatite reaction. It is generally accepted that for large alkalinity changes, the rest should be as anaerobic as possible to reduce the growth of acetobacter.

Acetic Acid ($C_2H_4O_2$)

Acetic acid is not very useful to the brewer because of the strong off-flavor it has. In fact, it is more commonly a contaminant due to acetic acid bacteria. However, it is also a product of *Brettanomyces* fermentation and can be desirable at low concentration in some beer styles. Acetic acid is a moderately strong monoprotic acid (one equivalent per mole, pK = 4.76). It contributes 59 mg/L of acetate ions per mEq of acid when added to water. The reaction of acetic acid in water for dealkalizing is shown below, except that the empirical formula of the acid has been replaced by the structural formula for clarity:

$$CH_3COOH \leftrightarrow CH_3COO^- + H^{+1}$$

$$CH_3COO^- + H^{+1} + HCO3^{-1} \leftrightarrow H_2CO_3 + CH_3COO^-$$

$$H_2CO_3 \leftrightarrow CO_2 + H_2O$$

Inoculation with acetobacter and aerobic rests after fermentation promote acetic acid formation. An alternative to performing these rests is to add glacial (i.e., concentrated) acetic acid in appropriately small doses to add the nuances of that character to the finished beer. The measured dosing of glacial acetic acid can be more consistent batch to batch than culturing acetic bacteria during the fermentation of the beer.

Citric Acid ($C_6H_8O_7$)

Citric acid was very popular in the early days of home brewing. Its popularity has waned, probably because of the relatively strong flavor of its anion. Citric acid is a weak polyprotic acid (but stronger than phosphoric, acetic and lactic, pK 3.14, 4.77, 6.39) that contributes between 2 and 3 equivalents per mole. It contributes about 96 mg/L of citrate ions per mEq of acid when added to water. The empirical formula for citric acid is $C_6H_8O_7$. The structural formula is unwieldy so the empirical is used below. The dealkalizing reactions, assuming 2 equivalents per mole, are as follows:

$$C_6H_8O_7 \leftrightarrow C_6H_6O_7^{-2} + 2H^{+1}$$

$$C_6H_6O_7^{-2} + 2H^{+1} + HCO_3^{-1} \leftrightarrow H_2CO_3 + C_6H_6O_7^{-2}$$

$$H_2CO_3 \leftrightarrow CO_2 + H_2O$$

Table 12—Summary of Methods for Reducing Alkalinity

Method	Efficacy	Safety	Comments
Dilution with RO (DI) water	Very Good	Low Hazard	Very effective. Potential corrosion issues for the raw RO water, even with stainless piping. PVC or CPVC is preferred.
Boil	Fair	Low Hazard	Reduces both hardness and alkalinity. High energy costs and decanting necessary before use. Deposits may be difficult to clean. Efficacy depends on water composition.
Lime Softening (slaked lime, $Ca(OH)_2$)	Good	Low Hazard	Effective at reducing alkalinity and hardness in water with high alkalinity and hardness. Best accomplished by third party in terms of cost and economies of scale.
Hydrochloric Acid	Good	Hazardous	Adds chloride to water. No effect on hardness.
Sulfuric Acid	Good	Hazardous	Adds sulfate to water. No effect on hardness.
Phosphoric Acid	Good	Moderate Hazard	Adds phosphate to water. Minimal effect on flavor. Can reduce calcium in water, depending on final pH.
Lactic Acid	Good	Low Hazard	Adds lactate to water. May affect flavor. No effect on hardness.
Acetic Acid	Fair	Low Hazard	Adds acetate to water. Will affect flavor. No effect on hardness.
Citric Acid	Good	Low Hazard	Adds citrate to water. Will affect flavor. No effect on hardness.

This acid may add fruity or ester perceptions to the beer that may benefit certain styles, such as Belgian Wit. Citric acid is reported to have a flavor threshold of about 150 ppm in beer[4]. That flavor threshold can vary between tasters and therefore, the 150 ppm threshold may not hold for all individuals. Typical beers can naturally have a low concentration of citric acid (typically 50–250 ppm) from fermentation byproducts and this may restrict further use of this acid in water treatment for brewing.

Acidification of Mashing and Sparging Water

Many brewers acidify their sparge water and/or mash water. At the beginning of the sparge, the mash pH should be at the target and the buffering conditions within the mash should be at full strength. As the sparging water rinses the bed, the sugars and buffers are rinsed away and the pH shifts towards the pH of the sparging water. If the sparging water is alkaline, the mash pH will rise, and the extraction of tannins, silicates and ash from the malt husks is more likely as it approaches a pH of 5.8. These compounds can ruin the taste of an otherwise well-brewed beer. The easy solution is to stop sparging when the pH hits 5.8, or when the specific gravity falls below 1.008, and top up the kettle with hot liquor alone. This will only cause a small drop in efficiency while preventing significant off-flavors in the beer.

However, an ounce of prevention is worth a pound of cure, as they say. The better solution is to acidify the sparge water to a pH in the mash target range, which should effectively prevent the pH of the mash from rising above 5.8; although as discussed in Chapter 5, the DI pH of the base malts may pull it higher. The rise in mash pH at the end of the sparge is more common to lower-gravity paler styles where the buffering systems in the mash are weaker and/or more dilute. It can also occur in low-gravity darker styles where the melanoidin concentration (a buffer) is actually low despite the high color wort.

Jim Mellem of Sierra Nevada Brewing Co. presented the following data (Table 13) at the MBAA South & Southeast Technical meeting in 2010. In the presentation, "Water Quality From a Craft Brewer's Perspective," he showed results from experiments they had conducted to compare their standard operating procedure of phosphoric acid acidification of all brewing water, with doubling the amount of calcium salts normally added to the mash and boil, as appropriate to the beer recipe.

Table 13—Experiments with Calcium Levels
(*Sierra Nevada Brewing Co., 2010*)

Special Description	Standard Brew/Acidified Water	Standard Salts/No Water Acidification	2X CaCl$_2$ In Mash/ No Water Acidification
Liquor pH	5.7	7.8	7.8
Mash pH	5.30	5.49	5.38
1st Runnings Lauter pH	5.24	5.36	5.27
Last Runnings Lauter pH	5.56	5.91	5.83
1st Runnings Gravity (°Plato)	17.8	17.5	17.7
Last Runnings Gravity (°Plato)	1.30	1.25	1.30
Lautering Time (minutes)	77	78	78
Final Wort pH	5.17	5.37	5.31
Final Wort Gravity (°Plato)	13.3	13.3	13.4
Final Beer pH	4.37	4.37	4.41
Final Beer Gravity (°Plato)	3.00	2.75	2.78
Bitterness Units	38	38	40
Color	11	12	13

Pale ale beers were brewed on a 10 barrel pilot system, each condition brewed twice to fill 20 barrel fermentors. To summarize the findings, the mash pH of all three conditions was within acceptable parameters, as was the extract yield and general parameters of the beers. The most significant difference between the trials was the last-runnings lauter pH, which rose to 5.91 for the standard salts without acidification, and 5.83 for the doubled calcium level without acidification. The pH for standard procedure condition (brewing liquor acidified to 5.7 by inline injection) only rose to 5.56 at the end of sparging. In triangle testing, 38 trained panelists determined that there was a statistically significant difference in taste between the three conditions (α=0.05) with regard to astringency, harshness and acceptability, and that the standard brew was superior in each attribute. The cause of this difference between the beers would seem to be the higher solubility of tannins, silicates, and ash due to the higher pH at the end of the lauter, compared to the standard brew, although higher wort pH during the boil will also extract a coarser bitterness from the hops.

Another example of this effect was a wheat beer brewed by one of the authors (C. Kaminski) at Downtown Joe's Pub in Napa, CA. The wheat beer (*Lazy Summer American Wheat*) is a standard product with 40% wheat malt, an OG of 1.040 and 10 IBU. It has been brewed with many different water profiles in the past 500 batches. (The water sources change monthly in Napa due to the seasonality and multiple source waters. Constant measurement and adjustment are required to maintain beer parity.)

Original Wheat Beer Water Profile (ppm)
139 Ca
41 Cl$^-$
252 SO$_4$$^{-2}$
10 HCO$_3$

The first water profile (above) resulted in a boil pH of "normal," according to the logbook. As you can see the calcium levels were very high and while the beer was acceptable, the comments received were that it was light, refreshing but minerally. A de-ionizing (DI) unit was installed to lower the alkalinity and a new search for the right water composition began.

The DI water profile gypsum and calcium chloride additions evolved over many batches into:

74 Ca
21 Cl$^-$
157 SO$_4$$^{-2}$
5.24 Boil pH

After a discussion of the effect of very low sulfate levels on light beers with A. J. deLange, it was decided to cut the sulfate entirely to make this ale more lager-like. The first attempt used 100 grams of calcium chloride and 10 mL of 85% phosphoric acid to acidify the 300 gallons of hot liquor. This water calculates to 24 ppm Ca and 42 ppm Cl⁻. The pH of the final runnings rose as can be seen in Figure 24. The sparge was stopped at that point. The boil pH for this batch was 5.47. The finished beer seemed to have the normal fermentation characteristics and typical FG, but had a distinct dry, harsh and almost ashy aftertaste.

The calcium was increased on the next batch to 36 ppm Ca, 64 ppm Cl⁻ with the same amount of phosphoric acid as the last, and the pH didn't rise at the end of the sparge. The finished beer did not have the harsh aftertaste.

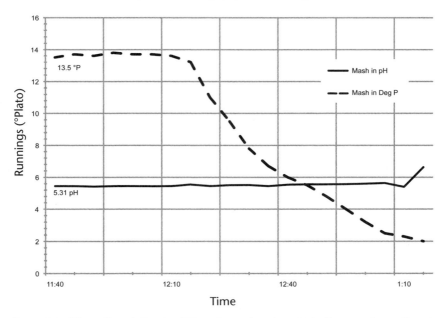

Figure 24—Wort pH and Gravity (°P) vs. Lautering time. This diagram shows the abrupt increase in mash pH at the end of the lauter as the gravity of the running fell below 3°P (1.012). Increasing the calcium content of the brewing water on the next batch prevented the rise at the same gravity.

Precipitation of Calcium Due to Phosphoric Acid

Acidification of brewing water is one of the trickier aspects of water chemistry. One issue to be considered when acidifying water with phosphoric acid is the precipitation of calcium phosphate, which changes the residual alkalinity equilibrium. How much does acidification with phosphoric acid change the calcium level in the water?

Several equilibria are affected by the change in pH. A. J. deLange tackled the chemical theory and hard math to determine the effect of acidification on calcium especially for this project. The result is a series of charts, presented in Appendix B, that describe the reduction of alkalinity as a function of acidification endpoint pH, and the saturation level of calcium as a function of acidification. The charts show that acidification to the typical mash pH range instead of to a higher pH such as 6.5 or 7.0 is better for calcium retention in the water. Several examples are presented to illustrate the use of the charts. These charts only address the acidification of the water, not acidification of the mash. However, the charts are an excellent tool for understanding the playing field if you plan to acidify your water for brewing.

Adding Alkalinity

Although most brewers are usually trying to reduce the alkalinity in their brewing water, there are times where a brewer actually needs to increase the pH in the mash in order to mash a darker, more acidic grain bill. However, it needs to be understood that we are never adding alkalinity to the sparge water. The alkalinity of sparge water always needs to be as low as possible to minimize or prevent pH rise in the grain bed during lautering.

There are different ways to add alkalinity to the mash: one is to add carbonate or bicarbonate, and the other is hydroxide. There is a big difference between adding alkalinity to the water versus to the mash, however. As we showed in Chapter 5, predicting the mash pH requires calculation of the total moles of carbonates (C_T), and then the Z alkalinity needs to be determined from Figure 22 (p. 26), based on the mash pH target. This Z method is a first-order approximation of what may actually occur in the mash. The actual chemistry is more complex and depends on the interaction of several components: the carbonate species, the phosphate species, the pH, and all the chemical constants that go with them, such as pK_1. However, we can start the discussion by looking at the simplest case: the addition of sodium bicarbonate to water.

Adding Sodium Bicarbonate

Sodium bicarbonate (a.k.a., baking soda) is very soluble in water, and reaches its saturation limit at about 9% by weight at 25°C (77°F), or about 1 pound per gallon. Therefore it can easily be added to the brewing water or the mash in order to raise the alkalinity. However, the carbonate system is a weak base, and therefore its charge (mEq/mmol) changes depending on the pH range it is moved through. This was explained in Chapter 5.

If we are adding the bicarbonate to water in order to raise the total alkalinity as $CaCO_3$, and thereby Kolbach's residual alkalinity, the only necessary adjustment to the salt contributions per gram (as calculated per Appendix C) is a slight reduction due to the definition of total alkalinity. As we have said before, total alkalinity is the amount of acid in mEq that is required to reduce the pH of the water to 4.3 by converting carbonates and bicarbonates to carbonic acid. However, at pH 4.3, there is still 0.01 charge on the carbonates, i.e., they have not been reduced to zero but to 1%. Thus to be more accurate, we need to adjust the bicarbonate addition by this 1% as well.

The way this works is that the charge of any bicarbonate addition starts out at 1 mEq/mmol, regardless of the water pH, because it is pure bicarbonate—it has 1 mEq/mmol. If 1 gram of sodium bicarbonate (mw=84 grams) were dissolved in 1 liter of water, it would equal 0.0119 moles per liter (or 11.9 mmol per liter). At a charge of 1 mEq/mmol, 11.9 mmol/L equals 11.9 mEq/L of total alkalinity, as measured by titration to an endpoint of 4.3 pH. However, this is where the 1% remainder comes into play. Therefore, the addition of 1 gram of sodium bicarbonate per liter only yields 99% of its 11.9 mEq/L to the total alkalinity, and the ppm of HCO_3^- needs to be adjusted accordingly. See Table 14 (p. 136).

The preceding is for calculating the effect of additions to either total alkalinity or residual alkalinity, but without regard to the eventual mash pH. It doesn't matter whether the additions are done to the water or the mash if you are only considering those parameters of alkalinity. On the other hand, if you are adding sodium bicarbonate with the intent of moving the pH to a particular target (Z pH) in accordance with the model presented at the end of Chapter 5, you now have to calculate the Z alkalinity of the addition.

Whenever a carbonate species is added to the mash for the purpose of adjusting the mash pH, the delta charge (Δc) must be calculated using

Figure 22 in Chapter 5, repeated below as Figure 25 for convenience. However, the Δc calculation is simplified by the fact that the starting point is ⁻1.0 (or ⁻2.0 in the case of carbonate). Therefore the respective Δc for a bicarbonate or carbonate addition with a Z pH of 5.4 would be:

⁻0.1 − ⁻1.0 = +0.9 mEq/mmol (bicarbonate)

⁻0.1 − ⁻2.0 = +1.9 mEq/mmol (carbonate—see Note below)

The Z alkalinity is equal to the net change in charge (Δc_Z), multiplied by the number of millimoles of total carbonates (C_T), i.e., Z alkalinity=$0.9C_T$ (for bicarbonate addition). Note that the 1% reduction does not apply here because we are not working with 'total alkalinity,' we are working with the actual alkalinity to the target pH; Δc_Z is the new reduction factor. See the end of Chapter 7, the brewing of a Foreign Extra stout, for an example.

Note: For the record, an addition of <u>dissolved</u> chalk (i.e., carbonate) to water, i.e., completely dissolved by bubbling CO_2 or sufficient overpressure of CO_2, would start at 2 mEq/mmol and the Δc_Z would still be calculated to the values on Figure 25, e.g., ⁻0.1 @ 5.4 pH. If any acid other than CO_2 were used to dissolve the chalk, such as hydrochloric acid, half of the alkaline charge would be used up converting all of the carbonate to bicarbonate, because the bicarbonate is the more soluble form, and the previously-described bicarbonate situation would apply. Undissolved chalk is a mess, as you will see in the next section.

An experiment conducted by deLange[9] using sodium bicarbonate and a caramel 80°L malt to verify the Z model demonstrated results that were consistent with the theory, but that also demonstrated the time factor inherent in carbonate reactions. The caramel 80°L malt sample had a DI mash pH previously determined to be 4.77, and an addition of sodium bicarbonate was calculated to bring the mash pH to 5.4, using the Z alkalinity concept. The pH was continuously monitored during the experiment. The pH started out very close to the DI mash pH, but climbed precipitously when the bicarbonate addition was made to the mash. At T=25 minutes, the mash pH had dropped back down to 5.56, at T=60 the mash pH was 5.51, and at T=135 the mash pH had dropped to 5.37, all of which are reasonably close to 5.4.

It should be noted that basing the sodium bicarbonate addition with respect to the total alkalinity would have resulted in a lesser addition that eventually would undershoot the mash target pH. Given the reaction kinetics, you may in fact wish to reduce the addition with regard to Z alkalinity, in order to spend the most amount of the total mash time in the optimum mash pH range. Balancing all of these factors for a specific recipe at a specific brewery will take experimentation, but at least the calculations discussed here help clarify what is actually occurring.

The only other issue with using sodium bicarbonate is the accompanying rise in sodium level—about 72 ppm at 1 gram per gallon. As will be noted in Chapter 7, sodium levels in excess of 100 ppm are generally not recommended, especially if sulfate levels are 300 ppm or greater, as it tends to give a metallic taste to the bitterness.

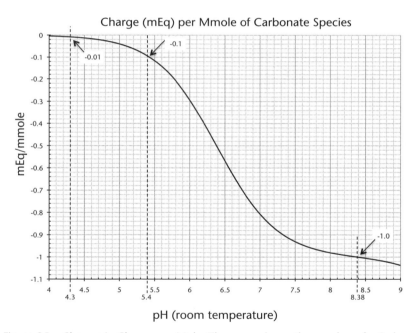

Charge (mEq) per Mmole of Carbonate Species

pH (room temperature)

Figure 25—Change in Charge per Mole. The curve shows the number of mEq/mmol as a function of pH for water. To calculate Δc when adding carbonates to the mash water, the initial charge is $^-1.0$ mEq/mmol for bicarbonates, and $^-2.0$ for carbonates (chalk). Therefore the Δc for a CO_2-dissolved chalk addition with a target mash pH of 5.4 would be: $^-2.0 - ^-0.1 = 1.9$ mEq/mmol. The Z alkalinity is equal to the net change in charge Δc, multiplied by the number of millimoles of total carbonates (CT). This chart does not apply to hydroxides, only to carbonate-based additions.

The Problems with Adding Chalk

In nature, the creation of a perfect alkaline ground water for a dark beer takes time, limestone, and high carbon dioxide partial pressure. It is not easily recreated in the brewery because the newly created solutions are not as stable as the natural water; the carbonate seems to have a higher tendency to precipitate out. As mentioned earlier in Chapter 4, the normal saturation level of calcium carbonate in water is very low, being only about 1 mEq/L or 0.05 grams per liter at typical atmospheric partial pressure of carbon dioxide. This equates to about 2 grams in 10 gallons of water! More calcium carbonate can be dissolved if carbon dioxide is bubbled into the water with constant stirring or supplied to a closed container under pressure, but the process is not very convenient or quick.

Conventional wisdom has been to add the chalk to the mash because the lower pH there would naturally dissolve the chalk more readily. However, anecdotal evidence has long pointed to chalk additions as not being very effective for adding alkalinity and raising pH. For example, Troester[5] compared the effect of chalk additions on the mash pH using chalk dissolved in de-ionized water with CO_2 overpressure vs. chalk that was not dissolved and essentially only suspended in the water. The same quantity of chalk was used in both solutions, and the titrated alkalinity was nearly the same due to the strong acid used for the titration. While the data was not conclusive, it suggested that the fully dissolved chalk had a greater effect on raising mash pH, but that the overall change was still not consistent with the amount of alkalinity added. The undissolved chalk solution only increased the mash pH by about 0.1–0.2 units, even when high chalk concentrations were provided. This suggests that the natural acids in the mash are not strong enough to dissolve suspended chalk, at least within the time period that the mash pH was observed (25 minutes).

A subsequent experiment by A. J. deLange[9], shed some light on the stoichiometry and a possible reason for poor performance of chalk additions. The mash contains a relatively high concentration of phosphates from the malt (about 1% by weight), approximately 30 times greater than a typical calcium concentration in the mash (about 100 ppm). The experiment consisted of adding known quantities of calcium carbonate slurry (i.e., suspended, not dissolved) to a solution of monobasic potassium phosphate (KH_2PO_4) comparable in concentration to the dibasic phosphate (HPO_4^{-2}) concentration in a typical mash, and monitoring the change in pH over time after each chalk addition. The rate of change of pH would correspond to the rate that the chalk absorbs the protons (acid). The results showed that the solution pH increased quite slowly as the chalk was added, typically 15–30 minutes for a 0.1 pH change in the range of 4.6–5.5 pH, and 30–60+ minutes for the same change in the range of 5.5–6. This suggests that it could take 3 hours to raise the pH from 4.9 to 5.4. In addition, the chalk seemed to be about 1/3 as effective as it should have been in raising the solution pH. In other words, the change in pH was about 1/3 of the expected result based on the quantity of the addition.

At the end of the experiment, there was a precipitate in the beaker that looked different from the chalk. The precipitate was fluffier, and tended to flocculate; whereas undissolved chalk is a fine crystalline powder, and if it does precipitate out, it takes a long time to settle. The flocculent was centrifuged from the solution and did not fizz when treated with a strong acid, as would happen if it contained appreciable calcium carbonate, but it did dissolve. The solution was then treated with a strong base to raise the pH to 14. A fine crystalline precipitate resulted. This reversal back to the original appearance confirmed that the calcium carbonate had been converted to apatite upon addition to the phosphate solution.

A Deeper Discussion of Carbonate Behavior in the Mash

The chemical equation that may explain these observations is similar to the apatite equation from Chapter 4. Whereas the apatite reaction takes existing calcium, bicarbonate and phosphate ions to produce apatite, carbon dioxide, water and 2 free hydrogen ions, the calcium carbonate reaction produces apatite, carbon dioxide, water, and 6 bicarbonate ions.

$$10Ca^{+2} + 12HCO_3^{-1} + 6H_2PO_4^{-1} + 2H_2O \rightarrow$$
$$Ca_{10}(PO_4)_6(OH)_2 + 12CO_2 + 12H_2O + 2H^{+1} \quad (Ch. 4)$$

$$10CaCO_3 + 6H_2PO_4^- + 2H_2O \rightarrow$$
$$Ca_{10}(PO_4)_6(OH)_2 + 10HCO_3^{-1} + 4H^{+1} \quad (theoretical)$$

$$10HCO_3^{-1} + 4H^{+1} \rightarrow 4H_2CO_3 + 6HCO_3^{-1}$$

$$4H_2CO_3 + 6HCO_3^{-1} \rightarrow 4H_2O + 4CO_2 + 6HCO_3^{-1}$$

The 10 bicarbonates and 4 hydrogen ions react to form 4 carbonic acid molecules and 6 bicarbonates, and the 4 carbonic acid molecules break down into carbon dioxide and water according to the pK_H constant. deLange's theory is that a suspended chalk addition to the mash (i.e., in the typical mash pH range) has a net effect of 0.3 equivalents of alkalinity for every equivalent of the initial addition. Note that 10 moles of calcium carbonate equals 20 equivalents of calcium carbonate because it has 2 equivalents per mole.

The carbonate species distribution depends on the pH as shown in Figure 13 in Chapter 4. The malt phosphate species (ex. H_3PO_4, $H_2PO_4^{-1}$, and HPO_4^{-2}), behave similarly, with the result that the number of protons actually released by the apatite reaction depends on their relative proportions, and therefore on the pH. The relationship between pH and protons released is shown in Figure 26. In the pH range of 4 to 6, the curve shows that a mean of 14 protons are released by the various phosphates per mole of apatite precipitated. In other words, going back to the equation above, 10 millimoles (20 mEq) of chalk react to produce 1 millimole of apatite plus a mean of 14 protons, i.e., 20 mEq of alkalinity reacts to release 14 mEq of *acidity*, neutralizing 14 mEq of the 20 mEq addition, leaving only 6 mEq of alkalinity left to affect the pH of the mash. This is 30% of the anticipated addition, and this is due solely to the calcium component of the addition reacting with malt phosphates. An addition of sodium carbonate (Na_2CO_3) would not experience this reduction, nor does sodium bicarbonate.

Number of Protons Released vs. pH

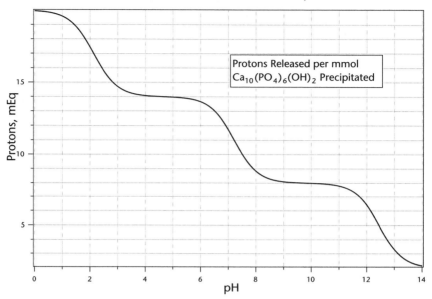

Figure 26—This chart shows the mean number of protons (or mEq of acidity) that are released as the result of the apatite reaction between calcium and malt phosphate as a function of pH. Note that the average number in the general range of mash pH (4–6) is 14 mEq/mmol. From deLange[9].

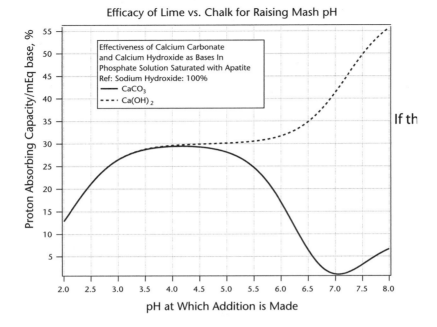

Figure 27—This figure shows the relative effectiveness of calcium carbonate and calcium hydroxide for absorbing protons in a simulated mash (i.e., raising alkalinity), based on the stoichiometric precipitation of apatite. Note that the value for both calcium carbonate and calcium hydroxide is about 30% of the mEq of the addition in the region of 4–6 pH, but that the hydroxide effectiveness actually increases at higher pH, unlike the carbonate. From deLange[9].

This means that 1 gram of calcium carbonate added to 1 liter of water in the mash would contribute 20 mEq/L of calcium and 20 mEq/L of carbonate, but the net effect is about 6 mEq/L of alkalinity from that 1 gram addition, (i.e., 6 mEq/L of hydrogen ions or acidity neutralized). The 6 mEq/L of alkalinity can be added to the C_T alkalinity in the mash. For the purposes of calculating the effect of the added calcium from the chalk addition on C_T RA, the calcium has gone away—it was precipitated as apatite—so only the net alkalinity is added.

Further experimentation by deLange[9] found that doubling the addition that led to the 30% hypothesis had no additional effect, and that a third addition several hours later actually resulted in a decrease in mash pH. The experimental results are valid, but unexplained.

deLange cautions that the '30% theory' is a relatively new finding, and should be used with discretion, if at all. While the above discussion is consistent with the observations of deLange and other brewers who have experienced a lack of response with chalk additions, there may be additional factors, or other explanations that are equally or more valid.

The bottom line is that chalk additions are *not recommended* for raising mash pH—it reacts slowly and is the least effective of the options.

Adding Calcium Hydroxide (Slaked Lime)

Calcium hydroxide can be added to either the water or the mash. If added to the brewing water, the addition can be calculated as a change to the Kolbach residual alkalinity because it adds both calcium and alkalinity as mEq/L. For an addition of 1 gram/liter of $Ca(OH)_2$ (27 mEq/L) this calculates as:

$$\Delta RA = 27 - 27/3.5 = 19.3 \text{ mEq/L or 965 ppm as } CaCO_3$$

This quantity is consistent with the observations of M. Brungard[10]. The numbers for 1 gram per gallon are 7.13 mEq/gal as total alkalinity and $\Delta RA = 5.1$ mEq/gal or 255 ppm as $CaCO_3$

If the calcium hydroxide addition is being made to the mash to adjust mash pH, then the addition needs to incorporate the concept of Z alkalinity as done in the case of sodium bicarbonate additions above. The moles of total carbonates (C_T) in the mash would need to be calculated based on both the brewing water pH and the mash target pH (Z pH). The ΔRA from calcium hydroxide (19.3 mEq/L or 5.1 mEq/gal) as calculated above would be added to the Z alkalinity of the water in the mash. Note that there is no Z adjustment for hydroxide; it is a strong base and always contributes 1 mEq/mmol, the same as a strong acid does.

In addition, the calcium from the calcium hydroxide addition to the mash might experience the same fate as that of calcium carbonate[9], when added to the mash. Kolbach's equation for residual alkalinity incorporates factors for calcium and magnesium reactions but the amount of reduction in the alkalinity per Kolbach (28.5% reduction) is not consistent with the stoichiometry of the apatite equation. The theoretical apatite equation for calcium hydroxide is:

$$10Ca(OH)_2 + 6H_2PO_4^- \rightarrow Ca_{10}(PO_4)_6(OH)_2 + 12H_2O + 6OH^{-1}$$

Here the reaction products are water and hydroxide instead of bicarbonate, but the net reaction is the same: 20 equivalents of alkalinity from the initial hydroxide become only 6 equivalents due to apatite precipitation, i.e., a 70% reduction in contributed alkalinity. We should note that this equation is simply one reaction out of several that may be occurring depending on the concentrations and forms of the phosphates present in the mash.

A series of experiments was conducted by deLange[9] with calcium hydroxide (slaked lime) using the same procedure as for the carbonates. Again, the 80°L caramel malt was ground fine and mashed with distilled water, and the DI pH of the mash was verified. Calcium hydroxide was added, and the change in mash pH was recorded over time. The rate of pH change was much faster; the hydroxide additions only took about 4 minutes for the 0.1 pH change to stabilize across the 4.6–5.5 range, where the reactions were quickest. At higher solution pH (5.5–6.0), the rate of pH change also slowed for hydroxide additions, but not by the order of magnitude exhibited by the carbonates. However, there was some question as to the purity of the calcium hydroxide used for the experiments[1*]. This set of experiments showed that reaction kinetics were better, but did not give a good indication of the number of mEq to be realized from the additions.

The question of how much reduction to expect was addressed by taking a high-purity calcium hydroxide solution of 116 mEq (calculated) and adding it to the 80°L caramel malt mash. Using the 30 minute titration curve for this malt as shown in Chapter 5, 116 mEq should have shifted the DI pH of this malt to about 6.40 pH at 48°C. The actual result at T=30 for that addition was a pH of 5.87, which corresponds on that curve to an addition of about 83.5 mEq or 72% of the total addition. Note that this is very close to the Kolbach prediction. At T=120 minutes, the pH had fallen to 5.78 or about 66% of the total addition, but this

---

[1*] The real source and purity of the calcium hydroxide was not known, having been purchased many years before at a homebrew supply shop. Titration showed that it only tested to 53% of the typical alkalinity of calcium hydroxide, and that it did in fact contain some measure of calcium carbonate and other impurities.

time period and result is outside the parameters of the titration response curve of the malt. The results suggest that Kolbach's equation is valid for calcium hydroxide additions, at least within the typical mashing time of 1 hour. As mashing time gets longer, more apatite-type reactions may occur that will pull the mash pH lower to the stoichiometric net 30% of the addition.

Adding Sodium or Potassium Hydroxide

The addition of sodium or potassium hydroxide to the mash or the water does not cause an apatite reaction, so the effect on mash pH is more direct. As will be discussed in Chapter 7, sodium levels above 100 ppm are not generally recommended, although people probably have different tolerances to sodium in beer, similar to tolerance for salt in food. Some references, such as Taylor[3], state that the off-flavor threshold for sodium is as high as 250 ppm. Other brewers, such as one of the authors, C. Kaminski, have recommended no more than 50 ppm as the guideline.

The potassium content of beer is commonly listed as being about 40 mg/100 grams or 400 ppm, and Taylor[3] states the potassium content from a 10°P beer made from de-ionized water as being 355 ppm. The potassium content of orange juice, for comparison, is commonly listed as being about 1,800 ppm. An 1,800 ppm potassium concentration in beer might not be palatable, but adding significant amounts (~200 ppm K^{+1}) of potassium hydroxide or potassium chloride to the water/beer would probably not be noticed.

One gram per liter of sodium hydroxide adds 25 mEq/L of alkalinity and 575 ppm of sodium. One gram per liter of potassium hydroxide adds 17.8 mEq/L of alkalinity and 697 ppm of potassium.

To make a 1 Normal solution:

> Dissolve 40 grams of sodium hydroxide in sufficient water to make a 1 liter solution. Dissolve 56 grams of potassium hydroxide in sufficient water to make a 1 liter solution.

Note: Both sodium hydroxide and potassium hydroxide are strong caustics and should not come in contact with the skin, even in dry form. Wear appropriate personal protective equipment and consult the MSDS before handling.

Table 14—Summary of Methods for Increasing Alkalinity

Method	Comments
Sodium Bicarbonate *Can be added to water or mash.* **Efficacy:** Good **Safety:** Low Hazard	For total alkalinity adjustment of water: 1 gram per gallon = 72.3 ppm Na^{+1}, 188 ppm HCO_3^-, 3.04 mEq/gallon alkalinity. 1 gram per liter = 273.7 ppm Na^{+1}, 710.5 ppm HCO_3^-, 11.8 mEq/liter alkalinity. For mash adjustment to Z pH: 1 gram per gallon = 72.3 ppm Na^{+1}, 3.04 mEq/gallon alkalinity. 1 gram per liter = 273.7 ppm Na^{+1}, 11.9 mEq/gallon alkalinity. See text for additions to mash and Z alkalinity.
Chalk *Can be dissolved in water with CO_2 over-pressure or acid.* **Efficacy:** Poor **Safety:** Low Hazard	Powdered chalk additions are not recommended. Results are unpredictable, but generally ineffective for increasing alkalinity and the mash pH. If dissolved in water prior to addition, it will behave like sodium bicarbonate. See text for full explanation.
Slaked Lime *Can be added to water or mash.* **Efficacy:** Good **Safety:** Moderate Hazard	1 gram per gallon = 142.9 ppm Ca^{+2}, 121.2 ppm OH^-, 7.1 mEq/gallon alkalinity 1 gram per liter = 540.9 ppm Ca^{+2}, 458.8 ppm OH^-, 27 mEq/gallon alkalinity DRA = 5.1 mEq/gal DRA = 19.3 mEq/L Can be added to water or to mash. Reaction rate is acceptable: 4.9 to 5.4 pH in 15–20 minutes.
Sodium Hydroxide *Can be added to water or mash.* **Efficacy:** Good **Safety:** Hazardous	1 gram per gallon = 152 ppm Na^{+1}, 112.3 ppm OH^-, 6.6 mEq/gallon alkalinity 1 gram per liter = 575 ppm Na^{+1}, 425 ppm OH^-, 25 mEq/liter alkalinity Dissolve 40 grams in sufficient water to make a 1 liter, 1N solution.
Potassium Hydroxide *Can be added to water or mash.* **Efficacy:** Good **Safety:** Hazardous	1 gram per gallon = 184.1 ppm K^{+1}, 80.0 ppm OH^-, 4.7 mEq/gallon alkalinity 1 gram per liter = 697 ppm K^{+1}, 303 ppm OH^-, 17.8 mEq/liter alkalinity Dissolve 56 grams in sufficient water to make a 1 liter, 1N solution.

References

1. Brungard, M., Water Knowledge, https://sites.google.com/site/brunwater/water-knowledge, 2013.

2. Latham, B., *Softening of Water*, Journal of the Society of Arts, Vol. 32, London, 1884.

3. *Handbook of Brewing, 2ⁿᵈ Ed.*, Priest and Stewart, *Chapter 4-Water*, D.G. Taylor, CRC Press, 2006.

4. Briggs, et al., Malting and Brewing Science, Vol. 2, Chapman and Hall, London, 1981)

5. Troester, K., The Effect of Brewing Water and Grist Composition on the pH of the Mash, Braukaiser.com, 2009.

6. Sykes, WJ, Ling, AR, Principles and Practice of Brewing, 3ʳᵈ Edition, Charles Griffin and Co. Ltd., London, 1907.

7. deLange, A. J., Alkalinity Reduction with Acid, wetnewf.org/pdfs/alkalinity-reduction-with.html, 2013.

8. Kolbach, P., *The Influence of Brewing Water on the pH of Wort and Beer*, VLB Monthly for Brewing, P Kolbach Ed., Vol 6, Number 5, May 1953, Berlin. Translated by deLange and Troester, wetnewf.org/pdfs/Brewing_articles/KolbachPaper.pdf

9. deLange, A. J., Chalk, www.wetnewf.org/pdfs/chalk.html, 2013.

10. Brungard, M., email communication, 2013.

7

Adjusting Water for Style

Adjusting the water for a specific beer is one of the more challenging parts of creating a recipe. There are a lot of decisions, a lot of choices and a lot of leeway. There is no single perfect water for a specific style, but brewing water and style choice can evolve hand in hand to reach a perfect recipe.

The primary requirements for brewing water are that it mashes in at the target pH range (typically 5.2–5.6 pH at 68°F) and that the water's flavor character should enhance the beer character and not detract from it. Many great beer recipes have been discredited because of a lack of understanding about the relationship between the style and the water choices used to create the recipe. Fortunately, it is now becoming more common for recipes to include water information.

Another common mistake is thinking that the water from a famous brewing region was not adjusted before use in the brewery. Brewers have been modifying (fiddling) with their water for hundreds of years. Private water consultants have been around for at least 100 years and likely much longer. In 1935, Wallerstein Laboratories published, *The Treatment of Brewing Water in the Light of Modern Chemistry*. In the summary they state, "Every brewing water must be carefully studied and treated according to its specific needs. For over 20 years we have made the treatment of brewing water our special study, supplying the brewer with the particular Wallerstein Burton Salts necessary to improve and correct his brewing water."

We are brewers—we experiment, we tweak, we never stop being creative.

How to Brew Seriously Good Beer

Step 1—Buy a pH Meter

We have not spent the first two thirds of the book defining pH, describing factors that affect pH, and discussing methods for adjusting mash pH, just to toss it all aside and say, "Don't worry about the mash pH, it will be close enough." That's the kind of thing you tell beginners: "Don't worry, everyone falls down at first; just have fun!" You are not a beginner. If you are serious about brewing good beer, then you need to be serious about measuring your results and reaching your goals. To be able to visualize a goal, plan a course of action, and consistently achieve the goal is the mark of the expert.

So to that end, go out and buy a good pH meter. Test strips are for amateurs. Be serious about your beer.

For more information on pH meters, see Appendix A.

Historical Waters, Treatments, and Styles

Water is one of the factors that make a region's beers unique. A great example is Pilsner-style beer. The very soft water from Plzen influenced every aspect of the style; malting, mashing, the resultant malt flavors, the selection of hop varieties and the hopping schedule that paired best with those flavors. Recreating a Pilsner with vastly different water is one of the greatest challenges a brewer can undertake. Now, with the ready availability of reverse osmosis systems, it is much easier to build the right kind of water for a particular style. But what is the right kind of water? Historically, brewers have looked to the water compositions of some of the famous brewing cities and sought to replicate those waters to brew the same style of beer. Books such as the *American Handy Book of Brewing, Malting, and Auxiliary Trades* (1902), the Wallerstein Laboratories book mentioned above, and *Malting and Brewing Science* (1981) have all included water compositions to help readers understand the relationship between water composition and beer style. The profiles in Table 15 are commonly cited examples, but we cannot take these numbers as gospel just because they have been published; we have to understand the circumstances and context under which the measurements are typically gathered.

Table 15—Water Profiles from Famous Brewing Cities

City/Style	Ca^{+2}	Mg^{+2}	HCO_3^{-1}	Na^{+1}	Cl^{-1}	SO_4^{-2}	RA*	Sum (+)	Sum (−)
Pilsen/ Pilsner	10	3	3	3	4	4	⁻6	0.9	0.2
Dublin/ Dry Stout	118	4	319	12	19	54	175	6.8	6.9
Dortmund/ Export Lager	225	40	180	60	60	120	⁻36	17.2	7.1
Vienna/ Vienna Lager	200	60	120	8	12	125	⁻80	15.3	4.9
Munich/ Oktoberfest	76	18	152	?	2	10	60	5.4	2.8
London/ British Bitter	52	32	104	86	34	32	29	9.0	3.3
Edinburgh/ Scottish Ale	125	25	225	55	65	140	80	10.7	8.4
Burton/ India Pale Ale	352	24	320	54	16	820	⁻3	21.9	22.8

* RA values are given as $CaCO_3$ in parts per million (ppm). RA is calculated from the profile and rounded to the nearest whole number. Sources: Burton—Malting and Brewing Science Vol. 1, Dortmund—Noonen, G., New Brewing Lager Beer, Dublin—The Practical Brewer, Edinburgh—Noonen, G., New Brewing Lager Beer, London—Westermann and Huige, Fermentation Technology, Munich—Malting and Brewing Science Vol. 1, Pilsen—Wahl-Henius, American Handy Book, Vienna—Noonen, G., New Brewing Lager Beer

The Balance of Milliequivalents

For a water composition to be valid, the sums of anion and cation charges should be equal (or nearly equal, to allow for small errors). The easiest way to evaluate this is by dividing all of the ion concentrations by the appropriate equivalent weight to convert each concentration to milliequivalents per liter. It is best if the alkalinity is represented as "total alkalinity as $CaCO_3$," because if the listing is only for bicarbonate, you will need to calculate the total alkalinity based on the water pH. If the water pH is about 8–8.6, then the bicarbonate is about 97% of the total alkalinity and you can use the simple conversion factor, Total Alkalinity as $CaCO_3$ = 50 x HCO_3/61, to convert between the two values with confidence. If the water pH is not given, you can assume for the sake of argument that the water pH is probably 7.5 to 8.5—most potable waters are—and proceed using the conversion factor above, but the total alkalinity may be under-represented. This is one area where small errors (<1 mEq) can manifest. For more information on milliequivalent balance and carbonate species distribution, see Appendix D.

If the difference between the sums is greater than 1 mEq, then the cause of the discrepancy might be because the report was compiled from different locations around the city, or at different times throughout the year, or because of some other reason.

For example, the Dortmund profile in Table 15 converts to the following milliequivalents per liter.

Dortmund (from Table 15)								
	Ca^{+2}	Mg^{+2}	HCO_3^{-1}	Na^{+1}	Cl^{-1}	SO_4^{-2}	Sum (+)	Sum (−)
mg/L	225	40	180	60	60	120		
mEq/L	11.25	3.3	3.6	2.6	1.7	2.5	17.2	7.8

Summing the cation mEq/L gives 11.25 + 3.3 + 2.6 = 17.2

Summing the anion mEq/L gives 3.6 + 1.7 + 2.5 = 7.8

The ion balance is quite far apart, and therefore the given ion concentrations are probably not representative of the real water, although they may be close. The following is another profile for Dortmund, from Table 16.

Dortmund (from Table 16)								
	Ca^{+2}	Mg^{+2}	HCO_3^{-1}	Na^{+1}	Cl^{-1}	SO_4^{-2}	Sum (+)	Sum (−)
mg/L	230	15	235	40	130	330		
mEq/L	11.5	1.2	3.8	1.7	3.7	6.9	14.5	14.4

Here you can see that the sums of the cations and anions are nearly equal, and the biggest differences between the two profiles are the chloride and sulfate levels. The first profile is not necessarily wrong, but it is imbalanced and therefore it is not an accurate description of a naturally-occurring water. A brewer trying to replicate the water would have a difficult time getting the same concentrations, but replication is not the actual goal; the goal is a good-tasting beer in that style. In addition, keep in mind that the brewers in that city may have modified the water as well.

The following profiles were carefully researched by Martin Brungard, a civil and environmental engineer who has long specialized in water resources engineering. These profiles should be more representative of the actual water composition in each city (or at least at one location in each city). Comparing the two tables shows some differences.

Table 16—Brungard's Ion Profiles from Major Brewing Cities[1].									
City/ Style	Ca^{+2}	Mg^{+2}	HCO_3^{-1}	Na^{+1}	Cl^{-1}	SO_4^{-2}	RA*	Sum (+)	Sum (−)
Plzen/ Pilsner	7	2	16	2	6	8	7	0.7	0.9
Dublin/ Dry Stout	120	4	315	12	19	55	170	6.9	6.8
Dort- mund/ Export Lager	230	15	235	40	130	330	20	14.5	14.4

Vienna/ Vienna Lager	75	15	225	10	15	60	122	5.4	5.4
Munich/ Dunkel	77	17	295	4	8	18	177	5.4	5.4
London/ Bitter	70	6	166	15	38	40	82	4.6	4.6
Edin- burgh/ Scottish Ale	100	20	285	55	50	140	150	9	9
Burton/ India Pale Ale	275	40	270	25	35	610	1	18.1	18.1

* RA values are given as $CaCO_3$ in parts per million (ppm). RA is calculated from the profile and rounded to the nearest whole number.

The Dogma of Virgin Water

One reason for the concentrations in Table 15 not summing equally might be that they are averages from several sources around the city. For example, take Burton-Upon-Trent: you have probably heard that Burton water is the ideal pale ale water, and probably think that you want to replicate this water exactly to best brew the style. However, digging deeper into the history of the region shows that the water was not always this hard or sulfuric. In the book, *IPA: Brewing Techniques, Recipes and the Evolution of India Pale Ale*, by M. Steele[2], the author states that the earliest breweries drilled shallow wells close to the river Trent, to a depth of about 30 feet (9m). However, as the population and brewing industry grew, the river and local wells became polluted with human waste. As a result, new wells were dug further away from the river and deeper (100–200ft/30–60m) to find clean water. Data from Worthington for shallow and deep wells shows a difference of nearly 3 times more "Sulfate of Lime" (gypsum) and half the "Carbonate of Lime" (calcium carbonate) in the deep wells versus the shallow.

Many modern water adjustment methods for ales can be traced to changes experienced at Burton-upon-Trent. Indeed, the term, "Burtonizing," was coined in 1882. In addition, the *IPA* book cites, "*A Systematic Handbook of Practical Brewing*," by Southby in 1885, and shows a table comparing several water sources around England, such as, "Burton Above Marl," "Burton Below Marl," "Thames Valley, Deep Well," and others. (Marl is a clay-like or silt-like deposit containing a high proportion of calcite or other calcium minerals.) Of interest are the parameters used to compare these sources: "carbonates of lime and magnesia precipitated on boiling," "lime not precipitated on boiling," "sulfuric acid," and "nitric acid." Clearly, the brewers in the Burton region were taking steps to evaluate and adjust each water source to suit their needs.

Therefore, blindly copying these water profiles by the numbers can be misleading. Nevertheless, understanding the history of the region can be a good start when trying to plan the water profile for a style.

The Role of Heating on Decarbonation

Heating and boiling can have a large effect on the hardness and alkalinity of water. As noted in Chapter 4, the temporary hardness (the bicarbonate in the water) will precipitate as calcium carbonate because the rise in temperature causes a shift in the equilibrium partial pressure of carbon dioxide, causing CO_2 to come out of solution, the pH to rise, the bicarbonate to convert to carbonate, and thus over-saturation of calcium carbonate in solution. Typically, calcium carbonate will precipitate until the first of either calcium or carbonate reaches a concentration of 1 mEq/L. For example, look at the Munich water profile from Table 16 excerpted below.

City	Ca^{+2}	Mg^{+2}	HCO_3^{-1}	Na^{+1}	Cl^{-1}	SO_4^{-2}	RA	Sum (+)	Sum (−)
Munich	77	17	295	4	8	18	177	5.4	5.4

The calcium and bicarbonate concentrations are high, and the residual alkalinity is comparable to Dublin, Ireland. How did this city become renowned for brewing pale Munich Helles, and amber Oktoberfest? One answer may be the decrease in alkalinity from pre-boiling the water, as discussed in Chapter 6. This mechanism can greatly decrease the alkalinity by precipitating the temporary hardness and decanting the water from the sediment. The typical solubility of calcium carbonate at normal atmospheric pressure (partial pressure of CO_2 = ~0.0003-0.0005 atmospheres) is about

1 mEq/L or 20 ppm Ca^{+2} and 50 ppm of CO_3^{-2}. Therefore, boiling will reduce the temporary hardness to approximately those levels, assuming ideal conditions. Calcium and bicarbonate react on a 1-to-1 mEq basis, so dividing the above concentrations by the equivalent weights gives 3.85 mEq/L of calcium and 4.81 mEq/L of bicarbonate. Assuming 1 mEq/L of calcium (i.e., 20 ppm) remains, that means that 2.85 mEq/L of calcium would react with 2.85 mEq/L of bicarbonate, and that would leave (4.81 − 2.85 = 1.96 mEq/L); about 120 ppm of HCO_3 left in solution. The approximate water composition after boiling would be:

City	Ca^{+2}	Mg^{+2}	HCO_3^{-1}	Na^{+1}	Cl^{-1}	SO_4^{-2}	RA	Sum (+)	Sum (−)
Munich	20	17	120	4	8	18	74	2.6	2.6

This is a large change in the residual alkalinity of the water, from 177 to 74, and it may have enabled the brewing of lighter-colored styles.

The Role of the Reinheitsgebot

The Reinheitsgebot, the German Purity Law adopted in 1516, made achieving the proper mash pH with light malts even more difficult. Only the use of water, malt, hops, and yeast were allowed in the making of beer. The addition of brewing salts was not allowed. The addition of mineral acids was not allowed. Instead, acidification of the mash was accomplished by the use of Sauermalz (sour malt, i.e., malt that is sprayed with lactobacillus-soured wort and dried) and the decoction mashing process (melanoidin development). A long acid rest at 86–126°F/30–53°C was also used by many breweries. The acid rest temperature promotes phytase enzyme activity and favors lactobacillus growth.

The Reinheitsgebot and Biergesetz of 1993 forbid additions to water, but they do not bar removing elements from the water, and decarbonation by heating and slaked lime treatment are both common in Germany. Decarbonation by slaked lime was patented in 1841 by Thomas Clark, a British chemist. Several similar patents were filed in later years as attempts to improve this method, but the basic Clark process has stood the test of time and is still in use today. Lime softening has the benefit of precipitating iron and manganese hardness as well as carbonate hardness. More information on lime softening is provided in Chapter 6.

The bottom line is that the specific ingredients and brewing methods affect the flavor of the beer. Making these choices and striking the right balance are part of the brewer's art.

Flavor Ion Effects

Assuming we have a water that achieves our target pH, the next item on the agenda is the flavor effects of the ions. In beer, some ions have strong flavors, like chloride and sulfate; others are fairly neutral, like calcium; and others are typically low enough in concentration that they remain below taste threshold, like bicarbonate. Sometimes a brewer can only perceive the difference an ion creates by how it affects the flavors of the hops or malt.

The ions we are most concerned with are, of course, calcium, magnesium, bicarbonate (alkalinity), sodium, chloride, and sulfate. It should be remembered that all ions are added in the form of a salt and you cannot add any single ion without adding the associated cation or anion. For example, when we add calcium chloride we are adding both calcium and chloride ions. It is difficult to add more alkalinity to a soft water without adding significant hardness or sodium as well. It is often a case of two steps forward, one step back.

Calcium

Calcium is the friend of all brewers who brew with alkaline water. The reaction with malt phosphates is one of the primary mechanisms for the mash pH drop. It is remarkably flavorless. It protects, stabilizes, and promotes enzyme activity in the mash. It aids in protein coagulation, trub formation, oxalate precipitation, yeast metabolism, and yeast flocculation. The calcium levels in the water need to be high enough to carry sufficient levels through the boil and fermentation. A range of 50–200 ppm in the water for the mash is recommended. An old brewer's rule of thumb when brewing with soft water was to add 2/3 of the mineral addition to the mash and 1/3 to the boil to ensure that sufficient calcium was present for good clarity, although the actual amount of the total addition for good clarity was not mentioned. Calcium (and carbonate) are not perceived to have flavor effects, like sodium or chloride, but are readily perceived as "minerally" at high concentrations (>200 ppm), in the same sense as bottled mineral water.

Magnesium

Magnesium is usually added in the form of Epsom salt ($MgSO_4$), which also contributes to the sulfate load of the beer. Magnesium works half as well as calcium in lowering mash pH due to the higher solubility of magnesium phosphates and magnesium hydroxide relative to hydroxyl apatite.

Magnesium is recognized as a necessary yeast nutrient at 5 ppm, but barley wort typically contains much more than the yeast would require (c. 100 ppm @12°P). Some sources indicate that 40 ppm should be the maximum concentration because it is said to have a bitter flavor. The *EBC Manual of Good Practice, Vol. 13—Mashing and Mash Separation*, states, "At low concentration (less than 7.1 mval of $MgSO_4$), it does not affect beer flavour. At higher levels magnesium ion can impart an unpleasant sour and bitter taste to beer." (Note: 7.1 mval = 7.1 mEq/L = 86 ppm of magnesium.) Some brewers believe that having a minimum level of Mg in the beer contributes greatly to the flavor. To the best of our knowledge, no studies have been done to determine this level, but one of the authors (C. Kaminski), swears by adding small additions of Epsom salt to dark beers, such as porter, to achieve a minimum of 30 ppm Mg in the water going into the mash.

Sulfate

Sulfate is a defining character of the water from Burton-upon-Trent. While the Burton-upon-Trent municipal supply is required by statute to not exceed sulfate levels of 250 ppm, some wells can be as high as 850 ppm. Sulfate can make the hop character more assertive, or dryer, but many brewers find at very high levels it reduces the quality of the bitterness and can taste minerally. In relatively moderate amounts (200–400 ppm) it is said to increase the "linger time" of the bitterness, and accentuate the hop flavor and aroma. However, many Czech and German lager brewers avoid sulfates entirely, because they find that it ruins the soft noble hop character of Pils and Helles style beers. The most common way to add sulfate is by adding gypsum.

Chloride

Chloride is a common addition for water and beer. It provides a rounder, fuller, sweeter quality to the malt character and the beer. It can be added to the water as $CaCl_2$ in order to add calcium to lower the residual alkalinity, or it can be added to the boil as $CaCl_2$ or $NaCl$ (use non-iodized salt, free of anti-caking agents) in order to round out the malt character.

Chloride is said to be corrosive to brewery equipment, including stainless steel, at concentrations greater than 100 ppm. Concentrations greater than 300 ppm can have negative effects on beer clarification, body, and colloidal stability. Concentrations above 400 ppm are said to have adverse effects on beer flavor. Fermentation rate is affected when concentration exceeds 500 ppm. We are recommending that the concentration in mashing water not exceed 200 ppm.

Sodium

Sodium would seem to be the bastard stepchild of the brewing ions, and in many ways, it is. It is difficult to add alkalinity to water without adding sodium, either as sodium bicarbonate, or as sodium hydroxide. It is a common byproduct of ion exchange water softening, and it is mostly unaffected by other water treatments—it is also difficult to eliminate from source water. There are potassium versions of the same salts, but barley wort contains high concentrations already (c. 400 ppm @ 10°P). At low concentrations, sodium is said to sweeten the malt character. According to the *EBC Manual of Good Practice, Vol. 13*, when sodium is associated with chlorides (no level given), sodium gives a salty taste at concentrations greater than 150 ppm. At lower concentrations (<150 ppm) it acts to improve mouthfeel and fullness in pale beers. The EBC manual further states that ale beers are less affected by sodium chloride than lager beers. We are recommending that the concentration in mashing water not exceed 100 ppm.

Sulfate-to-Chloride Ratio

The ratio of sulfate to chloride is said to greatly influence the hoppy-to-malty or dryness-to-fullness balance of the beer. It has also been suggested that the ratio is more important to the balance than the actual amounts. However, common sense tells us that a beer with a 5:1 ratio consisting 5 ppm of sulfate and 1 ppm chloride would be indistinguishable from the same beer with a 5 ppm-to-5 ppm ratio. Clearly, a minimum level of sulfate and chloride concentration must be present in the beer for it to have a noticeable effect, somewhere in the range of 50–150 ppm. Of course, the first thought you have when designing a new pale ale recipe is that you want a crisp hop character with a nice round malty finish, and you would be tempted to maximize both (e.g., 400 ppm). However, high levels of both can taste minerally and harsh. The author's experience (C. Kaminski) with pale ale, wheat, IPA, and other core products at his brewpub over the past ten years has demonstrated that the effect is real, if implemented within the following guidelines:

- The sulfate-to-chloride ratio is a useful means of leveraging the flavor balance of a beer. The useful range of the ratio is 9 to 0.5, predominately for ales. Pale and light lagers that depend on fine noble hop aroma are more sensitive to sulfate levels and lower levels of sulfate (<100 ppm) are generally recommended.
- The sulfate-to-chloride ratio is not magic—a ratio of 30:30 ppm is not equal to 300:300 ppm, despite published references that suggest it.
- Based on our experience, a minimum level of chloride to affect beer flavor is about 50 ppm, and the maximum should probably be 200 ppm.
- Based on our experience, a minimum level of sulfate to affect beer flavor is probably about 50 ppm, and the maximum should probably be 500 ppm.
- It should be noted that although some great beers have been made with sulfate levels exceeding 800 ppm, many people can be sensitive to high levels of sulfate and it can cause gastrointestinal distress.

The nice thing about experimenting with the sulfate-to-chloride ratio in a beer is that it can be done in the glass. An easy experiment is to take several glasses of beer and dose them with different amounts of $CaCl_2$ and $CaSO_4$. To do this, dissolve a teaspoon (a few grams) of $CaCl_2$ and $CaSO_4$ into separate glasses of warm water. $CaSO_4$ is hard to dissolve so stir thoroughly; most of it will eventually dissolve. Use a straw or eyedropper to add a few milliliters of one or the other solution and taste the beer. You will learn the difference the ratio can make firsthand.

Building Brewing Water from Scratch

Brewers have been adding mineral salts to brewing water for hundreds of years, and while the names of salts and the units may have changed, the intent hasn't: increase the calcium and control the alkalinity to improve the beer. Brewers today have a luxury that historical brewers did not: easy access to de-ionized or reverse osmosis water that lets the brewer build a desired mineral profile from scratch. Generally speaking, these water treatments remove almost all of the minerals from the water. However, if this water is left exposed to the air, carbon dioxide will dissolve in from the air and the pH of the water will gradually drop towards 5, just as it does with rainwater.

The addition of calcium and magnesium sulfate salts to brewing water is very straightforward—the ion contributions are listed in Table 17, and both act to lower mash pH. Calcium sulfate can be difficult to dissolve in water however, having a saturation level of about 1.9–2.1 grams per liter across the brewing temperatures. The maximum solubility occurs at 40°C/104°F.

Calcium chloride is another popular option for affecting mash pH and flavor, but there are two problems when calculating additions: 1) calcium chloride tends to absorb water and the powder must be kept tightly sealed to prevent it from forming into a solid crystal, and 2) commercial sources vary in purity. The dihydrate form is most common and can be purchased from scientific supply houses at a premium price. A commercial source for the food or water treatment industry is more likely to supply a product that is 75–80% $CaCl_2 \cdot 2H_2O$, with other components being $Ca(OH)_2$, $MgCl_2$, $NaCl$, and water. If it is intended for the food industry, it is obviously food grade, but the impurities may throw off your calculations.

The number of water molecules associated with calcium chloride powder is typically two, but it will tend to adsorb more if exposed to moisture. In fact, calcium chloride is deliquescent—it will absorb so much water that it will eventually form a solution. The point is that the weight of this water needs to be taken into account when calculating the ion contributions of calcium chloride and other hydrated salt additions. The ion contributions for common brewing salts, including the hydrated ones, are listed in Table 17.

The carbonate salts can also be problematic, but for different reasons. First, calcium carbonate (chalk) is practically insoluble in water; the solubility being only about 0.05 grams per liter at standard temperature and pressure. The solubility can be increased by increasing the dissolved CO_2 content as discussed in Chapter 4, but it is not very practical. Chalk is more soluble in the mash than in water, but dissolution in the mash results in almost immediate precipitation of hydroxyl apatite, which greatly reduces the contributed alkalinity. Experiments have shown that it is largely ineffective. This is discussed more thoroughly in Chapter 6. The main problem with using bicarbonate, in the water or the mash, is that the bicarbonate dissociates/reacts according to the pK values given in Chapter 4, resulting in a redistribution of the carbonate species, and a redistribution of the amount of charge (mEq/mmol). This is also described in Chapter 6. Calculating the precise amount of alkalinity contributed by bicarbonate additions depends on the water pH, target pH and other carbonates already in solution.

Table 17—Ion Contributions by Salt Additions

The contributions are listed equivalently as mg/L (ppm), mEq/L, or ppm as $CaCO_3$, as applicable. mw = mole weight, eqw = equivalent weight, Ceqw = Cation equivalent weight, Aeqw = Anion equivalent weight.

Brewing Salt (formula)	Concentration at 1 gram of salt per liter	Concentration at 1 gram of salt per gallon	Comments
Calcium Carbonate $CaCO_3$ mw = 100 (eqw = 50)	400 ppm Ca^{+2}, 600 ppm CO_3^{-2} 20 mEq/liter alkalinity	106 ppm Ca^{+2}, 158 ppm CO_3^{-2} 5.3 mEq/L alkalinity	Don't Use. See Ch. 6 for explanation.
Sodium Bicarbonate $NaHCO_3$ mw = 84 Ceqw = 23 Aeqw = 61	273.7 ppm Na^{+1} 710.5 ppm HCO_3^-@99% 11.8 mEq/liter alkalinity @99%	72.3 ppm Na^{+1} 188 ppm HCO_3^-@99% 3.04 mEq/L alkalinity @99%	Dissolves readily and effective at raising alkalinity. Z alkalinity depends on pH. See Ch. 6 for explanation.
Calcium Hydroxide $Ca(OH)_2$ mw = 74.1 Ceqw = 20 Aeqw = 17	541 ppm Ca^{+2}, 459 ppm OH^- 27 mEq/liter alkalinity ΔRA = 19.3 mEq/ liter	143 ppm Ca^{+2}, 121 ppm OH^- 7.1 mEq/liter alkalinity ΔRA = 5.1 mEq/ liter	Dissolves readily in water. Raises alkalinity, but see Ch. 6 for explanation. Pickling Lime seems to be acceptable purity.

Sodium Hydroxide NaOH mw = 40 Ceqw = 23 Aeqw = 17	575 ppm Na^{+1} 425 ppm OH^- 25 mEq/L alkalinity	152 ppm Na^{+1} 112.3 ppm OH^- 6.6 mEq/L alkalinity	Dissolves readily. Raises alkalinity. Caution! Hazardous material! Consult MSDS before use.
Potassium Hydroxide KOH mw = 56.1 Ceqw = 39.1 Aeqw = 17	697 ppm K^{+1} 303 ppm OH^- 17.8 mEq/L alkalinity	184 ppm K^{+1} 80 ppm OH^- 4.7 mEq/L alkalinity	Dissolves readily. Raises alkalinity. Caution! Hazardous material! Consult MSDS before use.
Calcium Sulfate $CaSO_4 \cdot 2H_2O$ mw = 172.2 Ceqw = 20 Aeqw = 48	232.8 ppm Ca^{+2} 557.7 ppm SO_4^-	61.5 ppm Ca^{+2} 147.4 ppm SO_4^-	Saturation at room temperature is about 2 grams per liter. Stir vigorously. Lowers mash pH.
Magnesium Sulfate $MgSO_4 \cdot 7H_2O$ mw = 246.5 Ceqw = 12.1 Aeqw = 48	98.6 ppm Mg^{+2} 389.6 ppm SO_4^-	26.0 ppm Mg^{+2} 102.9 ppm SO_4^-	Saturation at room temperature is about 255 grams per liter. Lowers mash pH.
Calcium Chloride $CaCl_2 \cdot 2H_2O$ mw = 147.0 Ceqw = 20 Aeqw = 35.4	272.6 ppm Ca^{+2} 482.3 ppm Cl^-	72.0 ppm Ca^{+2} 127.4 ppm Cl^-	Dissolves readily. Lowers mash pH. Food-grade salt may not be high purity.
Magnesium Chloride $MgCl_2 \cdot 6H_2O$ mw = 203.3 Ceqw = 12.1 Aeqw = 35.4	119.5 ppm Mg^{+2} 348.7 ppm Cl^-	31.6 ppm Mg^{+2} 92.1 ppm Cl^-	Dissolves readily. Lowers mash pH. Food-grade salt may not be high purity.
Sodium Chloride NaCl mw = 58.4 Ceqw = 23 Aeqw = 35.4	393.4 ppm Na^{+1} 606.6 ppm Cl^-	103.9 ppm Na^{+1} 160.3 ppm Cl^-	Dissolves readily. Avoid iodized salt and anti-caking agents.

Choosing a Water for the Style

There are rules, that are meant to enforce the guidelines, that are derived from the principles, which suffice until you really understand what is going on.
—J. Palmer

By now, you are saying that you just want the water to be wet and forget about all the rules and guidelines. Never fear, it is possible to choose a water profile for your recipe without having to get a degree in chemistry. Suggested water profiles for most of the usual beer styles, excluding sours and wood aged, are listed in Tables 18 and 19. These are suggested water profiles, based on the authors' experience and calculations. These suggestions are the opinions of the authors; they are not gospel. Take them with a grain of salt. Brewers should look at these profiles as an entry point for experimentation with the style.

The tables are organized by ale and lager, and by strength and general color. The tables give suggested ranges for calcium, total alkalinity, sulfate, chloride, and Kolbach's residual alkalinity. These ranges are ballpark—they are not meant to be inclusive of every permutation of the components. For example, a particular combination of calcium and alkalinity from their respective ranges may not produce a residual alkalinity value that is within the listed RA range. That's ok—either find a combination that does fall within the recommended RA range, or consider it an opportunity for you to showcase your brewer's art and make a fantastic beer, regardless.

You may have noticed that recommended sodium and magnesium concentrations are not addressed in the tables. The main reason was to conserve space in the table. The second reason is sodium and magnesium levels have historically never been associated with particular styles. Sodium affects flavor, but the amount necessary to affect flavor seems to depend on the individual, the same as with table salt and food. Low concentrations are said to enhance the beer flavor, and make the beer taste sweeter. High concentrations are said to cause a harsh bitterness or a metallic flavor. We are generally recommending not exceeding 100 ppm. Indeed, a recent survey of several styles of commercial beers by C. Bamforth[3] indicated that of 25 beers, only one exceeded the general range of 10–75 ppm, with an outlying value of 127 ppm. The mean value was 35 ppm.

There are no particular recommendations for magnesium water concentrations in brewing literature either. However, the same survey by

Bamforth determined that the magnesium concentrations in tested commercial beers ranged from 30 to 118, with the mean value of 74 ppm. There is no doubt in the authors' minds that the vast majority of this came from the malt. There is generally a small amount in most water supplies, so we assumed a nominal concentration of 15 ppm magnesium for all profiles and used that concentration in all RA calculations. The only exception to this general recommendation would be for porters and stouts, and perhaps similar dark lager styles, where a concentration closer to 30 ppm is recommended by the authors for better beer flavor based on experience. Take it with a grain of salt.

A Few Notes about Defining the Categories and Ranges

Strength:	Light = OG 30–45; Medium = OG 45–65; Strong = OG 65+
Color:	Pale = 0–9 SRM; Amber = 9–18 SRM; Brown = 18–35 SRM; Black = 35+
Bitterness:	Soft = 10–20 IBUs; Moderate = 20–35 IBUs; Assertive = 36–100
Total Alkalinity as $CaCO_3$:	Low = 0–40 ppm; Moderate = 40–120 ppm; High = 120–200
Residual Alkalinity: (Kolbach)	As indicated.
Acidify:	Yes = acid additions are generally needed to hit the target mash pH and/or acidification of the sparge water is recommended to prevent excessive tannin extraction. Maybe = acid additions are generally not needed for mash pH, but sparge acidification may be helpful, depending on recipe grain bill and sparge water alkalinity. No = acid additions to the mash and sparge are generally not needed. Sparge water acidification is always an option at the brewer's discretion.

Note: If you are building your water from an RO source, and not adding alkalinity to it, then acidification for sparging is generally not needed.

These descriptions are general—no beer categorization system is perfect. Assertive bitterness in one beer style may be moderate bitterness in another. Where a particular style is an outlier within its group, such as Dortmunder Export in the medium lager/pale group, it is bracketed by parentheses, as is the outlying parameter. Bohemian Pils was placed in the light lager/pale category even though its OG places it in the medium category, but it has always been in a class by itself. Same problem with American pale ale, extra pale, and IPA—they were finally placed in their own category. The extreme hoppiness of the styles really differentiated them from the other ales of similar gravity and color.

Organizing beer styles by color is tricky. A good system would probably break color down into 2–3 SRM increments, and perhaps eight different groups. We chose to use four, and combined them into three. The reason for this goes back to Chapter 5 and the investigation into the relationship between malt color and malt acidity. Pale beers are essentially base malt-only or may contain low percentages of lightly kilned specialty grains. The malt acidity studies by Bies and Troester (see Chapter 5) indicate significant variability within the 2–10 Lovibond region, but they were generally within the range of 5–15 mEq/kg with respect to a 5.7 pH titration endpoint. Amber colored beers (~9–18 SRM) typically have a high percentage of kilned or caramel malts, though it rarely exceeds 15%. The bulk of the specialty malts in amber beers are moderately kilned, like Munich, biscuit, C40, C60, and C80, and have an acidity in the range of

Table 18—Suggested Water Profiles for Lager Styles

Type	Color	Bitterness	Ca	Alkalinity	Sulfate
light lager	pale	soft	50	0–40	0–50
medium lager	pale	moderate (assertive)	50–75 (75–150)	0–40 (40–80)	50–150
medium lager	amber	soft, moderate	50–75	40–120	0–100
medium lager	brown/black	soft, moderate	50–75	80–120	0–50
strong lager	amber	soft, moderate	50–75	40–80	0–100
strong lager	brown/black	soft, moderate	50–100	80–150	0–100

10–50 mEq/kg when titrated to a 5.7 pH endpoint. The higher caramel malts, such as C90, C120, and Special B actually have some of the highest recorded acidity: 40–80 mEq/kg re. 5.7 pH endpoint, but these malts are typically used only in small percentages (<5%) in deep amber, brown, or ruby-black beers. Roasted malts generally see higher usage in a recipe than the dark caramel malts, but the proportion rarely exceeds 10%. The acidity of roasted malts looks to be more constant with respect to increasing color, at about 40–60 mEq/kg re. 5.7 pH endpoint. A more extensive malt titration analysis by deLange (see Chapter 5) determined that contributed acidity and buffering capacity of malts varies considerably as a function of the pH of the solution (mash) to which it is added.

Nevertheless, deLange's work confirms the general magnitudes and trends of acidity for the different malt types (base, highly-kilned, and roasted).

The result of these various acidity ranges, recipe percentages, and beer colors is that pale beers make up a general category of relatively low-acidity styles, amber beers are a medium-acidity category, and copper, brown and black beers generally make up the highest acidity category. Analysis of typical grain bills in deep amber, brown and black styles suggests that many of these beers have a similar composite acidity. There are exceptions to every generalization of course; your recipe may vary. The main point is that the tables give you logical starting point for designing a water for your beer recipe. In the next section we will use the tables and work through a few examples.

(All values in ppm or ppm as $CaCO_3$ for Alkalinity and RA.)

Chloride	Kolbach RA	Acidify	Styles
50–100	⁻60–0	Yes	Lite American Lager, Standard American Lager, Munich Helles, (Bohemian Pils)
50–100	⁻60–0 (⁻30–30)	Yes	American Premium Lager, German Pils, Classic American Pils (Dortmunder Export)
50–150	0–60	Maybe	Vienna, Oktoberfest
50–150	40–80	No	American Dark, Munich Dunkel, Schwarzbier
50–150	0–60	Maybe	Helles/Maibock, Traditional Bock, Doppelbock
50–100	60–120	No	Traditional Bock, Doppelbock, Eisbock, Baltic Porter

Table 19—Suggested Water Profiles for Ale Styles
All values are in ppm (i.e., mg/L) except Alkalinity and RA, which are ppm as $CaCO_3$.

Type	Color	Bitterness	Ca	Alkalinity	Sulfate
light ale	pale	moderate	50–100	0–80	100–200
light ale	amber	soft, moderate	50–150	40–120	100–200
light ale	brown/ black	moderate	50–75	80–150	50–150
medium ale	pale	soft, moderate	50–100	0–80	0–50
medium ale	pale	moderate, assertive	50–150	40–120	100–400
medium ale	amber	moderate, assertive	50–150	40–120	100–300
medium ale	brown/ black	moderate, assertive	50–75	80–160	50–150
strong ale	pale	moderate	50–100	0–40	50–100
strong ale	amber	moderate, assertive	50–100	40–120	50–100
strong ale	brown/ black	moderate-assertive	50–75	120–200	50–150

Chloride	Kolbach RA	Acidify	Styles
50–100	⁻60-0	Yes	Blonde Ale, American Wheat, Standard Bitter, Best Bitter
50–100	0–60	Maybe	English Mild, Scottish 60/70/80, Standard Bitter, Best Bitter
50–100	30–90	Maybe	English Brown, Brown Porter, Dry Stout
0–100	⁻30–0	Yes	Weizen, Witbier, Cream Ale, Blonde Ale, Kölsch
0–100	⁻30–30	Maybe	American Pale Ale, American XPA, Saison, American IPA, Double IPA
50–100	0–60	No	Altbier, California Common, ESB, Irish Red, American Amber, English IPA, Roggenbier, Belgian Pale, Saison
50–150	60–120	No	American Brown, English Brown, Brown Porter, Robust Porter, Dry Stout, Sweet Stout, Oatmeal Stout, Foreign Extra Stout, American Stout, Dunkelweizen
50–100	⁻30–0	Maybe	Belgian Blonde, Golden Strong, Tripel
50–150	0–60	No	Strong Scotch Ale, Bière de Garde, Dubbel, Old Ale, Barleywine
50–150	120–200	No	Baltic Porter, Foreign Extra Stout, American Stout, Russian Imperial Stout, Weizenbock, Belgian Dark Strong, Old Ale

Adjusting Water to Suit the Style

In this next section we will look at three styles of beer (American pale ale, Pilsner, and foreign extra stout) and discuss options for adjusting the source water examples to better suit each style based on the guidelines in Tables 18 and 19. Every brewing situation presents you with options, and we will discuss the pros and cons of these options in hopes that you gain a better understanding of how to adjust your brewing water. Evaluating options and making these decisions is all part of the brewer's art.

Before we get started however, keep in mind some golden rules:

1. The goal is good-tasting beer.
2. Less is more—do not over-mineralize your beer.
3. Do not expect to create the perfect pairing of recipe and water the first time. Typically, it will take 3–5 batches to dial in any recipe.
4. The target mash pH range is 5.2–5.6, measured at room temperature. Whenever you adjust your brewing water, you should verify that your mash/wort still meets the target range by using a calibrated pH meter on a cooled sample.
5. Final runnings typically need to be below 5.8 pH and above 1.008 gravity to avoid extracting off-flavors. You should verify your final runnings pH at the end of lauter by using a calibrated pH meter on a cooled sample.

There can be other guidelines as well, such as:

Discretion is the better part of flavor.

Do not try to make a square peg fit in a round hole.

Measure twice; add once.

Don't be afraid to get your feet wet, but don't go overboard.

Calculating Residual Alkalinity

The equation for Kolbach's residual alkalinity is defined as milliequivalents of alkalinity being neutralized as a function of milliequivalents of calcium and magnesium via the protons released by the phosphate precipitation reactions. Total alkalinity is typically quoted as "ppm as $CaCO_3$" which is milliequivalents of alkalinity multiplied by the equivalent weight of calcium carbonate (50).

Sometimes the "Total Hardness as $CaCO_3$" will be listed as well. Unfortunately, this quantity is not very useful because the effects of calcium and magnesium on residual alkalinity are not equal—magnesium is half as effective as calcium. The concentrations need to be listed separately on the water report as simply ppm (the concentration of the ion itself). To use these concentrations in the classic equation: RA=Alkalinity–((Ca/3.5)+(Mg/7)), however, they must be converted to ppm as $CaCO_3$ to match the alkalinity unit, or all the species must be converted to milliequivalents. The basis for these calculations is covered in the Appendices.

To make your life easier, the following equation has been converted to using the calcium and magnesium concentrations in ppm, and total alkalinity as ppm as $CaCO_3$, directly:

RA = Total Alkalinity – [Ca]/1.4 – [Mg]/1.7

Brewing an American Pale Ale

The first beer we will try to brew is an American pale ale. This would seem to be an easy and forgiving style to make, but it can be won or lost depending on the water. Assume the grain bill contains no more than 15% total specialty malts, such as Munich, biscuit, and light caramel (C40), with an estimated beer color of 7 SRM. The OG is 1.052 or 13°P.

The first step is to get a water report. The report for this example is shown below.

Water Report:
pH: 7.8
70 Ca
15 Mg
125 Total Alkalinity as $CaCO_3$
35 Na
55 Cl⁻
110 SO_4^{-2}
66 RA (calculated)

At first glance, this water seems to be acceptable as-is, no changes necessary. More than the minimum calcium, a good level of magnesium and the sulfate-to-chloride ratio is 2:1. The alkalinity is a bit higher than medium, but not by very much.

Looking at the suggested profile for a medium strength pale ale in Table 15 shows:

50–150 Ca (check)
40–120 Total Alkalinity (close enough?)
100–400 Sulfate (check)
50–100 Chloride (check)
⁻30–30 RA (high)

Acidify—Maybe (Acid additions are generally not needed for mash pH, but sparge acidification may be helpful, depending on recipe grain bill and sparge water alkalinity.)

You could brew this beer as-is, and many brewers would, but the alkalinity and RA of this water will probably prevent the mash pH from hitting the target (ex. 5.4). If the mash pH is high, the wort pH will be high, and a coarser bitterness will be created during the boil. A higher mash pH may cause a slightly higher beer pH as well, not an abnormal value, but enough of a difference to make the beer seem a bit lackluster instead of great. Getting the mash pH on target generally means that the wort and beer pH will be on target. Therefore, the question becomes a matter of how to reduce the alkalinity.

We have a few options:
1. Add more hardness,
2. Dilute the alkalinity and add back hardness, or
3. Acidify the water.

Option 1—Adding Hardness:

Adding more hardness is the easiest option. The sulfate-to-chloride ratio could be higher for a pale ale, as high as 3:1, and the current sulfate concentration is at the bottom end of the suggested range. Let's use calcium sulfate to bring up the calcium content to 100 ppm Ca and see where that gets us.

1. From Table 17, 1 gram per gallon adds 61.5 ppm of calcium and 147 ppm of sulfate, so we will need roughly a half gram per gallon to make up the difference (30 ppm).

   30 ppm / 61.5 ppm per gram = 0.49 grams (per gallon).
       (Let's use 0.5 gram.)

0.5 grams per gallon contributes 0.5 x 61.5 ppm Ca/gram =
31 ppm Ca
31 + 70 = 101 ppm total Ca

How does this affect the residual alkalinity?
RA = 125 – (101/1.4) – (15/1.7) = 44 ppm as $CaCO_3$

This is better, but still outside the guideline. The color of our beer is only 7 SRM; it is a very pale ale. We probably need to bring the RA down closer to the middle of the guideline to hit the target mash pH (5.4-ish) and get the best flavor expression.

2. Let's use the maximum calcium in the guidelines (150 ppm) and see what the RA is then.

   RA = 125 – (150/1.4) – (15/1.7) = 9 ppm as $CaCO_3$
   This value is much better.

   Necessary weight of calcium for 150 ppm =
   (150 ppm – 70 ppm)/61.5 ppm per gram = 1.3 grams (per gallon)

   1.3 grams per gallon of calcium sulfate will add 191 ppm of sulfate, making the total sulfate 110 + 191 = 301 ppm SO_4^{-2}.

   This value is within the guideline for a hoppy pale ale.

This water profile meets the guideline for the style better, and it would be worth brewing the beer with this calcium level to see how it turns out. It is very important to measure the mash pH and the beer pH as part of this trial. Mash and beer pH are difficult to predict due to the variability of base malt DI pH and the variability of specialty malt acidity between maltsters.[1] This adjusted water composition may deliver an awesome beer, and it may not*. The beer might still be a little bit dull tasting, or it may taste minerally. You need to brew it and decide.

---

* Chimay, Chimay not (brewers' joke.)

Option 2—Dilution and Adding Hardness

This option would consist of diluting the source water 1:1 with distilled or RO water and adding calcium salts to bring the hardness back within the guidelines.

1. The methodology would be very similar to Option 1, using this diluted water profile:

    Diluted water (50% RO water):
    35 Ca
    8 Mg
    63 Total Alkalinity as $CaCO_3$
    18 Na
    28 Cl^-
    55 SO_4^{-2}
    33 RA (calculated)

2. Adding 1 gram of calcium sulfate per gallon (61.5 ppm Ca, 147.4 ppm SO_4^{-2}) to this diluted water would create:

    Adjusted water:
    97 Ca
    8 Mg
    63 Total Alkalinity as $CaCO_3$
    18 Na
    28 Cl^-
    202 SO_4^{-2}
    $(^-)$11 RA (calculated)

Again, it would be worth brewing the beer with this water to see how it tastes and compare it to the first option. On the off-chance that the mash pH for this option might end up being too low by a tenth or two, given the low RA, the dilution rate could be reduced or a little bit of sodium bicarbonate could be used to raise the alkalinity. A test mash would determine if this is the case.

Option 3—Acidification

The third option is technically the most challenging, but acidification is often the first choice of many brewers if they have a reliable pH meter at the mash tun. The problem with the source water is that the alkalinity and the residual alkalinity are a little bit high, which will tend to raise the pH of the mash, and sparge, and may lead to duller, coarser, more bitter-tasting beer.

Starting water:
70 Ca
15 Mg
125 Total Alkalinity as $CaCO_3$
35 Na
55 Cl⁻
110 SO_4^{-2}
Water pH = 7.8 (from report)
66 RA (calculated)

1. Figures 44 (100 ppm alkalinity) and 45 (150 ppm alkalinity) in Appendix B show the remaining percentage alkalinity due to acidification based on initial water pH and the acidified pH. In this example, we are starting at the water pH of 7.8 and acidifying (for example) to pH 5.75 with sulfuric acid. The value on the Y axis for the sulfuric acid, 5.75 pH curve at 7.8 pH (X axis) corresponds about 20 ppm as $CaCO_3$ in Figure 44 and about 30 ppm for the same curve on Figure 45. Logically, the value for 125 ppm total alkalinity would be 25 ppm as $CaCO_3$. The curves can be similarly interpolated for other values of alkalinity. How much acid was required? The calculations are explained in Appendix B, but the short answer is that we started with a total alkalinity of 125 ppm as $CaCO_3$, and acidified to a total alkalinity of 25 ppm as $CaCO_3$. The difference is 100 ppm as $CaCO_3$ or 2 mEq/L of alkalinity that was reduced and therefore 2 mEq/L of acid was used. The calculations for determining the volume of a particular acid are also given in Appendix B.

2. Assuming for the moment that nothing else has changed, we can recalculate the RA of the water after acidification to 5.75 pH:

Adjusted water:
70 Ca
15 Mg
25 Total Alkalinity as $CaCO_3$
35 Na
55 Cl^-
110 SO_4^{-2}
Water pH = 5.75 (acidified)
RA = 25 − (70/1.4) − (15/1.7) = ($^-$)34

This is less than the guideline, but this scenario is not far removed from the brewing conditions used for Sierra Nevada Pale Ale. Give it a shot, measure the actual mash pH and see what you get—it may be your best beer yet.

Brewing a Pilsner Beer

Pilsner is one of the least forgiving styles of any beer. Historically it has always been made from the softest of water, nearly devoid of any minerals whatsoever. Looking at Table 14, we see that the recommended profile for this group is:

50 Ca (minimum)
0–40 Alkalinity
0–50 Sulfate
50–100 Chloride
$^-$60–0 RA.

This profile is a suggestion, based on a low-gravity beer (Pilsner being an exception), soft yet bright malt character, and soft bitterness with the flavor balance towards the malt. This would seem to be a reasonable description of the Pilsner style except that we know that overall the style is described as being rich, with a pronounced but fine bitterness, not like an IPA. The beer is soft and balanced without any trace of mineral character.

Based on this description, we will want to temper the suggested profile a bit. We know we need some calcium for good fermentation and clarification, but do we really need the entire 50 ppm? The lagering cycle will improve the clarity that using less than the suggested calcium level may not. Perhaps we can cut the calcium back to 30 ppm if we plan for no alkalinity in the water. We probably do not need to add any magnesium to the water because the malt supplies quite a bit (about 70 ppm at 10°P/1.040).

We know we want the hops to be assertive but fine, so therefore sulfate should be avoided. A rich malt character is desired, so some level of chloride is probably acceptable, but we will target the low end of the suggested range to keep the water character as light as possible.

There is really only one option available to most brewers trying to best brew this style, and that is to start with RO water and add small amounts of salts. The best way to add the calcium without adding sulfate is to use the chloride salt. While a style purist might shy away from adding significant amounts of calcium and chloride, those additions can help produce a richer beer and a clearer beer with less lagering time. Again, these decisions are part of the brewer's art.

Only Option—Build the Water
1. From Table 17 (p.153):
   1 gram of calcium chloride per gallon = 72.0 ppm Ca and 127.4 ppm Cl^{-1}

   If our target water composition is:
   30 ppm Ca^{+2}
   0 ppm Mg^{+2}
   0 ppm Total Alkalinity
   0 ppm Sulfate

Assume for this example that we want to treat 10 gallons of water. To calculate the weight of calcium chloride to get 30 ppm of Ca in 10 gallons:

   30 ppm / 72.0 ppm per 1g/gallon x 10 gallons
   = 4.17 grams or about 4.2 grams of calcium chloride.

How much chloride does this salt addition add to the water?
4.2 grams x 127.4 ppm per 1g/gallon / 10 gallons = 53.5 ppm Cl^{-1}

This chloride level is right at the bottom end of the suggested range, so we have hit our target.

The easy way to calculate these salt additions is to use a water spreadsheet like Bru'n Water by Martin Brungard, or recipe software such as BeerSmith or BeerTools.

This mash may require acidification to hit the target mash pH due to the light malts. In Germany, it is traditional to use Sauermalz to add acidity to the mash. A recommended dose is about 2% of the grain bill. Otherwise, acidifying with the aid of a good pH meter is recommended.

This water has no alkalinity, so the buffer capacity of the malt phosphates in the mash should hold the pH fairly steady during the sparge. If the final runnings exceed 5.8 pH, stop sparging and fill the kettle with the remaining liquor to make up the necessary volume. The loss in extract yield should be minimal, and the beer will taste better than if the sparge had continued. The next time you might want to add more grain to increase the yield or acidify the sparge water to prevent the pH rise. However, keep in mind that this is a lager beer and depending on the lagering cycle, the excess tannin should precipitate out and smooth the beer.

Brewing a Foreign Extra Stout

In general, we see dark beers brewed in regions of high alkalinity. This is because the high alkalinity is balanced by the acidity of dark malts. For this example, lets assume we intend to brew a foreign extra stout of 1.075 OG, with 7% medium caramel, and 7% roast malts. This beer is categorized as a strong ale, brown/black, with moderate bitterness.

Starting water:
40 ppm Ca
9 ppm Mg
100 ppm Total Alkalinity as $CaCO_3$
140 Na
60 ppm Cl^-
245 ppm SO_4^{-2}
pH = 9
66 RA (calculated)

Target water:
50–75 ppm Ca (low)
30 ppm Mg* (low)
<100 ppm Na* (high)
120–200 ppm Total Alkalinity (low)
50–150 SO_4^{-2} (high)
50–150 Cl^- (low)
120–200 RA (low)
Acidification is not recommended for this category.
*recommended from the text

This is an interesting case—low hardness, high sodium, high sulfate and moderate alkalinity. A quick review of the city's water quality report on the Internet reveals that the treatment plant uses ion exchange for water softening, replacing higher calcium and magnesium levels with sodium. Ion exchange softening is discussed in Chapter 8.

To brew a rich foreign extra stout, we need a fair amount of alkalinity in the water to balance the acidity of the caramel and roast malts. Otherwise, the mash pH might be too low (~4.9) and the beer will take on a one-dimensional roast character, acidic and coffee-like. This beer should be smooth and rich, sweet and beguiling. However, the high sulfate concentration is going to make that difficult too—the sulfate will make the hop profile of this beer more assertive and drier than it should be for the style.

To brew this beer right, we need to increase the total alkalinity and the residual alkalinity. In addition, it would be nice to raise both the calcium and magnesium levels to 50 and 30 respectively, but raising the hardness will not be addressed here. (It could easily be done, however, based on the American pale ale example; the new concentrations could be incorporated into the options for raising the alkalinity that will be shown below. But that exercise will be left to the reader.)

Options:

1. Increase the alkalinity.
    1a. Using Ca(OH)$_2$—Kolbach RA method
    1b. Using Ca(OH)$_2$—Z RA method
    1c. Using NaOH—Kolbach RA method
    1d. Using NaHCO$_3$—Z RA method
2. Brew a different beer.

Option 1a. Using Calcium Hydroxide—Kolbach RA Method

Adding alkalinity to raise the RA can be tricky. As discussed in Chapter 6, you basically have a choice between carbonate, bicarbonate or hydroxide additions. Calcium carbonate was shown to be ineffective, so that is out. Sodium bicarbonate can be added directly to the water or the mash to raise the alkalinity, but the sodium level in this water is high already. We will do an example with sodium bicarbonate, but we will use it later as Example 1d. Calcium hydroxide would seem to be a good option. The calcium hardness we add is going to take away from the alkalinity contribution, but the calcium concentration of the water is low—50 ppm is the recommended minimum.

Therefore, calcium hydroxide (slaked lime) seems to be the best option here. We will do two examples (1a and 1b) using calcium hydroxide, and then follow up with another example using sodium hydroxide (Example 1c) so you can see the differences. In Example 1a we will use Kolbach's RA, and in Example 1b we will use Z alkalinity to illustrate that difference. The purpose of these additions is to raise the residual alkalinity of the water to the suggested range of 120–200 ppm as CaCO$_3$.

In this first example, we will calculate the weight of calcium hydroxide to achieve a Kolbach RA of 150 ppm as CaCO$_3$.

1. The residual alkalinity of the water is 66 ppm as CaCO$_3$, or 1.32 mEq/L. We want to bring this to 150 ppm as CaCO$_3$, or 3 mEq/L so we need: 3 – 1.32 = 1.68 mEq/L

    1.68 mEq/L will be necessary to bring us to 150 ppm as CaCO$_3$.

2. From Table 17: 1 gram per liter of calcium hydroxide contributes a ΔRA of 19.3 mEq/g•L. Therefore, 1.68 mEq/L/19.3 mEq/g•L = 0.087 grams/liter calcium hydroxide. If our water volume is in

gallons, then multiplying by 3.785 liters per gallon will give us the addition in grams per gallon (0.33 grams/gallon).

The changes to the residual alkalinity from the calcium hydroxide is already incorporated into the ΔRA factor although you do need to calculate the final calcium and TA values for your own information. Adding 0.33 grams of calcium hydroxide per gallon to the original water (page 168) gives us a new calcium concentration of 87 ppm, and a new Total Alkalinity of 218 ppm as $CaCO_3$. From Table 17, 1 gram of calcium hydroxide per liter yields 27 mEq of alkalinity, and the equivalent weight for alkalinity as $CaCO_3$ is 50.

0.087 g x 541 ppm Ca = 47 ppm Ca
40 + 47 = 87 ppm Ca
0.087 g x 27 mEq/L = 2.35 mEq alkalinity = 2.35 x 50 = 117.5 ppm as $CaCO_3$
100 + 117.5 = 218 ppm Total Alkalinity as $CaCO_3$

The Adjusted Water:
87 ppm Ca
9 ppm Mg
218 ppm Total Alkalinity as $CaCO_3$
140 ppm Na
60 ppm Cl^-
245 ppm SO_4^{-2}
150 ppm Residual Alkalinity as $CaCO_3$

3. We can multiply these additions by the total volume of water to get the total weight of the salt addition for the batch.

Option 1b. Using Calcium Hydroxide—Z RA Method

The new Z model suggests that the Z alkalinity of the water to the Z pH needs to be taken into consideration to determine the right amount of additional alkalinity to hit the target mash pH, rather than the traditional total alkalinity. For this example, we will use a Z pH of 5.4.

1. The first step is to calculate the C_T for the water.

C_T = Total Alkalinity/50 ÷ Δc_0

The water pH was 9, so referencing Figure 25 (p. 127),
$$\Delta c_0 = {}^-0.01 - {}^-1.04 = 1.03$$

$$C_T = 100/50 \div 1.03 = 1.94$$

2. Calculate Z alkalinity and Z RA for the water.

$$Z_{5.4} = C_T \times \Delta c_Z = 1.94 \times ({}^-0.1 - {}^-1.04) = 1.82 \text{ mEq/L}$$

3. Calculate the mEq/L of calcium and magnesium.

$$\text{mEq/L Ca} = 40/20 = 2 \text{ mEq/L}$$

$$\text{mEq/L Mg} = 9/12.1 = 0.74 \text{ mEq/L}$$

4. $Z \text{ RA} = 1.82 - (2/3.5 + 0.74/7) = 1.14 \text{ mEq/L}$

We want to bring this to 150 ppm as $CaCO_3$, or 3 mEq/L, so we need $3 - 1.14 = 1.86$ mEq/L

1.86 mEq/L will be necessary to bring us to 150 ppm as $CaCO_3$.

5. Applying the same methodology as above in Option 1a:
From Table 17 (p. 152): 1 gram per liter of calcium hydroxide contributes a ΔRA of 19.3 mEq/g•L. Therefore, 1.86 mEq/L/19.3 mEq/g•L = 0.096 grams/liter calcium hydroxide.

If our water volume is in gallons, then multiplying by 3.785 liters per gallon will give us the addition in grams per gallon (0.365 grams/gallon).

Note that this amount is larger than the addition calculated in Option 1a.

Option 1c. Using Sodium Hydroxide—Kolbach Method

Sodium hydroxide is the strongest base and using it to raise the alkalinity will increase the sodium concentration the least. (Although you could use potassium hydroxide instead for zero increase, but where is the fun in that?)

1. We can use the information calculated in Step 1 of Example 1a to get us started. The change in RA needed to bring us to an RA of 3 mEq/L is 1.68 mEq/L.

2. Sodium hydroxide is a strong base and has a charge of 1 mEq/mmol. From Table 17 (p. 153), sodium hydroxide contributes 25 mmol/L per gram, and thus 25 mEq/g•L. Dividing 1.68 by 25 gives the weight of the addition in grams per liter of sodium hydroxide needed:

   1.68/25 = 0.067 grams per liter of sodium hydroxide is needed to increase the RA to 3 mEq/L.

3. Calculating the increase in sodium concentration,
   0.067 x 575 ppm = 38.5 ppm

   Note: This sodium hydroxide addition could also be done using a 1 Normal (N) solution, as described in Chapter 6 and Appendix C. A 1 N solution contributes 1 mEq/milliliter, so the necessary addition of 1.68 mEq/L would be accomplished by simply adding 1.68 milliliters of the solution per liter of brewing water.

Option 1d. Using Sodium Bicarbonate—Z Alkalinity Method

We will calculate a sodium bicarbonate addition just for the sake of example. We can use the C_T and Z alkalinity information from the previous example (1b):

$C_T = 100/50 \div 1.03 = 1.94$ mmol/L in the water

$Z_{5.4}$ Alkalinity $= C_T \bullet \Delta c_Z = 1.94 \bullet (^-0.1 - ^-1.04) = 1.82$ mEq/L

Z RA $= 1.82 - (2/3.5 + 0.74/7) = 1.14$ mEq/L

1. The Δc_Z for the bicarbonate addition is ($^-0.1 - {}^-1.0$) because bicarbonate always starts at $^-1.0$ mEq/mmol, regardless of the pH of the water. Therefore the $\Delta c_Z = 0.9$ mEq/mmol.

2. The C_T for sodium bicarbonate is 11.9 mmol/g•L. Multiplying C_T by $\Delta c_Z = 11.9 \times 0.9 = 10.7$ mEq/L of Z alkalinity per gram of $NaHCO_3$.

3. Again, we know from Example 1b that we need 1.86 mEq/L to bring us to 3 mEq/L, so we will divide 1.86 by the 10.7 mEq/L per gram of the $NaHCO_3$ to get the weight of the addition per liter:

    1.86/10.7 = 0.174 grams per liter.

4. 0.174 grams per liter gives us an additional 0.174 • 273.7 = 47.6 ppm + 140 ppm = 187.6 ppm Na, which is really pushing the envelope. If we had calculated the bicarbonate addition using the Kolbach method, per Example 1a, the sodium bicarbonate addition would have been 11.8 mEq/L instead of 10.7, and the resulting numbers would be 0.158 grams per liter and 43 ppm additional sodium.

As you can see, there are many different options and permutations of options when it comes to calculating alkalinity additions. The most straightforward is to use Kolbach. The most complex is to use Z alkalinity and sodium bicarbonate. The method you use is up to you. The method almost doesn't matter. What matters is that you are able to determine an estimate of what needs to be done, and then you brew that beer, measure the resulting mash pH, and taste the beer to evaluate your results. Set a goal, formulate a plan, measure your results, and repeat until you are satisfied.

Option 2—Brew a Different Beer

The water might work better for an American stout with its assertive hop character and the high sulfate in this water. However, the high sodium content combined with high sulfate has been known to create a harsh bitterness, so perhaps an aggressively hoppy beer is not a good idea either.

An American amber ale might be a good choice. Less hoppy than the American stout, this style still contains medium caramel malts for acidity, 13 SRM, and the RA range is 0–60.

Starting water:
40 ppm Ca
9 ppm Mg
100 ppm Total Alkalinity
140 Na
60 ppm Cl^-
245 ppm SO_4^{-2}
pH = 9
66 RA (calculated)

Target water:
50–150 ppm Ca (low)
40–120 ppm Total Alkalinity (check)
100–200 SO_4^{-2} (high)
50–100 Cl^- (low)
0–60 RA (high)
Acidification is generally not recommended for this category.

Now we have room to add calcium and chloride to increase hardness and balance the sulfate without negatively impacting the suggested RA range.

1. Let's start by adding 1 gram of calcium chloride per gallon (72 Ca, 127.4 Cl^-). This addition changes the water profile to:

Adjusted water (1):
112 ppm Ca
9 ppm Mg

100 ppm Total Alkalinity
140 Na
187 ppm Cl^-
245 ppm SO_4^{-2}
15 RA (calculated)
(see previous examples for calculations)

This water is better. It fits the suggested profile for residual alkalinity, but it is not *much* better overall. The calcium is now high, and the RA is now a bit low for the color we intend to have (15–18 SRM). The sodium, chloride, and sulfate concentrations are all high, which may make the beer taste minerally.

2. Let's try this with only 0.5 gram per gallon calcium chloride addition.

Adjusted water (2):
75 ppm Ca
9 ppm Mg
100 ppm Total Alkalinity
104 Na
89 ppm Cl^-
245 ppm SO_4^{-2}
40 RA (calculated)

This water is much better. The calcium and residual alkalinity are both now better matched with the intended color, and the chloride is in range. We have made the best of a poor situation. Brew the beer and taste the results before exploring other options (such as buying unsoftened water from the city).

Water Profiles and the Black Box

It is interesting that many aspects of brewing are left to art, instead of being engineered down to the last detail. Why do we only have general recommendations for ion concentrations in water? Why do we not know, in this golden age of technology, the specific quantities and types of ions that are utilized in the fermentation process? Why do we not have a complete list of every nutrient and ion cofactor reaction? Perhaps it is because fermentation works and there are bigger problems to solve. Perhaps there are an exceedingly large number of combinations of mineral contents and other parameters that will produce good beer. Whatever the reason, the mash and fermentation process have always been regarded as something of a black box when it comes to water composition. The term "black box" means that we can predict the output of a process based on the inputs, but we do not completely understand what happens inside the process. All we seem to know about brewing water is that certain ion concentrations are recommended; we don't seem to care what concentrations come out, or how finished-beer ion concentrations affect the flavor of the beer. We only seem to know the effect of the initial concentrations on the beer.

In addition, very little research seems to have been done on ion contributions from the malt on overall beer performance. The table below shows data presented by Taylor[4] where an all-malt 10°P (1.040) beer was brewed with distilled water. It is interesting to note that the magnesium concentration is 70 ppm in the wort and 65 ppm in the beer. Apparently, 5 ppm are consumed, misplaced, or thrown out along the way. Magnesium is said to be an important enzyme co-factor and nutrient for the yeast, and there is at least one paper that states that a minimum of 5 ppm is required for good yeast performance. Could a wort with only 5 ppm of magnesium mash and ferment just as well as this one with 70? Or is there a threshold—for example, a minimum level of 50 is needed in solution but only 4% will be consumed? At this point in time we don't seem to know definitively, and it would be interesting to find out more.

Ion Contents in Wort (10°Plato) and Beer Using Demineralized Water		
Constituent	Wort (mg/l)	Beer (mg/l)
Na^{+1}	10	12
K^{+1}	380	355
Ca^{+2}	35	33
Mg^{+2}	70	65
Zn^{+2}	0.17	0
Cu^{+2}	0.15	0.12
Fe^{+3}	0.11	0.07
Cl^-	125	130
$SO4^{-2}$	5	15
$PO4^{-3}$ (Free)	550	389
$PO4^{-3}$ (Total)	830	604

References

1. Brungard, M., "Water Knowledge." https://sites.google.com/site/brunwater/water-knowledge, 2013.

2. Steele, M., *IPA—Brewing Techniques, Recipes, and the Evolution of India Pale Ale*. Brewers Publications, Boulder, CO, 2012.

3. Bamforth, C.W., "Inorganic Ions in Beer—A Survey." MBAA TQ Vol. 49, 4:131–133, 2012.

4. Priest and Stewart, *Handbook of Brewing, 2nd Ed., Chapter 4-Water*. D.G. Taylor, CRC Press, 2006.

8

Source Water Treatment Technologies for the Brewery

Water is one of the most important raw materials to control in the brewery. It is the major constituent in beer, comprising at least 90 percent in most cases. It is vitally important that the brewer evaluates the water source when choosing a location for his brewery because once he has built his brewery, there is little or no chance of getting a different water source—he has to make the best with what he has. The brewer's responsibility for the quality of the water surpasses that for any other ingredient. In fact, it is the only primary ingredient for which the brewer is specifically responsible. A maltster is accountable for the malt. A hop grower/packager is responsible for the hops and typically a yeast lab is responsible for the pure culture. It is the brewer's responsibility to understand his water source and be able to modify it, as necessary, to consistently brew good beer, year round.

A brewer needs high-quality water that can be readily utilized for every brewery need, whether in the mash, the boiler, or for cleaning. The water must be free of off-flavors and odors or the brewer must have the tools to readily make it so. The key to having high quality brewing water is knowing the water source—being able to recognize changes and adapt to maintain beer quality. While this may be a daunting task for a novice brewer, with time, study, and experience it can become second nature.

The general requirements for the brewery water supply are simple. The water must be potable and free from contaminants. Today, potability is rarely a concern, but one reason for beer's popularity throughout history was the fact that the brewing process rendered the local water biologically safe for drinking. The most common water problem for brewers today is the potential for off-flavors in beer due to industrial/chemical contamination or water disinfection byproducts (DBP). The problem becomes twofold: 1) how to recognize contaminants, and 2) how to get rid of them.

Source water contaminants and effects were discussed in Chapter 3. This chapter will focus on the methods and tools to remove those contaminants. We will address them in the same order that they are addressed in standard water treatment: removal of suspended solids, removal of dissolved solids, and removal of liquid and gas contaminants.

Figure 28—Rotary Screen at Sierra Nevada Brewery

Removing Suspended Solids— Mechanical Filtration

Removing particulates is an important treatment step for both water pre-treatment and wastewater treatment. In the case of water pretreatment, raw water is typically fed through conventional rapid sand filters, or sand and anthracite coal filters. These are usually large installations, suitable for a town or city. If a brewery is having suspended solids issues, the solution is generally a smaller filter, typically made of granular media, polymer fibers, or other replaceable or rechargeable media. Filter cartridges can come in many forms, such as packed granules, flat sheet, tubular, or spiral wound. Granular filters utilize granular media, such as sand or diatomaceous earth, to create the filter bed. Spiral wound filters utilize fibers to create a matrix that traps and impedes the particles. Filters are rated as standard or absolute. A standard filter will trap 99% of particles in its size range; an absolute filter will not allow any particles to pass larger than its rating. Filters are also rated for temperature because very high temperatures can cause premature breakdown of the filter medium.

Monitoring for a significant pressure increase between a filter's inlet and outlet points can give you an indication of when the filter needs to be changed. Suspended-solids filters are commonly used to precondition water before charcoal and reverse osmosis filtration for typical potable water supplies.

Removing Dissolved Solids—Iron and Manganese

Iron and manganese can cause many problems in brewing beyond haze, off-flavors, and premature staling. Both ions are typically removed in the early stages of municipal water treatment by oxidation into their insoluble forms, which then allows them to be filtered from the water. However, even very small remaining concentrations of these ions can lead to deposition and corrosion problems in boiler systems and heat exchangers.

A simple way to remove iron is to bind it with phosphates. This is a weak bond that can be broken by heat or strong light, but it converts the iron into an insoluble form that can be either settled or filtered. Some small commercial breweries have been known to dose all incoming water with phosphoric acid and use it first in the chilled liquor system. This causes precipitation of the iron phosphate and it can settle overnight. Clean water can be drawn off the next day for use as hot liquor for the next batch. The settling vessel needs to have a bottom drain for draining of the precipitate and a side port for racking off the clean water. The precipitate in the bottom of the tank will contain iron and chalk so it is important to clean it out often.

A homebrewer can use this same method to settle iron from the brewing liquor by acidifying the water with phosphoric acid to a pH between 5.5 and 5.7, and refrigerating the container overnight. Care must be taken to not disturb the sediment when racking the clear liquor off.

Manganese is hard to oxidize with typical aeration. It usually requires a stronger oxidizer like chlorine/hypochlorite. This is why manganese oxide deposits are a problem in water-cooling systems, which use these chemicals to prevent bio fouling. The oxidation of manganese is auto-catalyzing, meaning that once formed, deposition accelerates. It is an extremely hard and tenacious deposit, requiring aggressive mechanical and chemical methods to remove. It is more noble than stainless steel, and will cause galvanic corrosion and pitting of the steel underneath the manganese deposits.

Manganese can be removed by greensand filtration. Greensand is a naturally-occurring substance, containing the mineral glauconite, which is capable of reducing iron, manganese, and hydrogen sulfide from water through oxidation. When the oxidizing capacity of the greensand bed is exhausted, the bed can be regenerated with a weak potassium permanganate ($KMnO_4$) solution.

Greensand-based manganese, iron, and hydrogen sulfide treatment systems are readily available. These are granular-media systems that can be monitored and maintained just like ion-exchange water softeners. Iron and manganese can also be removed by ion-exchange systems. In fact, all ions can be, one way or another.

Removing Dissolved Solids—Ion Exchange

Ion exchange systems utilize polymer beads that are manufactured to contain either cation or anion exchange sites within the polymeric skeleton. While the beads look solid under a microscope, their molecular structure more closely resembles a ball of yarn, achieving water permeability and a high surface area for ion exchange. During use, water flows through the media bed, and through the resin-impregnated beads, where the undesirable ions in the water are exchanged with those in the resin, and bound up in turn. These systems have the advantages of high flow rate, low back pressure, and relatively easy maintenance, though some are better at some tasks than others. A general disadvantage of ion-exchange systems is the concentrated brine waste produced by the regeneration process.

Figure 29—The Water Softener at Kinetic Brewing Co. in Lancaster, CA

Four types of ion-exchange resins are available: weakly acidic cation exchanger, strongly acidic cation exchanger, weakly basic anion exchanger, and strongly basic anion exchanger. Each type of exchanger has its advantages for different species that the brewer wants to remove. See Table 20. The nomenclature comes from acid theory, which states that the conjugate base of a strong acid is a weak base, and the conjugate acid of a strong base is a weak acid, and vice versa in both cases. In other words, if calcium hydroxide is considered to be a strong base (it is), then it is a weak acid. Likewise, sulfuric acid is a strong acid, and a weak base. A weak acid cation resin removes calcium and magnesium because these are the cations of the "weak acids" of calcium and magnesium hydroxide.

Table 20—General Pros and Cons of Ion Exchange Resin Types

Type	Pros	Cons
Weak Acid Cation (WAC)	Two types: H^{+1} and Na^{+1} Good for removing all divalent metal ions including hardness ions $^-Ca^{+2}$, Mg^{+2} and the objectionable Fe^{+2} and Mn^{+2} This type only removes temporary hardness, not permanent. High capacity Efficient use of regeneration chemicals	Regeneration is difficult to monitor. Prone to calcium sulfate fouling Sensitive to chlorine/ chloramine contamination
Strong Acid Cation (SAC)	Two types: H^{+1} and Na^{+1} Operates across entire pH range Most common—removing hardness (Na^{+1}) or all cations (H^{+1}) Long resin life of 10–15 years	Sensitive to chlorine/chloramine contamination Sensitive to thermal shock High sodium output for Na^{+1} type Prone to iron, calcium sulfate, and aluminum fouling
Weak Base Anion (WBA)	Removes most anions, but not CO_2 or SiO_2 More economical than strong base anion	Effluent still contains SiO_2, therefore not suitable for boiler use
Strong Base Anion (SBA)	Removes all anions, including CO_2 and SiO_2	Requires strong caustic for regeneration Shorter resin life of 2–5 years

Weak Acid Cation—Common Water Softeners

Weak acid cation and strong acid cation resins are very similar, the main differences being the extent of softening that each type can achieve. WAC systems will only remove calcium and magnesium associated with bicarbonate (ie., temporary hardness) and only under alkaline (i.e. potable water) conditions, whereas SAC will remove all of the calcium and magnesium at any water pH. WAC systems are commonly used for treatment of brackish water or polishing of lime-softening effluent. They are prone to the same degradation issues as SAC resins.

Strong Acid Cation—Complete Water Softening

A typical SAC water softener works by exchanging all divalent metal ions in the water for sodium ions. Na^{+1} type SAC softeners have a resin bed that is initially charged with Na^{+1} ions (monovalent). As divalent ions (typically Ca^{2+}, Mg^{2+}, Fe^{2+}, and Mn^{+2}) pass over the bed, they exchange with the monovalent ions due to their greater affinity with the resin. The water softener also contains a salt reservoir that must be replenished on a regular basis. Once the resin bed has been completely exhausted, it is flushed with the salt brine to displace the collected metal ions from the resin and the process can start over again. Although it is more expensive, potassium chloride (KCl) can be used in place of sodium chloride to avoid the negative health effects of added sodium.

SAC resins also come with H^{+1} as the exchange ion, and this form can remove all cations from the water while contributing only H^{+1} ions into the water. This makes them more suitable for high-purity water applications such as boiler feed.

Obviously, sodium-type SAC softeners should not be used in the brewery for the production of brewing liquor unless they are used as pre-treatment for a deionizer or reverse osmosis system. High sodium levels are preferable to high calcium levels in reverse osmosis treatment because sodium is highly soluble and less prone to precipitating on the membrane. Calcium carbonate is more likely to precipitate on RO membranes and lead to early system failure.

Weak Base Anion—Dealkalizing Treatment

Alkalinity reduction is the eternal quest of brewers, and ion exchange does provide a tried and true means of accomplishing it. SBA exchangers can also remove silica, which can be a particular problem in boiler/heat exchanger systems.

A WBA exchanger removes the anions of strong acids (Cl^-, SO_4^{-2}, NO_3^-) by using hydroxide. These units generate carbon dioxide, which must be vented or purged to prevent corrosion downstream, and they do not remove silicate.

A SAC and WBA pairing make a good combination to pretreat water for reverse osmosis systems. This combination has a large treatment capacity and efficient regeneration.

Strong Base Anion—Dealkalizing Treatment

This type of system removes both strong and weak acid anions, including carbonates, silicates, and nitrates (w/special resin option). SBA can be combined with SAC, and use the anion of the acid, or sodium hydroxide, for regeneration. An SAC/SBA combination will produce water that is suitable for high-pressure boilers. Assuming the proper attention to detail and upstream pretreatment, this process is capable of producing water with less than 0.01 mg/L. The downside of SBA is that it requires a lot more chemical for regeneration than a WBA system.

SBA systems are also available which use chloride as the exchange instead of hydroxide. These systems are not as chemical intensive, and work very well at reducing alkalinity. However, when combined with a SAC using sodium instead of H^{+1}, the output is a light saline that can be quite corrosive to stainless steel pipes. There is a cloud for every silver lining, as it were.

SBA resin is also particularly prone to fouling by organic molecules, not only industrial contaminants such as solvents and oils, but also naturally-occurring fulvic and humic acids from decayed vegetation in surface water. WBA units are much less affected by this type of fouling and may be used to remove the organics ahead of a SBA unit if needed.

Ion Exchange—Mixed-Bed Reactors

Although serial cation and anion exchange systems have been discussed, mixed-bed systems containing both SAC (H type) and SBA (OH type) are also available that combine the functionality of both: cations are exchanged for hydrogen ions; anions are exchanged for hydroxyl ions. If the cations and anions are balanced, the exchanger releases equal amounts of hydrogen and hydroxyl ions that combine to form water. The disadvantage of a mixed-bed system is that once the resins are spent it must be recharged by washing with both strong caustic and strong acid. This cycle can be expensive and not very environmentally sound. Mixed-bed units are most commonly used for small amounts of pure water. Some home brewers use this type of unit, obtained from reef aquarium hobby suppliers, to prepare brewing liquor. Small breweries (20 bbl and less) can purchase mixed-bed filters on an exchange basis. A typical leased mixed-bed filter will last for 800 to 2,000 gallons of water depending on the TDS of the source water. Companies will charge a lease and a replacement fee. The source water conductivity can be measured and compared to the output water conductivity to set a standard for a specific brewery or brand. The output water conductivity can be monitored to check when a deionizer needs to be recharged.

Removing Dissolved Solids—Nanofiltration and Reverse Osmosis

Figure 30—The Source Water Reverse Osmosis System at Stone Brewing Co., in Escondido, CA.

Microfiltration, ultrafiltration, nanofiltration and reverse osmosis are all referred to collectively as membrane technologies because they utilize a thin film to act as a filter for dissolved solids. The smallest particles of silt and suspended solids that sand filters can typically filter out are about 10 micrometers (0.0004") in diameter. Microfiltration can remove yeast cells and most bacteria down to 0.1 micrometers (4 microinches). Ultrafiltration can typically do ten times better, down to 0.01 micrometers (0.4 microinches), filtering out most viruses. Nanofiltration does 10 times better than ultra, and can filter out most proteins and some dissolved ions, but reverse osmosis beats them all, down to 0.0001 micrometers (4×10^{-3} microinches), and is able to filter out most dissolved cations and anions, but not dissolved gases.

These membranes can be made from cellulose acetate or polyamide composite film. The polyamide films are more effective at filtering silica and monovalent (small) ions, but also very susceptible to oxidation and polymer breakdown (holes) due to chlorine, chloramine, and other oxidizers. Cellulose acetate is a little more robust and is often used for high-fouling situations.

Osmosis is the diffusion of water across a semi-permeable membrane from a region of low solute concentration to a region of high solute concentration. Think of osmotic pressure as a force that tries to even things out, to bring two adjacent systems to the same concentration of solutes by pulling the water through the membrane to the "drier" side. (Actually the pressure is due to chemical potential differences rather than concentration, but you get the idea.) Reverse osmosis means that we are applying enough pressure to the high solute side to overcome the osmotic pressure and concentrate the solutes even more. Actually all of these membrane technologies depend upon applied pressure to overcome the natural osmotic pressure of any given system. The difference is the size of particle that is blocked by the membrane. Obviously, "reverse osmosis filtration" requires the highest pressure of any of the methods, typically in the range of 10–15 bar, depending on the solutes, temperature, pH, etc. (1 bar is roughly 1 atmosphere of pressure.)

Reverse osmosis systems can be quite simple (no moving parts), and small systems are sold at home improvement department stores and aquarium suppliers at reasonable prices. Larger systems are widely used in commercial brewing operations to treat high alkalinity or brackish water, especially in arid parts of the world such as Africa and the Middle East. The larger systems typically utilize high-pressure pumps and tiers of much larger membrane cartridges than the small systems.

The typical system first passes the water through a particle filter or filters (5 and 1 micron are common sizes) and then a carbon block filter. The carbon filter removes organics, chlorine and chloramine, which can foul or poison the RO membrane. The feed water then passes to a membrane cartridge. The cartridges use cross-flow filtration, where the permeate is drawn off to the side, while the majority of the water continues to the outflow (drain/waste) and carries away the concentrated ionic content. An outflow valve restricts the flow, maintaining high pressure on the membrane. An operator can control this valve to adjust the pressure and wastewater flow rate (referred to as the 'concentrate' or 'brine') for better efficiency.

Simple systems sold for home use do not have this feature. The cartridge housing has a fixed orifice to limit the waste flow and create the high reverse osmotic pressure on the membrane. The housing also includes an outlet port for the filtered water that permeates the membrane (i.e., the permeate). The permeate passes either to a pressure tank or open tank (atmospheric tank). Pressure tanks contain a pressurized bladder. As permeate flows into the tank, the air in this bladder is compressed and the pressure in the tank rises. When the tank pressure plus the osmotic pressure equals the feed side pressure, no more water permeates the membrane and collection stops. These systems usually have a pressure switch monitoring the bladder tank pressure that operates a valve to close the feed and/or concentrate lines when permeate is not being collected to prevent waste of feed water.

The advantage of the pressure tank on these small systems is that it can be connected to a convenient faucet to draw RO water for drinking or cooking. While the pressure tank system is handy for small volumes, it lowers the overall filtration rate because it reduces the pressure difference across the membrane as the tank fills. Water can be obtained more quickly by disconnecting the pressure tank or by leaving the faucet open and collecting the water in another open container.

Criticisms levied at RO systems usually involve the high ratio of concentrate to permeate production. Typically, less than 20% of the feed water is captured as permeate in the typical home systems. This means that for every gallon that goes into the HLT, 4 gallons go down the drain. This can be an important factor depending on the water source, whether it is a fresh water well, or the ocean. In more elaborate systems the recovery (the fraction of feed water recovered as permeate) may be appreciably higher—as high as 80% or even a bit more—but such high recovery rates come at the expense of higher permeate ion content and more concentrated brine. Brine disposal is often an issue, whether it is low volumes of high concentrate, or large volumes of low concentrate.

Other criticisms involve the high cost of membrane replacement. These can be ameliorated by proper membrane maintenance. Carbon pre-filter protection from chlorine and chloramine, and cation softening to prevent the deposition of calcium carbonate have already been mentioned. But other minerals become concentrated in the brine too and this, depending on the chemistry of the feed water, can impose limits of the maximum allowable recovery.

RO filters can become infected with microorganisms because the chlorine/chloramine residual disinfectant has to be removed from the feed water beforehand. A final pass through a sterile filter (micro or ultra) or UV light sterilizer is recommended, as well as a de-aerator if using the RO water for post-boil dilution is required. Tanks and plumbing after a RO filter should be made from plastic (PVC or PEX) because the deionized water is highly corrosive.

RO water is a good choice when the brewer needs to remove alkalinity. RO is also good for removing problem elements like manganese, silicates, and iron. However, some of these same elements are responsible for fouling the membranes, leading to high working pressures, high pressure drop across the membranes, and low permeate flow. Other foulants are organics, microorganisms, colloids, and carbonate scale. Having an ion-exchange unit ahead of an RO system to reduce the load on the membranes can improve overall efficiency and reduce the total maintenance.

Since modest concentrations of ions are desirable in brewing water, RO's ability to strip nearly all the ionic content from the water can be counterproductive. Why strip everything out and then add some of it back? The more permeable nanofiltration membranes are more energy and water efficient while providing effective alkalinity and hardness reduction. Nanofiltration is also known as membrane softening since these membranes are much better at rejecting the larger divalent ions (such as Ca^{+2} and SO_4^{-2}) while passing more of the smaller monovalent ions (such as Na^{+1} and Cl^{-1}).

Although the water quality from nanofiltration membranes is less pure than that produced by RO membranes, the final ion concentrations are still low. RO membranes typically reject 95 percent or more of all ions, while nanofiltration typically reject between 80 and 90 percent.

A nanofiltration system is typically capable of 80% reduction of sodium from an ion-exchanged feedwater, such as taking the level from <200 ppm sodium to <40 ppm sodium. Higher concentrations in the feedwater will result in higher concentrations in the permeate. All other ions in the permeate are likely to have much lower concentrations. If the sodium rejection is not sufficient to meet brewery needs, using either unsoftened feed water or RO membranes are alternatives to achieving purer water.

The advantage to nanofiltration is that it provides softened water for cleaning without significantly increasing the total dissolved solids in the waste stream, which can be a disposal problem for ion exchange and lime softening. In many cases, nanofiltration can provide acceptable brewing water quality with better overall economy. The economic difference will depend on the specific circumstances: TDS concentration, composition of the TDS, and acceptance limits on the permeate. Many large breweries now utilize nanofiltration instead of RO for their water needs.

Nanofiltration membranes are available for typical commercial equipment in the same 2.5, 4, or 8 inch diameter cartridges as are available for RO membranes. At this time, nanofiltration membranes are not available to fit the typical home RO systems. The relatively recent availability of affordable RO presents a tremendous opportunity to home and commercial brewers alike. Whereas in the past the emphasis has been on fixing water in the mash or at the kettle to make a suitable beer (and indeed much of the material in this book reflects this), the paradigm can now shift to preparing source water that is suitable for all the beers being brewed. Preparation is much simpler than troubleshooting.

Removing Liquid and Gas Contaminants—Chlorine

Microbiological contamination is the main concern of any municipal water supplier. These contaminants can be bacteria or other organisms such as cryptosporidium and giardia intestinalis. Residual disinfection is needed to provide constant protection after the water leaves the treatment plant. A good disinfectant is a strong and lingering disinfectant—one that doesn't lose effectiveness over time as the water sits in a tank or pipe.

Low-flow regions of piping or "dead legs" can be a particular problem in breweries because the chlorine/chloramine residual disinfectants have typically been removed to prevent off-flavors in beer, such as chlorophenols. Bacteria can form deposits or biofilms in low-flow regions that are subsequently hard to disinfect because the thickness of the deposit can prevent cleaners and sanitizers from reaching the entire colony.

However, with good sanitation practices in the brewery, getting rid of the chlorine and chloramine in the first place is the challenge. Chlorine disinfectant is either added as "free chlorine" or chloramine. Water may be chlorinated at several places in the initial treatment process and the chlorination level may be adjusted throughout the year. Free chlorine is the older method of chlorination that produces hypochlorite ion OCl⁻ in the water to oxidize and kill organisms.

When chlorine is dissolved in water the following reaction takes place:

$$Cl_2 + H_2O \leftrightarrow H^{+1} + Cl^{-1} + HOCl \text{ (hypochlorous acid)}$$

Water reports often list chlorine as, "free chlorine" or "residual chlorine." The definitions are as follows:

Free chlorine = $2[Cl_2] + [HOCl] + [OCl^{-1}]$

Combined chlorine = $[NH_2Cl] + 2[NHCl_2] + 3[NCl_3]$

Residual Chlorine = free + combined chlorine

At pH below 7.6, HOCl is prevalent over OCl^{-1}. HOCl is a better oxidizer and is better able to penetrate the cell membrane of microbes because of its neutral charge. It is, therefore, a better germicide. Hypochlorite is added to water by adding sodium hypochlorite, calcium hypochlorite, or by bubbling chlorine gas through the water. The hypochlorite ion (free chlorine) is highly volatile and can be removed from water by heating it or simply allowing it to sit at room temperature in an open container for a long period of time. Fortunately for brewers, simply heating the water to strike temperature in an open kettle will drive off most of the free chlorine. However, it only takes very small amounts of free chlorine in brewing water to produce discernible chlorophenols in beer.

Unfortunately, hypochlorite can also react with (oxidize) organic compounds from decayed vegetation to form potentially carcinogenic compounds—known as disinfection by-products (DBPs). Many of those organic compounds are naturally occurring and prevalent in surface water sources like lakes and streams. These DBPs are undesirable in potable water supplies and are controlled by environmental regulation and the Clean Water Act in the US. Chloramines are much less likely to form DBPs, so water companies frequently use chloramine in place of chlorine. Unfortunately, chloramine has a lower odor threshold (3–5 ppm) than chlorine (5–20 ppm), and is mostly responsible for that swimming pool odor. But, some of these DBPs, like THM and HAA5, have odor and flavor thresholds in parts per billion in beer, typically fishy or pond-like.

Chloramines are created by combining chlorine and ammonia in water. Chloramines exist in mono-, di-, and tri-chloramine forms, but the predominant form is monochloramine. It has been used for potable water disinfection since the early 1900s when it was found to provide a much more stable disinfectant in water distribution systems. Since the toxic effects of chlorine DBPs were discovered in the 1970s, chloramines have become a new standard for disinfection of water supplies containing significant organic content. It stays in solution longer, regardless of organic load and therefore works better as a residual disinfectant.

Chloramine is now used in the majority of large water treatment plants; though there is concern that chloramine still causes higher-than-desirable levels of DBPs. Thus other disinfection procedures such as ozonation and treatment with ultraviolet light are being used in some plants. Since boiling treatment requires fuel and time, the most cost-effective chlorine and chloramine removal options are UV degradation, activated carbon filtration (GAC), or metabisulfite treatment.

Chlorine/Chloramine Removal by Metabisulfite

Vintners have long used sodium metabisulfite and potassium metabisulfite (also known as Campden tablets) to suppress wild yeast in wine must. It is also useful as an anti-oxidant in beer. However, it is most useful for breaking down chlorine and chloramine in water. Metabisulfite forms sulfur dioxide when dissolved in water according to the equation:

$$K_2S_2O_5 + H_2O \rightarrow 2K^{+1} + 2SO_2 + 2OH^{-1}$$
(potassium form shown in this example)

It is the sulfur dioxide that reduces the chlorine to chloride, and in return is oxidized to sulfate.

The equation for chlorine breakdown by either sodium or potassium metabisulfite is:

$$Na_2S_2O_5 + 2Cl_2 + 3H_2O \rightarrow 2Na^{+1} + 2SO_4^{-2} + 6H^{+1} + 4Cl^{-1}$$

$$K_2S_2O_5 + 2Cl_2 + 3H_2O \rightarrow 2K^{+1} + 2SO_4^{-2} + 6H^{+1} + 4Cl^{-1}$$

Assuming 3 ppm of residual chlorine is present in the water, this reaction would use 4.7 ppm of $K_2S_2O_5$ and result in 3 ppm of chloride, about 4 ppm of sulfate, and about 6 ppm as $CaCO_3$ of alkalinity neutralized by the hydrogen ions.

The reaction of chloramine and metabisulfite is similar:

$$Na_2S_2O_5 + 2H_2NCl + 3H_2O \rightarrow$$
$$2Na^{+1} + 2SO_4^{-2} + 2H^{+1} + 2Cl^{-1} + 2NH_4^{+}$$

Again, assuming 3 ppm of residual chlorine, the reaction would require 9.4 ppm of $K_2S_2O_5$ and create 3 ppm of chloride, 8 ppm of sulfate, 1.5 ppm of ammonium, and about 4.2 ppm of alkalinity as $CaCO_3$ reduced. The ammonium ion is a yeast nutrient. Any residual metabisulfite/sulfur dioxide will not harm the beer, but act as an antioxidant. Treatment numbers are given in Table 21.

Table 21—Dosing Requirements for Metabisulfite Treatment
The units are volumeless, although if the free chlorine concentration is 3 mg/L (ppm) then the corresponding potassium metabisulfite requirement would be 3 x 1.564 x total liters to be treated. A fudge factor of 20–30% more may be used to assure completion.

Constituent	Per mg Free Chlorine	Per mg Monochloramine
mg of potassium metabisulfite required	1.564	3.127
mg of sodium metabisulfite required	1.337	2.674
mg of sodium added*	0.323	0.646
mg of potassium added*	0.550	1.100

mg chloride added	1.0	1.0
mg sulfate added	1.35	2.70
mg ammonia added	0	0.51
Alkalinity neutralized (mg as $CaCO_3$, not ppm)	2.11	1.43

If Used. (Calculations courtesy of A. J. deLange.)

Water systems that use chloramines may sometimes revert to chlorine disinfection during periods when their water supply has low organic content (typically spring or winter). Chlorine is more effective in killing microorganisms and is less costly than chloramine. The occasional disinfectant change helps maintain sanitary conditions in the distribution system. Water users may notice more chlorine aroma from the water when this change is performed.

Chlorine Removal—UV Degradation
A relatively new technology for dechlorination is ultraviolet light photolysis, in which high-energy photons break molecular bonds. UV light breaks down the chlorine and chloramine molecules into component ions, yielding chloride, ammonia, and water. Chlorine degradation is optimized at 180–200 nanometers (nm) and the chloramines are optimized across 245–365 nm wavelength. The typical dose recommended in the literature is about 20X the disinfection dose, i.e., about 600 millijoule (mJ)/cm^2, with the spectrum centered at 245 nm wavelength for combined breakdown.

UV also has the added benefit of killing 99.99% of bacteria and viruses at this level, and the complete breakdown of total organic carbon (TOC), typically non-polar molecules, into polar or charged species that are more susceptible to ion exchange removal. In other words, a UV dechloration treatment will also help prevent fouling of downstream processes, such as ion exchange and reverse osmosis treatments.

The energy cost may be high, but there are corresponding benefits in lower maintenance and replacement costs for ion exchange and membrane technology media.

Figure 31—The UV degradation system at Sierra Nevada Brewing Co. This unit is placed before granular activated carbon (GAC) filtration.

Removing Organic Contaminants— Activated Carbon

Granular activated carbon (GAC) is the most common method for removing chlorine and most organic contaminants, including DBPs. GAC differs from powdered activated carbon (PAC) by particle size—GAC typically being 1.2–1.6mm in diameter, versus less than 0.1 mm diameter for PAC. Carbon filtration works by taking a carbon source (typically wood, coconut husk, nut shells, coal, etc.) and "activating" its substrate by either heat (pyrolysis) or a combination of chemicals (oxidation) and heat. The pyrolysis process forms a high carbon content 'char'. The oxidation process selectively burns away portions of the carbon matrix, leaving behind a pure carbon shell that is very porous, giving it a very large surface area. Subsequent treatment may include impregnation with chemicals such as phosphoric acid, potassium hydroxide, zinc chloride, etc., to improve the adsorption properties for specific contaminants. Activated carbon filtration is not actually a filtration process, but is an adsorption process that causes molecules to stick to the carbon matrix. The very large internal surface area adsorbs a variety of volatile organic compounds from the liquid. GAC will remove many chemicals that cause off-odors and taste in water. GAC also serves as a catalytic media that oxidizes complex molecules such as hypochlorite and chloramines.

Granular activated carbon (GAC) filtration is utilized in most breweries to treat the incoming water supply. It removes free chlorine relatively quickly and chloramines relatively slowly. When a water supply is known to contain chloramines it is important to have proper dwell time within the carbon media. Using large filters or putting multiple filters in parallel will work to increase carbon media contact time. Increasing the carbon media contact time improves contaminant removal and improves the overall utilization of the carbon media. However, with filters in parallel, any single filter that becomes saturated and leaks (breakthrough) provides a path for contaminants to bypass the filter system.

The removal or oxidation of contaminants within a GAC media bed tends to occur in a limited zone. As the flow rate is decreased, that treatment zone narrows and the utilization of the GAC media increases. If the flow rate is high, the treatment zone may 'smear' across the entire depth of the GAC media, which will result in premature breakthrough of the contaminants. Low velocity through the media is critical to improving contaminant removal and extending the filter life.

The sizing of GAC filter units is based on the interior volume of the filter casing holding the GAC media. Empty bed contact time (EBCT) is the primary design parameter for activated carbon systems. EBCT is calculated by dividing the total volume of the vessel holding the carbon media by the liquid flow rate. This methodology simplifies the analysis by removing the porosity of the carbon media from the analysis. In the brewing industry, the EBCT for chlorine removal should be at least 2 minutes. The EBCT for chloramine removal should be at least 8 minutes with typical GAC media. It can typically be reduced to about 6 minutes when specially-treated media for chloramine destruction are used. A comparison for these EBCT design recommendations can be made with the kidney dialysis industry, which has more critical requirements for chloramine removal; that industry recommends a 10-minute EBCT. Their EBCT recommendation conservatively assumes typical GAC media.

GAC media is rated by several parameters, each being a different measure of the media's ability to adsorb a substance. The most basic parameter is the iodine number, which is a measure of the micropore content of the activated carbon (0–20 Angstrom (Å), or up to 2 nm) by adsorption of iodine from solution. It is defined as milligrams of iodine adsorbed by one gram of carbon when the iodine concentration in the residual filtrate is 0.02 N. It is a useful gauge of the media's ability to adsorb low molecular weight substances, like Trihalomethanes (THMs). The iodine number for carbon media used in the brewery should be at least 850 mg/g for fresh carbon, and preferably greater than 1,000 mg/g.

The molasses number is a useful parameter for gauging the adsorption of higher molecular weight substances. The test consists of measuring the decolorization of a standardized dilute solution of molasses as a percentage compared to a GAC standard. The tannin test measures the ability of the media to absorb tannins and is reported as ppm concentration. The hardness number is a measure of the media's resistance to attrition, or movement, such as bed expansion during backwashing. The hardness number depends on the carbon source used to make the media, and should be at least 70.

GAC systems can be sized for most any need, and home units are common. The 10-inch GAC cartridges for under-sink filters typically contain about 30–32 cubic inches of AC media. Using the EBCT guidance above, the flow rate through this AC filter should be limited to about 0.065 gallon/minute for chlorine removal and about 0.016 gallon/minute for removal of chloramines. However, much shorter EBCTs for chlorine removal have been proven suitable in practice. A one gallon/minute flow rate through a 10-inch AC filter can provide adequate removal performance and filter life.

Common problems with GAC filters are microbial contamination and contaminant breakthrough due to lack of maintenance. Carbon filters are a perfect home for bacteria and other microorganisms after the chlorine/chloramine has been removed. Other organic contaminants that are trapped by the filters can provide a convenient food supply. GAC filters need regular steam or chemical backwashing to clean and refresh the media, and kill any microorganisms present.

You can easily measure the chlorine levels using any of several simple test kits sold by aquarium hobby shops or manufacturers of water testing equipment (Hach, LaMotte). Note that 'free chlorine' test kits measure only hypochlorite ion and not chloramines. If chloramines are used in the water supply, a 'total chlorine' test kit is required. Measurement of other contaminants, such as THMs, requires the use of a gas chromatograph or spectrophotometer. If any residual is detected, the carbon should be replaced. Large-scale GAC canisters include sample ports at various depths within the carbon bed for the purpose of measuring the progress of GAC consumption within the canister. All GAC media eventually needs to be replaced, even with regular maintenance.

Removing Dissolved Gases—Deaeration

Oxygen is the bane of brewers and brewing, with the sole exception of utilization by yeast for sterol synthesis. It's little wonder that substitutes like olive oil have been tried in the effort to remove it from the brewery entirely. Numerous oxygen reduction methods have been tried and many are in regular use to limit the effect of oxygen in each stage of the brewing process. Unfortunately, even 1 ppm in the finished product is a big problem. Current industry maximum acceptable levels of oxygen in finished beer are always less than 0.05 ppm, usually less than 0.03 ppm, and the goal for many brewers is less than 0.01 ppm. Generating and maintaining those levels in the water/beer during any transfer operation and packaging requires very low oxygen to begin with. How do we get there?

Deaeration is limited and/or controlled by both Dalton's Law and Henry's Law. Henry's law states that solubility of a gas is directly proportional to the partial pressure of the gas above the liquid. Dalton's law states that the total pressure of a gaseous mixture is equal to the sum of the partial pressures of the component gases. To deaerate water, the ratios of the partial pressures must be shifted so

Figure 32—Deaeration column at Sierra Nevada Brewing Co.

that the partial pressure of oxygen is as small as possible. This can be accomplished by increasing the partial pressure of another component gas to offset it, by increasing the vapor pressure of the water, or by reducing the total pressure of the system.

The original vacuum deaeration technology works by spraying the water into a mist in a partially evacuated chamber. The high surface area of the mist allows the oxygen and other gases to more easily be drawn out of solution in the partial vacuum and removed. This method has the option of using a stripping gas like CO_2. This technology typically achieves 0.07–0.1 ppm oxygen content and is adequate for boilers.

Membrane technology can also be used to remove oxygen and other gases. The membranes are typically hollow fibers connected to a low-pressure chamber to draw off the gases as they diffuse through the membranes. These systems can typically reduce residual oxygen down to 0.02 ppm, but they have some drawbacks. The fibers are relatively expensive and difficult to maintain.

The current technology of choice in the brewing industry is a column deaeration system, in which tall columns packed with a proprietary media assure high surface area contact between the water and the stripping gas (carbon dioxide or nitrogen). The water trickles down through the column while the stripping gas rises to the top. Most of the stripping gas is dissolved into the water, and the rest (including scrubbed oxygen) is vented. Cold-column systems in which the water is not heated can typically reach less than 0.03 ppm residual oxygen. By then heating the water to below boiling point using heat exchangers, this level can be further reduced. These hot-column systems can achieve residual oxygen below 0.01 ppm (less than 10 parts per billion). Other advantages of column systems are low energy use, high flow rates, and low maintenance. Units can be sized to deliver 5,000–80,000 liters per hour (40–680 barrels per hour).

Summary

In this chapter we have looked at most of the currently practical technologies for removing solids, liquids and gases from source water in order to prepare it for use in the brewery. These processes are usually combined in some way to make treatment more effective and efficient. For example, carbon filter cartridges with SAC resin to reduce hardness and heavy metals, ion exchange preceding reverse osmosis to improve the membrane service life, or UV dechlorination followed by GAC to adsorb any residue. There are many ways to combine these technologies to work better for you. In the next chapter, we will discuss the requirements for different service water uses in the brewery, and the use of the material presented in this chapter will be evident.

9

Brewery Process Waters

For many brewers, the brewing liquor is the only water that needs attention. However there are many tasks that water performs in the brewery and there are other reasons to treat water. It is important to have the ability to minimally process water for each task it is required to perform. Work smarter, not harder, as they say.

All water entering the brewery should meet some baseline water quality standard for potability. It is unrealistic to rely on the water supplier to provide water that is perfectly suitable for brewing. However, it is also unrealistic to plan to use brewing liquor for every brewery water use. Since we have discussed water for wort production extensively in earlier chapters, this chapter will focus on the other brewery uses; where factors such as scale formation and chemical costs are more important.

We have said it elsewhere in this book, but one of the most common pieces of advice from pro brewers, large and small, is to taste your water every day. This basic step can alert the brewer to changes in the water— changes that may affect the flavor of the beer, but also changes that can affect brewery process water. Successful breweries like Sierra Nevada Brewing Co. of Chico, California test their water at several points in the process. They smell and taste the source water, they smell and taste it after dechlorination, and after GAC filtration. Do not discount this simple test—it can save a lot of remediation.

Brewing Water

Generally, the first treatment step for brewing water consists of chlorine/chloramine breakdown, often by activated carbon filtration or metabisulfite addition. However, this removes residual disinfectant from the water, and that can lead to other problems, especially if there is a restaurant attached to the brewery. UV disinfection ahead of a carbon filter can serve two purposes: 1) it highly disinfects the water and helps prevent bacterial contamination of the carbon filter, and 2) it breaks down organics like chloramine ahead of the carbon filter, reducing the adsorption load and reducing the risk of contaminant leakage.

Water for domestic usage, such as cooking, lavatories, etc., should not have the residual disinfectant removed, and this water use should be split off from the main supply before brewery treatment. See Figure 33 for an example of water distribution and treatment in the brewery. The order of treatment should be adaptable to changes in needs, but brewers are cautioned against creating splits and legs in the flow stream ahead of actual need, because these dead legs can provide a haven for bacterial growth.

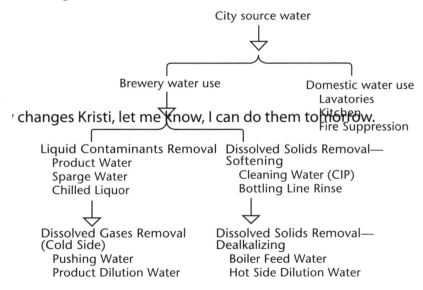

' changes Kristi, let me know, I can do them tomorrow.

Figure 33—An Example of Water Distribution and Treatment in the Brewery. Water treatment measures should not be wasted on water that doesn't need it, but should be used where it makes economic sense.

Cleaning and Rinsing Water

Most brewery water is used for cleaning. An ultra-modern brewery may use only 1 barrel of cleaning water to make 1 barrel of beer, but older, less-efficient breweries may use 3–8 barrels for cleaning per barrel of beer produced. Currently, a good total water use per barrel of beer production is about 4.5–5 barrels on average. This usage would typically break down to about 2–3 barrels of wastewater, 1 barrel lost to spent grain, yeast, evaporation, etc., and 1 barrel to the product. Higher brewery production actually helps improve water usage due to economies of scale. The largest breweries in the United States have set a total usage goal of about 3.5 barrels per barrel of beer production. However, it can be difficult to reduce usage to less than 4.5 barrels per barrel of beer production if the brewery is producing less than 10,000 barrels annually.

Cleaning water should have low calcium and magnesium hardness (<50 ppm total hardness recommended) to make the most efficient use of detergents and caustics. In hard water conditions, a portion of the cleaning chemicals will be bound up (essentially neutralized) by the calcium and magnesium in the water, so more chemicals are needed for any given task. Softening the water reduces this problem and can therefore save money. In addition, when more cleaner is used, more water is needed to rinse it away.

Softened water is therefore good for cleaning, and it will leave less carbonate scale behind as it dries. Softened water is also good for rinsing—but the problem is, many emulsifiers, dispersants, and surfactants use sodium or potassium in their chemistry. These ions are highly soluble in water and aid in the dissolution of the cleaner. Rinsing is more difficult with a solution that already contains a relatively high concentration of the solute. (Just like sparging with wort is less effective for extraction than sparging with water.) So, while softened water is generally less effective at rinsing than un-softened, there is still a net savings in using softened water for rinsing due to the reduced cleaning chemical usage. Even partial softening of moderately hard water can still reduce caustic usage significantly. One brewery with 75 ppm total hardness was able to reduce its chlorinated caustic usage by 50% after a softener was installed. Softening the cleaning water can quickly pay for itself in saved chemical costs and saved labor, even in a small brewery.

Cleaning and Rinsing Water Notes

- Cleaning and rinsing is typically the largest water use in the brewery: 3–8 volumes per volume (v/v) of beer.
- Softened water is recommended for cleaning and rinsing (<50 ppm hardness is best).
- Softened water can reduce cleaning chemical cost and usage.

Silicates

One problem that can be a big headache for brewers is silicates. Silica (SiO_2) is present in most water supplies in the range of 1–100 ppm, but it doesn't respond to most softening/dealkalizing treatments. Silica can polymerize to insoluble colloidal silica or silica gel. Silica becomes more soluble with increasing pH, dissociating into SiO_3^{-2}. Unfortunately magnesium silicate becomes less soluble at higher pH (>8.5) and is very difficult to remove without mechanical action. If the water is softened, and a white haze forms on tank surfaces upon drying, it may be sodium or potassium silicate. These salts are less soluble in acidic solutions, and can be best cleaned by caustic followed by a high-purity water rinse.

Water that is high in silica (>25 ppm) should not be used for boiler feedwater due to the high potential for scaling.

Chilled Liquor

Water used for cooling in heat exchangers and fermenters is often referred to as chilled liquor. It can be either brewing product water that is being heated for the next batch, or it can part of a closed-loop system utilizing propylene glycol. It is common practice to use the brewing liquor as the chilled liquor in the heat exchanger for wort chilling and thereby heat it for the next batch. This can be a big savings in energy costs. If the tap water is not cool enough to take the wort temperature to pitching temperature, a second stage of cooling may be required using glycol.

Figure 34—The main heat exchanger at New Belgium Brewing Co., Fort Collins, CO.

The cold side of the exchanger is not as susceptible to carbonate scaling because most calcium salt additions are typically made later at the mash or kettle. In addition, the water still contains dissolved carbon dioxide; so dissolved carbonates are more stable. This brewing water is typically filtered and dechlorinated, but is not otherwise treated.

Fermentors and bright tanks typically have glycol jackets for cooling because these provide better control over temperature than pure water-cooling methods. Propylene glycol solutions have lower freezing points than water and therefore are less likely to freeze in the lines and shut down the cooling system. Glycol manufacturers recommend that distilled water be used to create the solution, but it is not common practice among brewers to do so. Most breweries just use city water for dilution, although water sources with high hardness are not recommended. Glycol cooling system manufacturers recommend that the propylene glycol content be at least 30% (by volume) so that the freezing point is 20–25°F (11–13°C) below the lowest thermostat setting in use at the brewery—this is the typical margin to prevent freezing of the coolant in the system. See the propylene glycol sidebar for more information.

Residual disinfectants and biocides are needed in open-air cooling systems, such as cooling towers, to prevent growth of micro-organisms. Biocides are also recommended for closed-loop glycol systems because glycol can be a food source for some bacteria. Peracetic acid (CH_3CO_3H) is a common biocide choice because it is effective at very cold temperatures. However, it is a strong oxidizer, is highly corrosive, and can be hazardous when inhaled. Care must be taken when handling and using peracetic acid.

Chilled Liquor Notes

- Brewing liquor is often used in first stage heat exchangers to remove and recover the heat content from the boiled wort, effectively pre-heating the brewing liquor for the next batch. A second stage glycol-chilled heat exchanger is often used to further cool the wort to pitching temperature.
- Propylene glycol is added to lower the freezing point of water. Thirty to 35% (by volume) is the typical glycol concentration used in glycol cooling systems.
- Low hardness and iron content for glycol systems is desirable, but not required.
- Residual disinfectants or biocides are recommended for glycol systems.

Propylene Glycol Properties

Propylene glycol is on the FDA Generally Recognized as Safe List and while every effort is made to not contaminate beer with it, it is safe to ingest in case of a leak. It is very effective at lowering the freezing point of water, but also reduces the specific heat, i.e., the chilling power of the solution. Therefore, the propylene glycol concentration should be only high enough to prevent freezing at the intended system minimum operating temperature (plus safety factor). Its concentration can easily be measured with a brewing refractometer or hydrometer. It is quite expensive, so every effort must be made to avoid leaks in the system.

Propylene Glycol Solution Properties

Volume %	Freezing Point °F (°C)	Refractometer Reading (Brix) @68°F (20°C)	Specific Gravity* @70°F	Specific Heat BTU/(lb-°F) @70°F
10	26 (-3.3)	8.5	1.006	0.986
20	18 (-7.8)	16	1.015	0.968
30	8 (-13.3)	22.5	1.024	0.939
32	6.6 (-14.1)	24	1.025	0.932
34	3.9 (-15.6)	25.5	1.026	0.924
36	0.8 (-17.3)	26.5	1.028	0.917
38	-2.4 (-19.1)	28	1.030	0.908
40	-6 (-21.1)	29	1.031	0.900

* Specific gravity is generally not recommended because density increases, then decreases with increasing percentage of glycol in solution (>60%). Glycol solutions do not follow the same relationship for refraction vs. gravity as sugar solutions do. Same instrument—different utilization.

Boiler and Boiler Feedwater

Steam is commonly used for heating the mash tun and kettle, and for sanitizing heat exchangers. Boiler and steam systems require water with low total dissolved solids (TDS) because the solids accumulate as scale that can insulate and plug the system. Boiler water refers to the water in the boiler reservoir, where the solids accumulate. Feedwater is the makeup water that is added to the boiler as steam is lost to the system over time. TDS measurement via water conductivity is the best way to monitor boiler water quality. Boiler water that exceeds the general industry guideline of 1,000 ppm TDS is removed from the boiler during blowdown/maintenance. Low silica content is an especially important criterion because it forms a very tenacious scale at higher concentration.

Figure 35—The Boiler at Heretic Brewing Co., Fairfield, CA.

Proper boiler water composition can extend the life of a steam system significantly. The boiler's internal environment can be highly corrosive, so water composition and treatment are very important. Whenever water is lost from the system, whether by leaks or during the normal blowdown process to remove accumulated solids, more water must be added. The feedwater should be low in TDS (low hardness and carbonates), and have very low levels of oxygen and carbon dioxide. RO or distilled water is commonly used to make boiler feedwater. Condensate from the kettle can also be utilized as feedwater if it is pure enough.

Minerals in boiler water are responsible for scale, and dissolved gases in the water will cause corrosion of the steam piping and boiler components. Carbonates in the water will decompose into carbon dioxide at high temperature and pressure, according to the reaction:

$$Ca(HCO_3)_2 \text{ (heated)} \rightarrow CaCO_3(ppt) + CO_2(g) + H_2O$$

The carbon dioxide dissolves into the steam and condensate to form carbonic acid. Although carbonic acid is weak, it is strong enough in the condensate environment to drop the pH below 5. Carbonic acid causes pitting in steels by forming ferrous bicarbonate, which is quite soluble. Once a pit has formed, it is the most likely place for further corrosion to occur and it is a source of free iron to spread corrosion throughout the steam system.

Oxygen corrosion occurs in a similar manner, forming ferric hydroxide and causing pits. The combination of oxygen and carbon dioxide appears to increase corrosion up to 40% more than either gas would alone. Higher water/condensate pH (>7) slows the rate of corrosion somewhat.

Chloride ions are corrosive to all steels, but chlorine (Cl_2) is the more stable form at pH 10 and above. The National Board of Boiler and Pressure Vessel Inspectors (NBBI) recommends that boiler water should be maintained at 11 pH, and that condensate should be maintained between 7.5–8.5 pH to best prevent corrosion problems.

Recommended additives are caustic for pH control, phosphates for scale control, and sodium bisulfite for oxygen control. Another common treatment is the addition of filming amines (e.g., octadecylamine). These long chain amino acids are added to boiler water. When heated, they evaporate and coat the surfaces of the steam system with a waterproof coating, protecting the steel from corrosion. The requirements are very boiler-specific depending on size, pressure, and system variables. Breweries should contact a boiler specialist for more detailed information.

Caustic embrittlement is another potential problem for boilers and it occurs where the local concentration of caustic (i.e., hydroxide) is greater than ten percent, such as in crevices from rivets or fittings. This type of embrittlement is very similar to stress corrosion cracking, where cracks propagate due to relatively low combinations of stress and a corrosive agent. Sodium metabisulfite and phosphate additives may be used to mitigate caustic embrittlement.

Problems Caused by Poor Boiler Water Treatment
- Scaling and accumulation of solids decreases efficiency.
- Excess gases, carbonates, and caustic can cause corrosion.
- The pH of boiler water should be maintained at 11 to minimize corrosion risk.

Boiler Water Requirements
- Boiler water should be made from softened and dealkalized water, or from RO or distilled water.
- Suggested upper limits for boiler water from the MBAA's Practical Brewer (3rd Ed.):
  3,500 ppm TDS
  1,000 ppm hardness
  700 ppm alkalinity
  300 ppm suspended solids
  125 ppm silica

Boiler Water Additives
- Chelating agents (i.e. EDTA) for calcium removal
- Phosphates for calcium removal
- Oxygen scavengers (i.e. sodium bisulfite)
- Filming amines to prevent corrosion
- Sludge conditioners to precipitate carbonates to be removed by blowdown

Boiler Feedwater Requirements
- Low carbonates (less than 50 ppm as $CaCO_3$)
- Low chloride (Cl^-) (less than 50 ppm)
- Deaeration is required (O_2 should be less than 20 ppb).
- Silica concentrations should be very low (25 ppm max).
- Consultants are often used to set up and check boiler water.

Packaging

Softened water is used in many places in packaging operations. Softened water is preferred because it rinses cleanly and leaves little residue. For general cleaning around a bottling line, softened water with a chlorine-residual disinfection is adequate. Breweries with naturally soft water often use the water as-is. Practices for bottle rinsing vary; sometimes the rinse water is softened only, and sometimes it is GAC-filtered with the addition of a no-rinse sanitizer such as chlorine dioxide or ozone. The same water may be used for fobbing the beer (i.e., to cap on foam), although some brewers prefer RO and/or deaerated water for this final contact to minimize the potential for oxygen pickup during packaging.

Figure 36—One of the bottling lines at Sierra Nevada Brewing Co., Chico, CA.

Scaling and corrosion are prime considerations for a pasteurizer line. The water used in pasteurizers is softened and often includes corrosion inhibiters similar to the boiler water/ feedwater treatments.

The keg washing and packaging operations can be a bit different than bottling. Kegs have a greater likelihood of picking up carbonate scale and beerstone, so softened or even deionized water use is more common. Stainless steel kegs can be steam sanitized, but no-rinse sanitizers are common too.

Packaging Water Notes
- Softened water is the minimum recommended treatment for general cleaning.
- GAC or RO filtration is recommended for rinsing and fobbing water.
- Deaerated water offers better protection for reducing oxygen pick-up during packaging.

Pushing Product

A lot of beer can be lost in transfer piping, hoses or WIP (wort in progress). Using water to push product through long lines can provide significant savings in a large brewery. With good flow or volume control, very little wort is wasted when transferring wort to the fermenter or when pushing finished beer to a bright tank or the bottling line.

Sterile, dechlorinated water is required to push wort. Deaeration is not required for wort transfer, because yeast will consume any added oxygen during fermentation. Deaerated water is highly recommended for pushing beer though, and ideally, this would be the same water used for post-fermentation dilution. However, since the interface between the beer and water is small and the contact time is short, many brewers simply stop the wort transfer a little early and consider the small amount of product lost to be insignificant to the overall gain.

Pushing Product Water Notes
- Sterile, dechlorinated water is best for pushing wort.
- Sterile, deaerated water (<15 ppb) is best for pushing beer.
- However, with accurate flow/volume control, less rigorous requirements are acceptable because the small volume of interface wort/beer can be discarded.

Dilution Water

It is common practice to brew to a couple points higher than the target gravity and dilute a little at the end of boil to hit the target. In some cases, brewers boil at 30% or more above the target gravity, which is known as high-gravity and ultra-high-gravity brewing. This practice ensures a consistent starting gravity, which is essential to creating a consistent product. It is important that this pre-fermentation dilution water have the same or higher calcium content than the brewing liquor to promote calcium oxalate precipitation before it gets to packaging. Higher calcium content promotes calcium oxalate precipitation earlier in the brewing process. Generally, the calcium concentration in the brewing water should be at least three times the oxalate concentration listed on the malt analysis. If the calcium oxalate precipitates in the bottle, it can cause gushing, where the entire bottle turns to foam upon opening. In aging and bright tanks calcium oxalate (beer stone) causes extra labor and expense in cleaning cycles.

There are two methods of high-gravity brewing: the first dilutes the wort before fermentation, and the second dilutes the beer after fermentation. Pre-fermentation dilution is most often used for low-gravity beers when the fermentation capacity exceeds the boil capacity. It is simpler than diluting post-fermentation because deaeration is not required. Pre-fermentation water must be sanitized, and the most common methods are sterile filtration, UV sterilization and heat sterilization. It is strongly recommended that this dilution percentage not exceed 30%.

Post-fermentation dilution water has the strictest requirements of any water used in the brewery. It must be sterile, just like the pre-fermentation water, but must also be deaerated to prevent staling the beer. Different deaeration methods have different capabilities—boiling the water at normal atmospheric pressure only reduces the dissolved oxygen level to about 4 parts per *million*. This level of oxygen in packaging may have been acceptable 50 years ago, but is not acceptable today.

The current industry guideline for maximum acceptable oxygen level in packaged beer is less than 50 parts per *billion*. Levels are typically less than 30 ppb, and the goal for many breweries is less than 10 ppb. If the product is carbonated, then the dilution water must be carbonated as well. Fortunately, hot-column deaerators use carbon dioxide as a stripping gas; so residual CO_2 is not an issue there. Post-fermentation dilution is usually done on the way to the bottling line and can result in extensive savings on storage equipment and refrigeration costs. It is very important that post-fermentation water have a lower calcium concentration than the beer in order to prevent oxalate precipitation and gushing in the bottle. The calcium level in the beer may be one-third of the original calcium level in the brewing water, so it is important to be sure of the margin to prevent precipitation.

Dilution water considerations
- Calcium content should be adjusted as necessary to prevent oxalate precipitation in the package.
- Sterilization is required.
- Carbon filtration to remove all organic odors and residual chlorine is common.
- The less dissolved oxygen, the better.
- Dilution water may be carbonated if diluting inline at packaging.

Summary
This chapter is intended to give an overview of the additional ways water is used in a brewery. There are many ways to design water quality into brewery operations. Often logistical and monetary considerations are large factors in designing water treatment systems. The idea is to set up treatment processes in a natural progression so that water of appropriate quality is available where needed, at the most economical cost, and high-quality water is not wasted where it isn't needed. That would be money down the drain.

"Use as much water as you need but not a drop more."

–Brewer's Proverb

10

Wastewater Treatment for the Brewery

It's the end of the day at the brewery: the wort is made, the beer is fermenting, other beer has been packaged, and all the equipment has been washed down or cleaned up. The wastewater has gone down the drain. The job is done. Or is it? Wastewater just goes down the drain, right? Excess wort from spent grains? Down the drain. Wastewater from CIP operations? Down the drain. The city will take care of it, right?

For many small brewers, this is indeed the case. The city sewer/water treatment system can handle 100–500 gallons of water or wort at a time without much trouble. But as a brewery gets larger (the issue of size depends on the city or treatment plant), the brewery may be responsible for higher fees to have its wastewater treated, or may have to treat the wastewater itself before discharging it.

This chapter is intended to be an introduction to brewery wastewater treatment. It is not intended to be completely comprehensive or to recommend a best approach. There is no single answer when it comes to choosing among wastewater treatment options. Determining the best approach will require a thorough review of all the local, state, and/or national requirements, the affordability of options, and consultation with more knowledgeable people than the authors of this book. The purpose of this chapter is to educate you on what wastewater is, why it needs to be treated, and how it can be treated.

What is Wastewater?

Any water that is adversely affected in quality by human use or utilization is called wastewater. Quality in this definition refers to drinking water quality. Wastewater can contain suspended solids, dissolved solids, and/or dissolved liquids and gases. Brewing can be a very wasteful activity: typical water usage is 5–8 volumes of water per volume of beer produced and about 3 pounds of saturated spent grain per gallon of beer. Additional waste, mostly proteins and spent hops, are produced as trub in the whirlpool and fermentors. Some of this waste can be collected and disposed of as solid waste, but a lot of it makes its way to the drains. Most brewery wastewater comes from cleaning operations, and will contain caustic cleaners, sanitizers, acids, and brewing residue. The strength of these effluents can be measured in several ways, but two of the most common are biological/biochemical oxygen demand (BOD) and chemical oxygen demand (COD). The BOD test gauges the amount of biodegradable organic compounds in water by measuring the amount of oxygen consumed by bacteria in an incubator during a five day period, expressed as mg/L of O_2. The COD test is quicker; it measures both biodegradable and non-biodegradable organics by measuring the amount of a strong oxidizer (typically potassium dichromate) that reacts with the sample. The COD test overestimates the amount of organic contaminant in the water compared to the BOD test, but its speed and consistency make it valuable in planning water treatment needs. Other common methods for determining organic content of water are color (for tannins and humic matter), solvent extraction, and total organic carbon (TOC). The TOC test is an atomization and combustion procedure that measures total carbon as CO_2, including alkalinity in the water (although alkalinity is typically subtracted). The most relevant measure for brewery waste is BOD, and likely may be the only measure that you actually use. The other definitions are included for your information, just in case.

It is primarily the organics in wastewater that need to be treated, and by treated, we mean removed. The organics in wastewater from breweries are typically not chemical contaminants like oils or solvents, but rather proteins and carbohydrates that provide food for bacteria and molds. If discharged untreated into streams or rivers, this effluent provides sufficient nutrition for microorganisms to strip all available oxygen from an ecosystem, effectively killing it.

Why Do We Treat Wastewater?

Brewery waste is a particular problem for a city waste treatment plant because of its strength. Typical brewery wastewater can contain suspended solids in the range of 400–800 ppm, and BOD of 2,000–3,500 ppm. The temperature of the wastewater can exceed 140°F. The pH of the discharge can easily exceed the 5–11 pH limits due to the cleaning caustics and acid rinsing. The yeast load can potentially out-compete the treatment facility's digestion bacteria. Residual sanitizers can also damage or kill the digestion bacteria and shut down the treatment operation.

The discharge of a brewery will vary depending on the particular brewing activity at the time, i.e., emptying the mash tun, cleaning out the fermentor, or washing down equipment. Brewery waste can be more effectively handled by first diverting it to a holding tank where it can be diluted with other wastewater, and then fed at a more uniform rate to the sewer over an extended period of time. An equalization tank is therefore the first step of any waste management system.

The national requirements for wastewater discharge to surface water in the United States are listed in Table 23. The Clean Water Act via the National Pollutant Discharge Elimination System (NPDES) of 1972 imposed these limits. Any wastewater that exceeds these limits must be treated (i.e., contaminants removed by a waste treatment plant) before discharge back to the environment.

Table 23—NPDES Requirements for Discharge to Surface Water Sources

Waste Parameter	Limit
pH	6-9 pH
Temperature	100°F (38°C)
BOD	30 ppm
TSS	30 ppm
TDS	(varies)
Phosphorus	(varies)
Ammonia	(varies)

The discharge requirements from the brewery to the local sewer and waste treatment plant vary with the location, due to local laws and needs. Typically, the sewer requirements are much less restrictive than the environmental requirements for BOD and total suspended solids (TSS). Typical effluent requirements for discharge to sewers in the US are shown in Table 24.

Table 24—Typical US Sewer Discharge Limits

Waste Parameters	Limit
Flow	<25,000 gallons per day*
Temperature	140°F (60°C)
pH	5–11
BOD	250 mg/L
TSS	250 mg/L
Fats, Oils, Grease	100 mg/L

*Flow rates greater than 25,000 gallons per day are considered to be Significant Industrial Users, subject to higher fees and requirements.

The load that the treatment plant sees at any given time is a combination of the volume of the wastewater and its strength. A large volume of low strength waste can be handled with relative ease, and in fact this condition could be considered typical for daily processing. A small volume of high strength waste can be diluted by other waste streams before or immediately after entering the plant and can be accommodated without too much trouble. However, a large volume of high strength waste (ex. high BOD) can be a real problem. In addition, any facility that discharges more than 25,000 gallons per day is considered to be a Significant Industrial User by the US EPA, and is subject to higher rates and more restrictive requirements. Assuming a fairly typical wastewater to beer ratio of 4:1 for mid-size breweries, this would equate to an annual production of about 75,000 barrels a year.

How is Wastewater Treated?

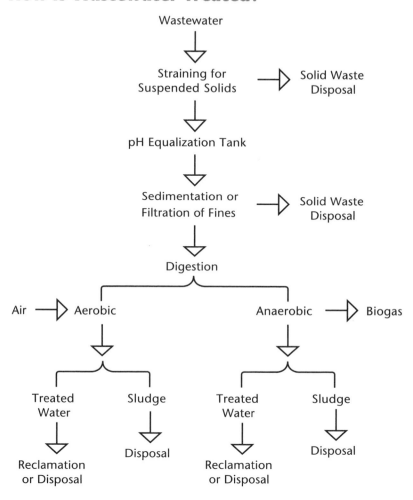

Figure 37—Schematic Diagram of Basic Wastewater Treatment Steps. The first step is suspended solids removal, then filtration of fine particles, pH equalization, and then actual treatment of the BOD in the wastewater by aerobic or anaerobic digestion.

The order of operations for wastewater treatment is nearly the same, whether it is conducted at a brewery, factory, or municipal treatment plant. First the suspended solids are removed by screens or sedimentation. These can be anything from wood, toys, shoes, or dead animals, to food scraps and particulates that are too large for later process treatment steps to handle. The screening step is usually only capable of removing the big pieces, though. The next step is to remove any remaining suspended solids that have passed through screening or filtration (i.e., fines), and the dissolved solids. Typically, the fines and dissolved solids must be reacted or consumed to take them out of the waste stream. This is particularly true in brewery waste where the density of the fines is nearly the same as water, making sedimentation a time-consuming process. Dissolved solids are in solution and generally cannot be removed by filtration, although activated carbon filtration can be useful for some contaminants. The pH of the wastewater is usually adjusted before proceeding to any chemical and/or biological processing steps, so that those processes can run more consistently and effectively. After the dissolved solids have been eliminated, or reduced and concentrated, the sludge (residue) is collected and sent to a landfill or otherwise disposed. Partially purified water is typically reclaimed at one or more points during processing and may be further purified by a variety of methods, including reverse osmosis. Each of these major process steps will be reviewed in more detail below.

Removal of Suspended Solids

Brewery wastewater usually contains a high volume of suspended solids that should not be in the wastewater stream. These solids can include spent grains, spent hops, spent yeast, proteins, tannins, broken glass and bottle caps. The openings in the filtration screens at municipal water treatment plants tend to be approximately 6mm spacing or diameter (0.25 inch). However, brewery screens need to be finer, and are typically less than 2mm spacing or diameter (0.08 inch). The waste stream is screened and continues on to the next step, typically a holding or equalization tank where the pH is adjusted and the flow rate is regulated to the next process(es).

The screens for removal of suspended solids can be either static or rotary, but both need a method of removing the trapped solids and cleaning the openings to maintain flow. Static screens usually have some sort of rake, scraper, or wiper to keep the screen clean. Rotary screens rotate to constantly dump the collected solids and continually present a clean surface to the waste stream.

The recovered solids from the screens can be used in composting or mulch for outdoor garden areas, or sent to a landfill, depending on their composition.

Figure 38—The Rotary Screen in use at Sierra Nevada Brewing Co., Chico, CA.

pH Adjustment/Equalization Tank

The next step after screening is typically the equalization tank. An equalization tank serves two purposes: it acts as a reservoir to accumulate and dispense the wastewater at a controlled rate, and it is typically where the pH of the wastewater is adjusted to suit downstream processes like digestion. The first function is probably obvious to most brewers, as it is similar in purpose to a lautering grant—slugs of flow are detained and metered out of the tank at a more even flow rate. The pH adjustment is understandable as well, given the pH differences between acid washdown and caustic CIP cleaning solutions. Some breweries have automated acid and caustic dispensing systems to monitor the pH of the tank, while others will have a single agent for dosing systems. If the tank is large enough, slugs of acid- or caustic-laden flow can be moderated without intervention. The point is that the pH of the effluent needs to be controlled to a range so that it does not disrupt downstream processes. If the effluent from a small microbrewery is simply being sewered to a local treatment plant, then any pH between 5 and 11 is probably acceptable. If the wastewater volume is much larger, or requires further treatment in-house, then a pH range of 6–9 is better. If the waste is going to be digested, as discussed below, then even tighter control may be needed.

A steady flow of consistent-strength waste is easiest to manage for everyone.

Filtration of Fines

Many of the suspended solids in brewery wastewater streams are very fine, often less than 1mm in diameter (.04 inch). These fines can be carbohydrates, proteins, silica from beer filtration, or yeast. While the organic compounds can be digested by other processing downstream, it is useful to extract purified water from the stream and reduce the volume of wastewater that needs to be treated.

Sedimentation is usually the preferred method for separation of suspended solids in most other industries, but brewery solids are more problematic. The particle density of grain, hops, and trub is very nearly the same as water, so solids don't settle very quickly—large settling ponds would be required to give the material sufficient time to fall out. Coagulants and flocculants can be used, but these chemicals can often be expensive. These sorts of particles can often be settled out in reverse, by dissolved air flotation, but again, brewery waste tends to be problematic. The high volume of fines, high dissolved oxygen, and traces of spent yeast can create a rampant fermentation in the separation chamber, and a messy waste product!

Fortunately there are other technologies available to concentrate these fines, and one of the most popular is microfiltration using membrane technology. Microfiltration uses a microporous membrane to filter purified water from the wastewater. Microfiltration is often used in membrane bioreactors (MBR) in aerobic digestion systems, and this will be discussed further in the next section.

Microfiltration is generally capable of filtering out yeast and bacteria, and this type of filter is commonly used for bottled water processing to eliminate microorganisms. Yeast cells are typically 0.005–0.010 mm (0.0002–0.0004 inch), and bacteria may be 10 times smaller. The range of pore size available for microfiltration membranes is 0.1–10 micrometers (i.e., the same range as typical bacteria and yeast). The membranes can be hollow fibers, flat sheets, tubes, or spiral-wound cartridges. In continuous processing, it is useful to have the membranes arranged in racks or similar geometry for easier maintenance.

During filtration, a pressure difference is often applied across the membrane, typically suction, to pull filtrate water away from the effluent. The difference between the pressure on the feed side of the membrane and the filtrate side of the membrane is called the trans-membrane pressure, or TMP. Typical operating pressure is 2–4 psi (14–28 kPa). The TMP will rise as the feed side of the membrane becomes fouled with solids. Agitation of the feed side is provided by air or liquid washing to maintain low TMP and prevent solids accumulation on the feed side of the membrane fibers. For example, coarse bubbles, generated by a diffuser below the membranes, create a scouring effect that reduces the accumulation of solids on the outer membrane surface.

The use cycle includes a relaxation step, or soak step when the pressure differential is reduced or zeroed. The filtration stops for a short period of time (minutes) during the relaxation step to allow the scouring effect to remove particulate matter more effectively. This process can cycle several times per hour, depending on demand.

Periodic maintenance typically includes a weekly chemical backwash to remove stubborn deposits. Typically a low concentration of chlorine solution or other cleaner is injected to the filtrate side of the membranes at a low flux for a set amount of time. The chlorinated solution soaks in the membrane fibers and pores, breaking down any foulants that were not removed by normal scouring. A no-pressure relaxation step can then be used to remove the loosened foulants, and normal operation can resume.

Digestion

The fines and dissolved solids can be broken down by aerobic or anaerobic digestion using microorganisms ('bugs'). These microorganisms can be any variety of bacteria, protozoa, fungi, algae, rotifers, and even worms, depending on the type of waste that needs to be reduced. For brewery waste, they primarily consist of bacteria.

The microbes are sensitive to temperature and pH, thriving best at 85–95°F (30–35°C), and 6.5–7.5 pH. The pH range can be broader, 5–9, but 6.5–7.5 is optimum. The pH can drop quickly in digestion systems due to generation of CO_2 and nitrates, though this depends on the bacteria in the system. If the pH drops, it should be adjusted quickly to prevent biological die-off and a halt to treatment. The low alkalinity water typically preferred in brewery operations is prone to wider pH swings due to its relative lack of buffering.

The nutritional needs of the microbes can't be ignored either. Usually the brewery waste supplies everything they need (phosphates, calcium, magnesium, sulfate) but sometimes extra ammonia nitrogen is required to maintain healthy growth, the same as for yeast. Generally the microbes require a waste BOD/nitrogen/phosphate ratio of 100:5:1 for best performance. A snapshot of typical brewery waste is given in Table 25. Brewery waste can vary considerably in strength depending on the process du jour. Generally a COD of >5,000 mg/L is considered high-strength waste.

Table 25—Typical Brewery Waste Strength

Parameter	Concentration (mg/L)	Typical Production
Total COD	3,000–5,500	2.5–7.5 lbs./bbl
Total BOD	2,000–3,500	--
Total Suspended Solids	400–800	0.3–1.1 lbs./bbl

There are two options for digestion: aerobic and anaerobic. Aerobic microbes use gases (mainly oxygen) to foster their growth and digest the effluent. Anaerobic microbes digest the effluent in the absence of oxygen and produce gases (primarily methane). Both processes can consume nearly all of the brewery's BOD waste and produce a sludge biomass that is very low in BOD. In other words, it is fairly inert and can be landfilled or used for compost. Sludge from other industries can have traces of heavy metals or other hazardous waste that can be more difficult to dispose, but brewery sludge has the potential to be a useful commodity.

Aerobic Treatment

Aerobic treatment methods and equipment are fairly simple: build a large tank or pond, install aerators, add microbes, and pretty soon you are reducing BOD. The aerated mixture of wastewater and microbes digests the BOD in the wastewater. The biomass is then sent to a clarifier where the treated wastewater is separated from the microbes and the microbes are returned to the inlet of the aeration tank to maintain the balance of biomass to wastewater. Aerobic systems handle low- to medium-strength waste best.

Beware of Hop Oils and Sanitizers!

The microbes in digesters are no more immune to hops and sanitizers than other beer spoilage microbes. The relatively recent emphasis on IPAs and dry hopping has caused problems for several breweries that treat their own waste, as hops can inhibit both bugs and treatment. The best solution for this is to take extra steps to keep spent hops out of the wastewater stream (better screening).

Sanitizers are of course anti-microbial, but you would expect them to be de-activated in the equalization tank. Unfortunately, this is not always the case. Peracetic acid sanitizers seem to have the longest residual activity and extra steps should be taken to neutralize them before they enter the digester. A caustic addition can help deactivate peracetic acid in wastewater.

Figure 39—Aerobic Digestion Tank at Sierra Nevada Brewing Co., Chico, CA.

Figure 40—Aerobic Digestion Pond at New Belgium Brewing Co., Fort Collins, CO.

Clarifiers can be tanks or ponds. Tanks can be circular with a center inflow point and outflow around the tank perimeter, or rectangular with an inlet at one end and an outlet at the other. The distance between the tank inlet and outlet provides time for the now-heavier biomass to settle out of the wastewater flow. Clarified water discharges at the top of the tank, while the sludge biomass collecting at the bottom of the tank is pumped back to the aeration tank to digest more BOD. The treated sludge is discharged from the system and typically dewatered so that it can be better handled and disposed. There are several sludge disposal options available, including land application, composting, and landfilling.

The advantages to aerobic systems are that they are easy to set up and operate, and can be readily expanded. When operated correctly, the odor from the aerated tank or pond is minimal with most of the gases consisting of CO_2 and water. If operated incorrectly, the bacteria can die, the tank may go anaerobic, and foul odors will blanket the area. The current economics of treatment suggest that aerobic systems are best suited for loadings of up to 5,000 pounds of COD per day. Beyond that load, anaerobic systems may be more economical.

Some of the disadvantages of an aerobic treatment system are the high energy requirements for the aeration, a large processing footprint for the tank(s)/pond and clarifier, and a high biomass yield (i.e., treated sludge). Expandability (building more aeration tanks or ponds) is a nice feature but it uses a lot of the available space. Often the sheer volume of wastewater can overwhelm the treatment system, not by its strength, but by its volume. This is where dewatering becomes important. Membrane filtration can help dewater the waste stream and this is where membrane bioreactors come into play.

Membrane Bioreactors (MBR)

The MBR process replaces the typical sedimentation clarifier. MBR units have dramatically smaller footprints, often 5% or less of the original tank. An MBR is essentially a cabinet filled with racks of microfiltration filaments or sheets. The MBR can be placed inside or next to the digester tank, and works by filtering out excess water while keeping the biomass in the tank. The membranes can be either microfiltration (~0.1 micrometer pores) or ultrafiltration (~0.01 micrometer), depending on the need, and can achieve almost complete particle separation from the water. The permeate water is typically microbe-free and clear, with few suspended solids (e.g. tannins). The water will still contain all of the inorganic dissolved solids (minerals), and some undigested organics (residual phosphates, tannins, etc), but at much reduced levels. Meanwhile, the more concentrated effluent is retained for further breakdown in the aeration tank.

A bubble stream along the exterior of microfiltration filaments or sheets of the MBR unit helps prevent fouling. Stone Brewing Co. has used this sort of system alongside their aerobic digestion tank for years and it has proven very reliable and low maintenance. An MBR reduces the overall volume of water in the treatment system, and provides a water source that can be readily used as wash down water for non-critical equipment. The water is biologically pure, and potable, but without a residual disinfection agent. It has more dissolved phosphates (~50 ppm) and tannins than the original source water but much less than the raw wastewater. The water has the color of tea (or beer) and a slightly dry, earthy odor. At Stone, most of this reclaimed permeate is fed to a reverse osmosis system for further purification. Considering the cost and scarcity of water at Stone's Southern California brewery, the opportunity for water recycling is appealing.

Anaerobic Treatment

Aerobic digesters are simple and efficient, but are relatively large and energy expensive to run. On the other hand, anaerobic digesters have smaller footprints, are more complicated to run, but can pay for themselves with biogas production that can be used as fuel. Anaerobic digesters are currently the best available technology for treating brewery wastewater. This technology uses sealed vessels to keep air out of the process to create the anaerobic condition. The most common design of anaerobic digesters in US breweries today are the UASB type (Upflow Anaerobic Sludge Blanket), but there are other types in use at breweries as well, such as the EFB (Expanded Fluidized Bed) where liquid turbulence gets the biomass agitated. These systems use specialized tanks and require careful operation. Another option uses a typical sealed tank with forced circulation to keep the contents well mixed. Linear Motion Mixing (LMM) is a recent energy-efficient mixing technology which uses a slow-moving plunger to keep the tank contents mixed. Each of these digester systems performs the same task: converting a large amount of strong BOD waste into methane gas, while producing less sludge volume than an aerobic process.

All anaerobic digesters use methane-producing bacteria to reduce the waste. Acetogens (acetate-forming) can be present as well, but are usually not needed to break down brewery waste. Acetogens like warmer temperatures than methanogens (methane-forming). Methanogens like 85–95°F (30–35°C). The anaerobic bacteria are very sensitive to the environment, and they can be overwhelmed by yeast. The process can be finicky and requires constant attention.

The benefit of anaerobic digestion is the methane gas that it produces. Nominally you have three options with the gas: you can flare it to the atmosphere (burn it), you can clean it and use it in the brewery, or you can clean it and sell it. The biogas contains other gases besides methane, which is typically 50–70% of the total. Most of the rest of the gas is carbon dioxide and water vapor, but there are traces of hydrogen sulfide, and other hydrocarbons. Cleaning consists of removing these contaminants. Once cleaned, the methane gas can be used in boilers or engines. The heating value of the biogas after drying is typically 500–700 BTU/ft^3, compared to about 1,020 BTU/ft^3 for natural gas, and about 2,500 BTU/ft^3 for propane gas. Drying is accomplishing by pressurizing and condensation.

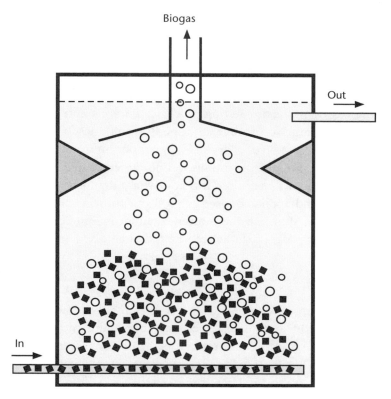

Figure 41—Upflow Anaerobic Sludge Blanket Digestion System. The biogas is collected from the center.

Figure 42—The Top of the Anaerobic Digestion System at New Belgium Brewing Co., Fort Collins, CO. An anaerobic system must be closed off from the surrounding air, so there is not much to see from the outside.

Sludge Dewatering

The sludge or biomass that is produced from these digesters is nutrient poor and has little odor. The water should be removed from the sludge to aid disposal and save shipping costs. The water can be removed by filtration or decanter centrifuging. Polymer coagulants can be added to the sludge to aid in the dewatering process and improve its handling. For example, the decanter centrifuge at Stone Brewing doesn't run every day of the week, and produces a dry (18% water) crumbly sludge with low odor (smells like dirt). Most landfills will not accept liquid wastes, so dewatering sludge may be required if that is where the material is directed. If the sludge is land-applied or used as a soil amendment, then dewatering may be optional. Although the nutrient content is significantly reduced by the treatment process, sludge can be a desirable soil amendment for agricultural lands.

Summary

Breweries use a lot of water, and as water resources become more scarce, water conservation and management are becoming more important. Treating wastewater in the brewery can be handled in several ways, often with easy steps. The first step for any brewery, even small ones, is to install an equalization tank to moderate the strength and volume of the waste. This can be a big help to avoid fines when sewering wastewater with a city or treatment plant. Later, as the brewery grows, it is the first step for in-house treatment. As wastewater volume increases and surcharges from the wastewater utility grow, it becomes more economical to pre-treat brewery wastewater. Yes, it costs time and money to take on these tasks, but the effort is never wasted. Ask any mid-size brewery about the investment in in-house water treatment, and the most common response is, "We did it to save money."

Chemistry Glossary
and Primer

The purpose of this appendix is to provide a glossary and primer to facilitate the discussion of water and brewing throughout this book. Therefore, this glossary is not a general dictionary of words associated with water, or brewing terms. If you cannot find the term you were looking for, check the Index; the term may be defined in the text.

Δc_0—Delta C nought: the change in charge from the initial water pH to 4.3 per a total alkalinity titration.

Δc_Z—Delta C Z: the change in charge from the initial water pH to the target mash pH (Z pH).

°L—Degrees Lovibond for malt color.

Acid—An acid is a proton donor, according to the Brønsted-Lowry definition. When an acid donates a proton, the remainder of the molecule is called the conjugate base. For example, the ionic compound HCl is an acid, and donates a proton; the remainder, Cl^{-1}, is the conjugate base. A monoprotic acid has one proton to donate, and a polyprotic acid has more than one.

Acid/Base Pair—The associated acid and conjugate base, or base and conjugate acid, are referred to as acid/base pairs.

Acidity—The quantity of base necessary to change the pH of a substance by a defined amount. Acidity must always be defined with respect to specific pH endpoint or magnitude of pH change.

Alkali—A substance that is a base, or more specifically, a basic ionic salt of an alkali metal or an alkaline earth metal (i.e., the first two columns on the periodic table of elements).

Alkalinity—The quantity of acid necessary to change the pH of a substance by a defined amount. Alkalinity must always be defined with respect to specific pH endpoint or magnitude of pH change.

Amine—An amine is a chemical structure derived from ammonia (NH_3) where one or more of the hydrogens has been replaced by an akyl or aryl group. An amino acid is an amine consisting of carboxylic acid and various side chain organic molecules. A chloramine is an amine where one (or more) of the hydrogens has been replaced by a chlorine atom.

ASBC—American Society of Brewing Chemists.

Atom—Atoms are the basic building blocks of all solids, liquids, and gases in our world. An atom is the smallest unit of an element, such as an atom of oxygen, iron, or carbon, as opposed to a molecule. See Molecule.

Atomic Mass—The fundamental atomic scale unit of mass is the *unified atomic mass unit* symbolized by "u" and sometimes referred to as a Dalton (abbreviation Da), especially by biochemists. The atomic weight of an atom is its weight expressed in u or Daltons. A Dalton or u is defined as $1/12$ of the mass of the Carbon 12 atom. One Dalton is equal to a mass of about 1.6605×10^{-10} grams.

Both protons and neutrons have an atomic mass of about 1u. To be precise, the mass of a proton is defined to be 1.00727647012u, and neutrons are 1.00866490414u. The mass of an electron is 5.48579903 x 10^{-4} u. This is about 0.05% of the mass of a proton, and this is why the mass of electrons is not considered to be significant in most calculations.

Atomic Number—The number of protons in the nucleus of an atom. The atomic number differentiates and defines each element in the periodic table.

Atomic Weight—The atomic weight of an element is the weighted average of the masses of the isotopes of an element. The atomic weight on an element is used for calculating molecular weights, equivalent weights, etc. See Atomic Mass and Isotope.

Avogadro's Constant—6.022 x 10^{23} "things" per mole. Considered to be dimensionless, but was derived to describe the number of atoms in 1 gram-mole of oxygen, i.e., the number of oxygen atoms in 1 mole of oxygen weighing 16.00 grams. One mole of bananas would be approximately 6.022 x 10^{23} bananas, give or take a bunch. See Mole.

Base—An acid is a proton accepter, according to the Brønsted-Lowry definition. When a base accepts a proton, the remainder of the molecule is called the conjugate acid. For example, the ionic compound $Ca(OH)_2$ is a base, and accepts protons; the remainder, $Ca+$, is the conjugate acid.

Biocide—A pesticide or antimicrobial agent that can deter or disable any harmful organism by chemical or biological means. A disinfectant or sanitizer.

BOD (Biological Oxygen Demand)—The BOD test gauges the amount of biodegradable organic compounds in a wastewater sample by measuring the amount of oxygen consumed by bacteria in an incubator during a five day period, expressed as mg/L of O_2.

Buffer—A buffer is either a weak acid or a weak base that reacts to moderate the change in pH of a solution. The way it works is that the dissociation constant of the buffer is near the pH of solution, such that when another chemical is added, such as a strong acid or base, the buffering agent dissociates or re-associates according to Le Chatelier's principle to maintain the equilibrium, and thereby minimizes the change in pH. A buffer is most effective when the pH is near the pK of the buffering compound and when it has one or more ions in common with the chemical(s) being added to the solution.

Buffering Capacity—The buffering capacity of a substance is its ability to resist a change in pH, in mEq/pH•L or mEq/pH•kg, depending. The quantity of acidity or alkalinity of a substance is equal to the buffering capacity of the substance multiplied by the change in pH. Very similar to the relationship between current, resistance, and voltage, with regard to Ohm's Law ($I = R \times E$).

Burtonization—The act of adding salts, principally sulfate salts, to brewing water to mimic the famous water of Burton-upon-Trent in the UK.

Carbonate Species—Sometimes referred to as *carbo*, or the *carbo system*, the carbonate species are any of the three forms that occur in natural water: carbonic acid (H_2CO_3), bicarbonate (HCO_3^-), and carbonate (CO_3^{-2}). The sum of these species is often quantified as C_T or the Total Alkalinity as $CaCO_3$. See C_T and Total Alkalinity.

Charge—The valence charge on an ion and/or the number of equivalents per mole that the ion represents. A strong acid or base has a constant charge, but the charge per mole of a weak acid or base can vary with pH as in the case of carbonate and bicarbonate, and weak polyprotic acids such as phosphoric acid.

Chelation—A type of molecular bond between metal ions and other molecules. It is a looser bond than ionic or covalent molecular bonds, where the metal ion is only strongly associated with the chelating agent, and can be separated without requiring a chemical reaction. It could be compared to using duct tape rather than welding two parts together.

Chemistry—Chemistry is, very broadly speaking, the science that describes matter and the way it behaves under particular conditions. It is a broad subject, encompassing sub-disciplines such as general chemistry, analytical chemistry, biochemistry, physical chemistry, electro chemistry, organic and inorganic chemistry, quantum chemistry, polymer chemistry, molecular biology and nuclear chemistry. Water chemistry touches on a few of these: general chemistry, inorganic chemistry and physical chemistry.

General chemistry is concerned with the fundamental makeup of matter: electrons, protons and neutrons, and the ways in which they combine to form the various chemical elements, ions, and compounds.

Organic chemistry is concerned with compounds of carbon (whether from living things, as the name suggests, or synthetic) and inorganic chemistry covers everything else. The study of brewing water falls primarily under inorganic. A lot will be said about carbonates, which do, of course, contain carbon—but calcium carbonate is a mineral and is therefore not considered organic. Physical chemistry deals with the properties of solutions and gasses, the extent to which things dissolve, how acids and bases act as a function of pH, and chemical equilibria, which are very important to water chemistry.

Chemical Equation—A chemical equation describes the reactants and products of a chemical reaction, in the general form of A + B $\leftrightarrow$ C + D. The extent of the reaction is described by the reaction or equilibrium constant. See Equilibrium Constant and Stoichiometry.

CIP—Clean-In-Place.

COD (Chemical Oxygen Demand)—The COD test measures both biodegradable and non-biodegradable organics by measuring the amount of a strong oxidizer (typically potassium dichromate) that reacts with the sample. The COD test overestimates the amount of organic contaminant in the water compared to the BOD test, but its speed and consistency make it valuable in planning water treatment needs.

Compound—A compound is a unique and identifiable chemical substance composed of two or more elements. A compound is formed and can be broken down by chemical reactions, and has a defined structure held together by chemical bonds.

C_T—The total moles of carbonate species (H_2CO_3, HCO_3^-, CO_3^{-2}) in solution. The alkalinity of water due to carbonates is equal to C_T multiplied by the change in charge as a function of pH. See Chapter 5 for explanation.

Da (Dalton)—See Atomic Mass.

Dalton's Law—The total pressure in a system is the sum of the partial pressures of the gases in the system.

DBP (Disinfection Byproduct)—A byproduct of the chlorine disinfection process such as THM or HAA5.

DIY—Do-It-Yourself

Dispersant—A dispersant acts to lower the surface tension of the liquid or otherwise acts to make a substance more wet-able, such as a surfactant, but also acts as a deflocculant to prevent a substance from clumping in the presence of a liquid.

DI—De-ionized water.

Dissociation Constant, Acid—An acid dissociation constant is a type of equilibrium constant describing how strongly dissociated the acid molecule is; this is a measure of the strength of the acid. For example, phosphoric acid is a polyprotic acid and has three dissociation constants, one for each proton. The first (pK_1) is 2.14, the second (pK_2) is 7.20, and the third (pK_3) is 12.37. One criterion for an acid to be considered strong (or strongly dissociated) is if the pH of the solution is at least two units higher than the pK of the acid. Therefore, the first proton from H_3PO_4 is strongly dissociated at mash pH, as can be seen in Figure 47, Appendix B. The second proton would not be strongly dissociated unless the mash or solution pH was at least 9.20 or higher. For the third proton to be strongly dissociated, the pH of the solution would have to be 14.37 or higher, which is difficult to create.

EBC—European Brewing Convention.

EBCT—Empty bed contact time, i.e., the amount of time that a particular volume of water actually spends within the carbon filter.

EDTA—Ethylenediaminetetraacetic acid, a chelating agent commonly used to dissolve carbonate scale.

Element—Elements are identified by the number of protons (positively charged particles) in the nucleus; this is known as the atomic number. For example, carbon has 6 protons, oxygen has 8, and gold has 79. If an atom has a different number of protons in its nucleus from another atom, then it is a different element. If you have a carbon atom and manage to pull out one of the protons in the nucleus, then it no longer carbon, but boron—atomic number 5.

Emulsifier—An emulsifier acts to stabilize an emulsion, which is a non-stable mixture of two liquids, such as vinaigrette salad dressing, or mayonnaise.

EPA—The United States Environmental Protection Agency.

Equilibrium—A chemical equilibrium is a state in which the concentrations of reactants and products do not change with time. A system is also at equilibrium when the forward reaction proceeds at the same rate as the reverse reaction. The reaction rates of the forward and backward reactions are generally not zero, but equal. Thus, there are no net changes in the concentrations of the reactant(s) and product(s).

Equilibrium Constant—An equilibrium constant (K) should properly be the ratio of the chemical activities of the reaction products over the reactants, but can also be described by the concentrations of the products and reactants, where the concentrations are typically raised to a power according to the chemical reaction coefficients.

$$aA + bB \leftrightarrow cC + dD$$
$$K = ([A]^a \times [B]^b) / ([C]^c \times [D]^d)$$

Equilibrium constants can be very small numbers, such as 1.6×10^{-9} and are therefore often quoted as pK, where the constant is the negative logarithm of the number, as in pH.

Equivalent—An equivalent is the amount of a substance that will react with or supply one mole of hydrogen ions (i.e., protons) to a chemical reaction.

FDA—The United States Food and Drug Administration.

GAC—Granular activated carbon. See Chapter 8.

Grist Ratio—More specifically the water-to-grist ratio, it is a weight ratio of kilograms of water to kilograms of grist (i.e., liters to kilograms), and is therefore normally quoted without units. If the ratio is being discussed in other units, such as quarts per pound (qts/lb) then the units must be included. The general conversion between quarts per pound to liters per kilogram is 1 qt/lb = 2 L/kg.

HAA5—Haloacetic acids. (Yes, there are 5 of them.) See Chapter 3.

Henry's Law—At a constant temperature, the amount of a given gas that dissolves in a given type and volume of liquid is directly proportional to the partial pressure of that gas in equilibrium with that liquid.

Ions—Normally, the number of electrons in an atom equals the number of protons in the nucleus, and an atom is therefore considered electrically neutral. An atom with a different number of electrons than protons is not neutral, and is called an ion. Ions are naturally created during chemical reactions with other elements and/or compounds. Ions can be either elements or compounds. The difference in electron charge of the ion to the base element/compound is called the valence, and indicated as a superscript, e.g., Ca^{+2}, Na^{+1}, or SO_4^{-2}. Electrons are negatively charged particles and therefore an atom/compound that loses electrons becomes more positive, whereas an atom/compound that gains electrons becomes more negative. Anions are negatively charged ions and cations are positively charged.

Isotope—An isotope of an element is an atom with a different number of neutrons in the nucleus than is considered typical, although this is misleading. There is no single 'correct' proportion of neutrons for an element, (just like there is no single 'normal' style of beer) but some isotopes occur more frequently than others in nature. An element can have several isotopes. The most common example is Uranium (atomic number 92), which has 3 isotopes that occur in nature, U238, U235, and U233. U238 has 146 neutrons in its nucleus, U235 has 143, etc. The most common isotope of an element is typically not labeled as being an isotope, e.g., "carbon" for Carbon 12, as opposed to "Carbon 14," which is understood to be a less-common form of carbon.

Le Chatelier's Principle—This principle can be summarized as follows: An equilibrium will react to a change in concentration, temperature, volume, or pressure to either maintain the equilibrium or establish a new equilibrium, depending on the type of change. It generally means that if the concentration of chemical reactants is increased, the concentration of reaction products will increase, in accordance with the equilibrium constant.

Maillard Reaction—The process for the non-enzymatic browning of foods is named for French chemist Louis-Camille Maillard, who first described it in 1912. The chemistry of the process was later defined by American chemist John Hodge in 1953, wherein an amino acid and a sugar react to produce any of hundreds of compounds, many of which have flavors and aromas associated with food. See Melanoidin.

MBAA—The Master Brewers Association of the Americas.

MBR—Membrane Bioreactor. See Chapter 9.

MCL—Maximum Contaminant Level. See Chapter 3.

MCLG—Maximum Contaminant Level Goal. See Chapter 3.

Melanoidin—Melanoidins are red and brown-pigmented polymers that are formed by Maillard reactions of aldehyde-type sugars and amino acids. They are responsible for many of the signature flavors and aromas of baked and roasted foods.

millival—A term for milliequivalent per liter, mostly European.

Molar (M)—A unit of concentration: one mole of solute per liter of solution.

Mole—The term "mole" is derived from "gram molecule" and is used to describe an equal quantity of chemical "things." These things can be atoms or molecules (or ions or electron charges) and it is useful to chemists for describing the quantities of things involved in a chemical reaction. Therefore, we can say that 2 moles of hydrogen react with 1 mole of oxygen to produce 1 mole of water. However, the mole was developed with the advent of atomic theory as scientists were quantifying atomic mass, and there were at least three candidates for the standard, namely hydrogen, oxygen, and carbon. Eventually, the isotope carbon 12 was chosen, and a mole was defined as the number of atoms in 12 grams of carbon 12. Accordingly, Avogadro's number was defined as being the number of atoms in 1 mole of carbon 12, and that number has since been experimentally determined to be $6.02214078 \times 10^{23}$ +/- 1.8×10^{17}.

An isotope of an element has the same number of protons in its nucleus as the parent element, but a different number of neutrons. Isotopes are identified by the total number of protons and neutrons in the nucleus. For example, the nomenclature Carbon 12 means that the atom contains 6 neutrons in addition to the 6 protons, signified by its atomic number, 6.

Molecular Weight—The molecular weight, sometimes referred to as the formula weight of a substance equals the total weight of all the atoms that comprise it. The molecular weight of water is 18 grams per mole, composed of 2 hydrogens and 1 oxygen. One mole of water weighs 18 grams and consists of Avogadro's number of water molecules. The molecular weight of a hydrated salt such as calcium chloride includes the weight of the two water molecules that are associated with it.

Molecule—A molecule is the smallest unit of a recognized polyatomic substance, consisting of two or more atoms of the same or different elements.

NOM—Natural organic matter.

Normal (N)—A unit of concentration: one equivalent of solute per liter of solution.

NTU—Nephelometric Turbidity Unit.

Oxalate—Oxalate or ethanedioate, has the chemical structure $(COO)_2^{-2}$ and in association with calcium, is responsible for kidney stones and beerstone. The precipitation of calcium oxalate crystals in packaged beer can create nucleation sites for the rapid evolution of carbon dioxide bubbles, called gushing. The factors affecting the levels of oxalate in malt are not well understood.

Oxidation—Oxidation is not just rusting or corrosion of metals. It is actually the loss of electrons or an increase in the oxidation state of a molecule, atom or ion. The loss of electrons can also be considered as the gain of a proton, i.e., proton acceptance, such as by a base.

Oxidane—The formal chemical name for water.

PAC—Powdered activated carbon.

PCE—Tetrachloroethylene.

pH—In chemistry, pH is a measure of the activity of hydrogen ions in solution, based on the concentration. The concept was first introduced by Danish chemist Søren P. L. Sørensen at the Carlsberg Laboratory in 1909, and revised to the modern usage in 1924. Current usage in chemistry equates the terminology to the negative logarithm of dissociation constants as in (pK).

pH meter—A good pH meter will typically cost a few hundred dollars, but most of that cost is in the electrode. The meter electronics tend to be similar these days. You want to get a meter that has at least +/-0.05 pH accuracy, if not +/-0.02, and ATC. ATC keeps the probe in calibration when the temperature of the sample is several degrees off from the calibration temperature. Two-point calibration capability is preferred over single point. A good electrode can be either sealed or refillable and will have a resolution of +/-0.02 pH or smaller. A double junction electrode is less prone to contamination than a single junction electrode, which is important when working with sticky viscous solutions like wort and beer. Some electrode models have flushable junctions, which allows for easier cleaning and longer life.

pK—The negative logarithm of an equilibrium constant K. See Equilibrium Constant or Dissociation Constant.

ppb—parts per billion.

ppm—parts per million; equivalent to milligrams per liter for dilute solutions such as water and wort.

Residual Alkalinity—See Chapter 4.

Reduction—Reduction is the gain of electrons, or decrease in the oxidation state of a molecule, atom, or ion. The gain of electrons can also be considered as the loss of a proton, i.e., proton donation, such as an acid.

RO—Reverse osmosis.

SAC—Strong acid cation, i.e., ion-exchange resin type. See Chapter 8.

Salt—A salt is an ionic compound (i.e., held together by electrostatic charge difference) that can result from the neutralization reaction of an acid and a base. Calcium carbonate is a salt of carbonic acid and calcium hydroxide. Calcium sulfate is a salt of Sulfuric acid and calcium hydroxide. Table salt is the salt of hydrochloric acid and sodium hydroxide. The acid and base can be any type; these examples just happen to use hydroxide forms.

SBA—Strong base anion, i.e., ion-exchange resin type. See Chapter 8.

Scientific Notation and Significant Digits—Scientific notation provides a convenient way of expressing very small and very large numbers. Scientific notation simplifies a number by expressing it as a decimal (called the mantissa) multiplied by a power of 10 (the exponent). Typically, the mantissa is written with only one digit to the left of the decimal, and the rest behind. As examples: 150 billion yeast cells can be written as 1.5 x 10^{11}, or a calcium concentration could be written 155 ppm, which is the same thing as saying 155 x 10^{-6}, but could be written 1.55 x 10^{-4} which equals 0.000155. It is also common to write the exponents in multiples of 3, i.e., thousands, millions, billions, and this is referred to as engineering notation. So, 150 billion would be written as 150 x 10^{9}.

The number of digits, including zeros, that follows the decimal indicates the degree of precision of the number, and these are called significant digits. Significant digits are important in weights and measures because they tell the resolution of the measurement. The rules for significant digits are as follows:

1. Any non-zero number is significant, e.g.155 has 3 significant digits.

2. A zero between two non-zero numbers is significant, e.g. 107 also has 3.

3. Any zeros behind the decimal point are significant, e.g. 1.4100 has 5 significant digits.

4. A number containing trailing zeros without a decimal point is ambiguous. For example, the number 1,500 would appear to be a round number, e.g., about one and a half thousand. Further precision could be indicated if the trailing zero were underlined, or by addition of a decimal point, for example, 1,5<u>0</u>0 (3) or 1,500. (4).

These rules apply to scientific notation as well. The number 1.500 x 10^{3} has 4 significant digits, versus 1.5 x 10^{3} having only 2.

Scientific notation also simplifies calculations. To multiply two numbers in scientific notation, multiply the mantissas and add the exponents. To divide two numbers in scientific notation, divide the mantissas and subtract the exponents: e.g. $2 \times 10^{11} / 4 \times 10^2 = 0.5 \times 10^9 = 5.0 \times 10^8$.

SMCL—Secondary maximum contaminant level. See Chapter 3.

SRM—Standard Reference Method of the ASBC for determining beer color.

Stoichiometry—Stoichiometry is the branch of chemistry that deals with the relative quantities of reactants and products, such that a balanced equation typically forms positive integer ratios. A balanced reaction equation does not have an excess or deficiency of reactant. For example:

$$Ca^{+2} + 2HCO_3^{-1} \leftrightarrow CaCO_3(ppt) + CO_2(g) + H_2O$$

In other words, one mole of calcium ion (Ca^{2+}) reacts with two moles of bicarbonate ions ($2HCO_3^-$) to yield one mole of calcium carbonate precipitate (ppt), one mole of carbon dioxide gas (g), and one mole of water. Note that the number of calcium atoms on each side of the equation is the same (1), the number of carbon atoms on each side is the same (1), the number of oxygen atoms on each side is the same (3) and the number of hydrogen atoms on each side is the same (2). Also the sum of the charges on the left side (+2, 2 of $^-$1 = 0) is equal to the sum of the charges on the right side (0). This equation is balanced. The charges are balanced. In addition, if we count all of the atoms on one side of the arrow we have the same number on the other side. This is the definition of a balanced equation. As with sentence structure, a balanced equation is not always correct but an unbalanced one is always incorrect.

Surfactant—A surfactant acts as a wetting agent, decreasing the surface tension between a liquid and a solid.

Taylor Series—A Taylor Series is a mathematical expansion representing a function as an infinite sum of terms that are calculated from the values of the function's derivatives at a single point. The equation describing a line from a *polynomial curve fit* is an example of a Taylor Polynomial, where a finite sum of terms (a subset) are used to generally describe the function.

TCE—Trichloroethylene, an industrial solvent.

TDS—Total Dissolved Solids, i.e., anything that is dissolved in water, such as sodium chloride or sugar or calcium carbonate, etc.

Titration—A common laboratory procedure for determining an unknown concentration of a known solute. It is also known as quantitative or volumetric analysis because volume measurements play a critical role. In acid-base titrations, a reagent, typically a strong acid or base, is prepared as a standard solution. The specific quantity of reagent (volume x concentration) used to change the pH of the solution to a specified endpoint determines the unknown concentration of the solute. Titrations often use a color changing dye, called an indicator, to visually determine when the endpoint has been reached, although the use of digital pH meters to monitor progress is becoming more common.

TOC—Total organic carbon.

TTHM—Total Trihalomethanes, a DBP.

UASB—Upflow Anaerobic Sludge Blanket. See Chapter 10.

UV—Ultraviolet light.

WAC—Weak acid cation, i.e., ion-exchange resin type. See Chapter 8.

WBA—Weak base anion, i.e., ion-exchange resin type. See Chapter 8.

Z Alkalinity—Z stands for the German word "Ziel", meaning goal or target, and indicates that the alkalinity of carbonates are calculated with respect to a target mash pH, rather than standard titration endpoint of 4.3 or 4.5 for determination of total alkalinity. Z alkalinity is always smaller than total alkalinity for the same water. See Chapter 5 for explanation and usage.

B

Acidification of Sparging or Brewing Water

Note: Whenever acidification of brewing water was discussed in correspondence the question that most often arose was, "What happens to the calcium?" In response, A. J. deLange generously contributed the following.

A model for estimating mash pH was presented in Chapter 5, where the influence of each of the malts and the water was tabulated and summed to determine either: a) the mash pH that best fit the zero sum condition, or b) the number of milliequivalents of acid or base necessary to zero the final sum with respect to a target pH (Z).

This Appendix will focus on water, and present charts and methods to determine the effect of acidification on the total alkalinity in the water if a strong acid is used to take it to a particular pH in the general mash range (5.2, 5.5, 5.75, and 6.0). The charts also estimate the effect on calcium levels in the water if phosphoric acid is used for acidification, as opposed to lactic or hydrochloric acids, for example.

Brewers must overcome two sources of buffering to change the mash pH from an initial value to the target value Z: bicarbonates in the water, and acid/base pairs in the malt.

The buffering capacity of the acid/base pairs in any given malt is best expressed by titration curves such as those in Chapter 5.

When we acidify the brewing or sparging water ahead of the mash, we are only concerned with the buffering capacity of the water and the mEq/L of acid to overcome it. If we were going to acidify the water to a pH of 4.3, then the buffering capacity of the water would be the total alkalinity of the water in mEq/L divided by the change in pH:

mEq/L Acid = buffer capacity (pH_2–pH_1)

The amount of acid we would need to acidify the water to the mash pH (ex. 5.5) is therefore less than the total alkalinity mEq—typically 10 to 20 percent less. This is where the concept of Z alkalinity comes in, as introduced in Chapter 5. Logically, once we bring the water to mash pH, no additional water treatment is required, and the only remaining concern is the buffering of the malts (where, admittedly, more research is needed).

This approach suggests that incremental curves for 50, 100, 150, and 200 ppm total alkalinity as $CaCO_3$ would be quite useful in planning water treatment. The easiest way to explain how to use these graphs is by example.

Example 1—Determining Acid Additions to Reduce Alkalinity and Lower pH

Let's assume we have a water that has the following composition:
- 16 ppm Ca
- 50 ppm total alkalinity as $CaCO_3$
- pH of 7.5
- small amounts of magnesium, sodium, chloride and sulfate

Our goal is to acidify the water to the target mash pH of 5.5. How much acid do we use? And how much alkalinity do we neutralize?

Look at Figure 43 (p. 257)—Alkalinity 50 ppm as $CaCO_3$. The legend for the graph is divided into four pH levels for three conditions. The four levels of pH are 6.0 (*circles*), 5.75 (*triangles*), 5.5 (*squares*), and 5.2 (*inverted triangles*). The three conditions are:
- Sat. Ca+2; H_3PO_4; pH (X) = Calcium saturation at pH (X), using phosphoric acid (*dotted lines*)
- Rem. Alk.; H_3PO_4; pH (X) = Remaining alkalinity after acidifying with phosphoric acid to pH (X) (*dashed lines*)
- Rem. Alk.; H_2SO_4; pH (X) = Remaining alkalinity after acidifying with sulfuric acid to pH (X) (*solid lines*)

The lines with squares are for pH 5.5. The solid line with squares is the third condition, "Rem. Alk. H_2SO_4; pH 5.5," indicating that this is the curve that shows the effect of acidifying to pH 5.5 using sulfuric acid. Actually, this curve works for any strong acid, such as lactic or hydrochloric acid—same curve. Phosphoric acid has its own curve (2nd condition) because it is a weak acid and doesn't fully protonate (more on this later).

The way this works is we go to the intersection of our curve (Rem. Alk., H_2SO_4, solid with squares) and the starting water pH of 7.5, and read the remaining alkalinity (ppm as $CaCO_3$) off the left side scale. The value is about 6. Note that the scale is logarithmic, i.e., that the values go from 2 to 10 ppm and 10 to 50 ppm. The answer to our second question, "how much alkalinity did we neutralize?" is 50–6=44 ppm as $CaCO_3$.

And this answer is what allows us to answer our first question, "how much acid do we use?"—by dividing the change in alkalinity by its equivalent weight, 44/50=0.88 mEq/L.

Thus, 0.88 mEq of acid (per liter) is needed to neutralize the alkalinity. Assuming that we have prepared a 1 Normal solution of sulfuric acid (i.e., 1 N=1 mEq/mL), this would require 0.88 milliliters of 1 N acid per liter of water that we wanted to acidify. Table 26 lists acid concentrations and volumes for preparing 1 N concentrations.

Table 26—Preparing 1 Normal Solution of Common Acids

Acid	Stock Solution w/w %	Density (kg/L)	Molarity (M)	mLs of acid to prepare 1L of 1 Normal (N) Solution
Hydrochloric	10%	1.048	2.9	348
Hydrochloric	37%	1.18	12.0	83.5
Lactic	88%	1.209	11.8	84.7
Sulfuric	10%	1.07	1.1	458.3
Sulfuric	98%	1.84	18.4	27.2
Phosphoric	10%	1.05	1.1	935*
Phosphoric	85%	1.69	14.7	68*

*Phosphoric is approximately monoprotic at mash pH.

The reason we seem to be solving this problem backwards (i.e., finding the remaining alkalinity and then determining how much acid we used to get there) is because the chemistry is complex, requiring iterative calculations to solve. Therefore, we have solved the equations for specific conditions in order to generate curves that allow us to interpolate values for most conditions.

Example 2—Determining Phosphoric Acid Additions to Reduce Alkalinity and Lower pH

Now let's repeat Example 1 using phosphoric acid. Phosphoric is a weak acid that does not fully protonate. In other words, the number of hydrogen ions released (or the charge per mmol) changes depending on the pH of the solution, as carbonates do. The degree of protonation (i.e., mEq) is given as a function of pH in Figure 47. Note that the value ranges from 1 to 1.35, despite phosphoric acid (H_3PO_4) having 3 hydrogens available—it is a weak acid.

We do the same thing as before, except that we use the dashed curve with square symbols attached (2nd condition). Note that the phosphoric acid line is above the strong acid line. This means that phosphoric reduces less alkalinity for the same drop in pH as a strong acid does. This is because the anions of phosphoric acid are stronger bases than the anions of hydrochloric, sulfuric, or lactic acids.

In this example, the remaining alkalinity is 9 ppm as $CaCO_3$ at the intersection of the curve (Rem. Alk., H_3PO_4, dashed with squares) and the starting water pH of 7.5. This time only 41 ppm of alkalinity was reduced.

Dividing the change in alkalinity by its equivalent weight,

$41/50 = 0.82$ mEq/L

Thus, 0.82 mEq of acid (per liter) was used to neutralize the alkalinity. Figure 47 shows how many mEq of protons are contributed by each millimole of phosphoric acid in arriving at a particular pH. The mEq value at 5.5 pH is 1.02. Assuming that we have prepared a 1 molar solution (note difference) of phosphoric acid (i.e., 1 mmole/mL), we would need $0.82/1.02 = 80$ mmoL of phosphoric acid for each liter of water.

Example 3—Determining Calcium Loss from Phosphoric Acid Additions

There is a potential complication when adding phosphoric acid to water before the mash. Calcium and phosphate form the compound *hydroxyl apatite*, or $C_{10}(PO_4)_6(OH)_2$, which precipitates to release hydrogen ions and lower the mash pH. The phosphates in phosphoric acid can also react with the calcium in the water and could potentially precipitate it before the water even gets to the mash. The question is, "How much calcium is removed from the water by acidification with phosphoric acid?"

We can't predict apatite precipitation as a function of phosphoric acid addition because the mechanisms of apatite precipitation are very hard to model. However, we can calculate the saturation levels of calcium that can be tolerated before the onset of precipitation as a function of pH. This saturation limit is conveyed by the dotted lines, "Sat. Ca^{+2}; H_2PO_4; pH (X)." Going back to the conditions of Example 2, the intersection of the pH 5.5 line (squares, dotted) at initial pH 7.5 indicates a concentration of slightly more than 400 mg/L on the calcium scale on the right side of the chart. Below this level, the solution is not saturated with respect to calcium and apatite precipitation won't occur. This means that the 16 mg/L calcium content of our water will not be affected and we can use phosphoric acid to acidify it to pH 5.5 without calcium loss.

These charts show us how to avoid calcium loss, but they also reveal two trends that you may not have realized:

- The saturation limit for calcium increases the more you acidify. This is logical from the standpoint that calcium salts are more soluble in more acidic solutions. However, it may be counter-intuitive for those of you who have worried in the past about acidifying the sparge water too much, and have therefore acidified only to a pH of 6.0, just to "take the edge off" the alkalinity. The calcium saturation limit at pH 6.0 is quite low, only about 4 ppm for the conditions we have been discussing.
- The calcium saturation limit decreases with increasing total alkalinity level. Refer to Figures 43 and 45, where the saturation limit for endpoint pH 5.75 is about 100 ppm for 50 ppm Alkalinity, while the limit for the same endpoint pH is about 40 ppm for 150 ppm Alkalinity (assuming initial water pH of 8.0 for both).

Therefore, if you are going to acidify with phosphoric acid, make sure you take this trade-off between alkalinity, calcium, and endpoint pH into account. This situation does not occur when acidifying with other acids.

Example 4—Addition of Calcium to Acidified Water

Now let's assume that we want to brew a pale ale with this same water. The suggested water compositions in Chapter 7 indicate that we would want 50–150 ppm of calcium in the water so that its residual alkalinity better matches the pale color of the style and achieves the right mash pH range, etc. So we plan to add enough calcium sulfate to the hot liquor tank to bring the calcium level to 100 ppm. This is fine, since the calcium saturation limit for this water at pH 5.5 is about 400 ppm. However, we need to realize something: that adding calcium to this already acidified water will probably lower the water pH further by some small, difficult-to-predict amount.

Therefore, it is better to add the calcium sulfate to the water before acidifying with phosphoric to 5.5 pH. This way we know that the 100 ppm of calcium in solution is stable, and we know the pH of the acidified water. Of course, if you have a pH meter and are using it to measure your results, then you know your final water pH no matter what order of addition you use. The point is that if you are doing this for the first time and trying to predict your addition quantities and results, you should add the salts first and the acid second.

General Usage Notes

Charts for water with alkalinities of 50, 100, 150 and 200 ppm as $CaCO_3$ are presented in this Appendix. But suppose your water has a total alkalinity of 75 ppm as $CaCO_3$. Can you still use the charts? Yes, the results for this and other alkalinity levels can be determined by interpolation. Compare the 5.75 acidification lines for the 50 ppm and 100 ppm charts. Using an initial water pH of 7.5 as our basis of comparison, and acidifying to 5.75 with strong acid, the curves show about 9.5 ppm alkalinity remaining on the 50 ppm chart, and about 20 ppm on the 100 ppm chart. As 75 is half way between 50 and 100, it stands to reason that 75 ppm alkalinity is reduced to halfway between 9.5 and 20 or about 15 ppm.

Interpolation also works for saturation calcium levels, but results in more of a rough estimate due to the logarithmic scales and the chemical assumptions we had to make. Notice that the value of 3 on a logarithmic scale is about halfway between the values of 1 and 10, and that 30 is about halfway between 10 and 100. This is because in a log scale, LOG of 3=.477, LOG 5=.699, etc. Keep this in mind when eyeballing the values between the marks on the scale—what looks like two and a half is actually ~2.3, and what looks like two and three fourths is actually ~2.56.

For 50 ppm alkalinity with a 5.5 pH endpoint, the calcium saturation level is about 430 mg/L for pH 7.5 water and about 170 mg/L for the same conditions at 100 ppm alkalinity. The simple average of these two numbers is 300, suggesting that the saturation calcium level for 75 ppm alkalinity water should be close to this number. In fact it is 257 mg/L, so that the linear interpolation for saturation is at best a rough estimate. But these charts are only for rough estimation anyway, for reasons we will discuss below.

The strong acid curves are fairly robust, which means they should give you reasonable estimates. However, when it comes to the precipitation of apatite, more generalizations had to be made, and the numbers are less robust. Without going into agonizing detail, the probability of precipitation occurring depends on many factors. The most important factor is the solubility product of the solid being formed. We used the value of pKs=117 for hydroxyl apatite (taken from Stumm and Werner). Solubility products are very difficult, if not impossible, to measure precisely, so there is uncertainty in all the saturation numbers. Also, if the solution is not "ideal" (and it's not), we have to consider that the presence of other charged ions can *electrically* shield calcium and phosphate from one another and reduce the likelihood of attraction and precipitation. We have used the modified Debye-Hückle theory here to produce these charts, but this theory has its own limitations. Third, we have not considered the solubility limitations of other salts such as the primary and secondary phosphates of calcium.

So, in order to come up with the saturation curves we set up a hypothetical solution of given alkalinity at given pH in a computer model, and then incrementally added calcium to the solution, checked the ion product to see if it was less than the saturated value, and then repeated these steps until the saturation ion product was reached. (No animals were harmed during this process, although the cat was definitely getting on my nerves.)

But you can't add just calcium cation, you must also add an anion to keep the electrical balance neutral. We used sulfate because high permanent hardness is more commonly associated with sulfate than chloride. Sulfate has a stronger effect on ionic strength than chloride does and thus, had we used chloride, the saturation of calcium levels would have come out lower. However, the corollary to this assumption is that if you are working with or building a water that has a sulfate-to-chloride ratio of less that one, such as 1:2; or no sulfate at all, such as water for a Pilsner lager, then we suggest cutting the calcium saturation value in half to be on the safe side.

Summary

These curves can be used to give you a good idea of what to expect when acidifying water with phosphoric acid or other strong acids. The estimates for strong acid have better confidence than the estimates for phosphoric acid. The estimates from the curves should be verified by measuring dissolved calcium levels after the addition of phosphoric acid if there is any question that calcium precipitation may have occurred.

If calcium precipitation is possible, acidifying to a lower pH will reduce that likelihood. However be aware that in doing so, you may overshoot your mash pH target to values below 5, inhibiting proper conversion and reducing yield. Your results may vary.

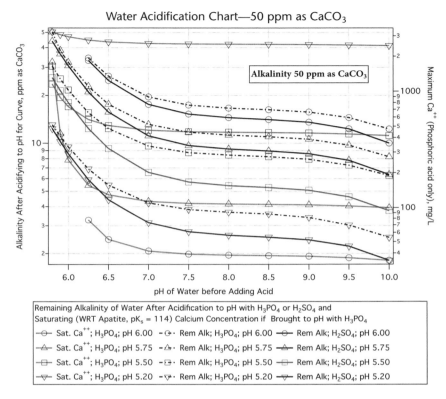

Figure 43—Remaining Alkalinity and Calcium Saturations After Acidification: 50 ppm Total Alkalinity as CaCO₃.

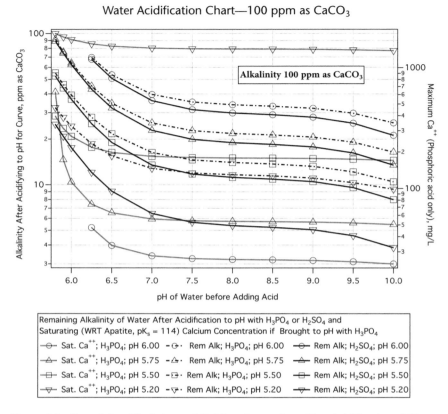

Water Acidification Chart—100 ppm as CaCO₃

Figure 44—Remaining Alkalinity and Calcium Saturations After Acidification: 100 ppm Total Alkalinity as CaCO₃.

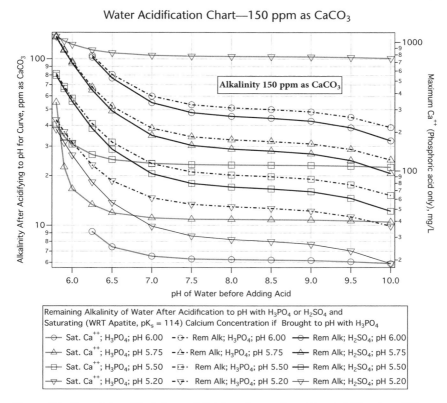

Figure 45—Remaining Alkalinity and Calcium Saturations After Acidification: 150 ppm Total Alkalinity as CaCO₃.

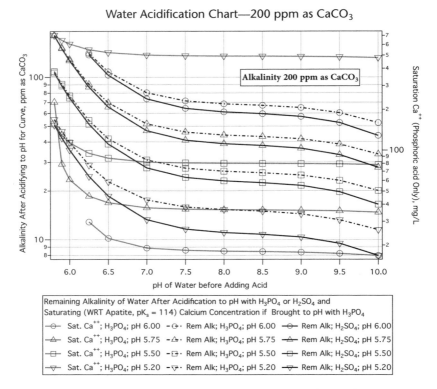

Figure 46—Remaining Alkalinity and Calcium Saturations After Acidification: 200 ppm Total Alkalinity as CaCO₃.

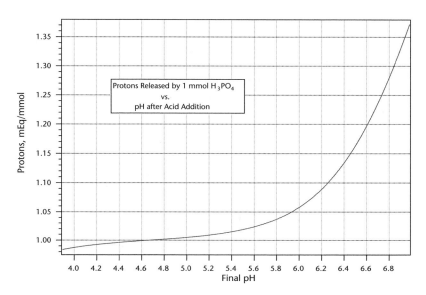

Figure 47—mEq Protonation per mMole Phosphoric Acid, as a Function of Acidification Endpoint.

Ion, Salt and Acid Calculations

Salt Concentrations

The procedure to calculate the ion contributions from adding a weight of a particular salt to water is very easy once you break it down into steps. The first step is to divide the weight of the salt you are adding (typically 1 gram) by its molecular weight to calculate the fraction of 1 mole of that salt that you are adding to water. The molecular weight of the salt should include the number of attached water molecules if the salt is hydrated, such as calcium chloride, which typically has two waters ($CaCl_2 \cdot 2H_2O$). Next, you calculate the weight fraction of the cation and the weight fraction of the anion that make up the molecular weight of the salt, and multiply each of those fractions by the mole fraction of the addition. Perhaps it would be easier to show you with an example.

Problem

If 1 gram of Calcium Chloride ($CaCl_2$) is added to 1 gallon of water, how much will that addition increase the concentration of Ca^{+2} and the Cl^{-1} ions?

Solution

First we have to calculate the molecular (molar) weight of calcium chloride. The container of calcium chloride should have the molecular formula $CaCl_2 \cdot 2H_2O$ on it. This formula means the molecular structure includes two water molecules and the molecular weight of the water needs to be included in the molecular weight of the salt. To calculate the molecular weight of a substance, we look up all of the atomic weights of the elements from the Periodic Table of Elements:

Ca = 40.078
Cl = 35.453
H = 1.00794
O = 15.9994

We don't need high accuracy for this, so we can round them to:

Ca = 40
Cl = 35.5
H = 1
O = 16

The total molecular weight of $CaCl_2 + 2(H2O)$ is:
$40 + (2 \times 35.5) + 2 \times ((2 \times 1) + 16) = 147$ grams/mole

The next step is to calculate the mole fraction of calcium and chloride in the compound.
The mole fraction of calcium in $CaCl_2 \cdot 2H_2O$ is:

$40 \div 147 = 0.272$

The mole fraction of chloride in $CaCl_2 \cdot 2H_2O$ is:

$(2 \times 35.5) \div 147 = 0.483$

The rest of the molecular weight is water.
Once we know the mole fractions, we can determine the weight of each ion contribution. So, if 1 gram of calcium chloride is dissolved into 1 gallon of water, we can say that the weight fraction of calcium is 1 gram x 0.272 = 0.272 grams or 272 milligrams (mg) Ca^{+2}.
Likewise, for chloride, 1 gram x 0.483 = 483 milligrams Cl^{-1}.

But how do we get from milligrams to concentration?

This is where the metric system makes things easier: 1 liter of water weighs 1 kilogram according to the original definition of a kilogram from 1799 (at the reference temperature of 4°C). The official weight today is a tiny bit different, but it is insignificant for our purposes here.

Therefore, 1 gram dissolved in 1 liter of water is the same as saying 1 gram dissolved in 1,000 grams of water. Going back to the weight fraction of calcium, 1 gram of calcium chloride contains 272 mg of calcium, which if dissolved in one liter of water, would equal 272 mg/L or 272 ppm.

mg/liter is the same as ppm,
because $1 \times 10^{-3} \text{ g}/1 \times 10^{3} \text{g} = 1 \times 10^{-6}$ or 1 part per million.

Therefore 1 gram of calcium chloride dissolved in 1 liter of water equates to:

272 ppm of Ca^{+2} and 483 ppm of Cl^{-1}

Going back to the original problem (1 gram of calcium chloride dissolved in 1 gallon of water), this becomes a matter of simply dividing that concentration by the extra volume.

1 gallon of water = 3.785 liters, so instead of being 272 mg/1 liter, the concentration becomes 272 mg/3.785 liters, or:

$272 \div 3.785 = 71.8$ ppm Ca in one gallon of water

$483 \div 3.785 = 127.6$ ppm Cl in one gallon of water

This is how salt contributions are calculated.

Swapping Calcium Chloride for Gypsum

Problem

Suppose you have built up a water recipe using distilled water and want to change the sulfate-to-chloride ratio without changing the total calcium concentration in the water. The current water recipe is 200 grams of gypsum and 100 grams of calcium chloride in 300 gallons of water. This gives ion concentrations of:

65 ppm Ca
98 ppm SO_4
42 ppm Cl
Sulfate-to-chloride ratio = 2.3:1

Without using a spreadsheet, how do you calculate a new sulfate to chloride ratio of 1:1?

Solution

First, go to Table 17 in Chapter 7 for the contributed ion concentrations in ppm from calcium sulfate and calcium chloride.

At 1 gram per gallon, calcium sulfate gives 61.5 ppm Ca and 147.4 ppm SO_4^{-2}.

At 1 gram per gallon calcium chloride gives 72.0 ppm Ca and 127.4 ppm Cl^{-1}.

The solution to this problem is a case of 2 equations and 2 unknowns. The unknowns are the gram weights of calcium sulfate (X) and calcium chloride (Y) such that:

a) the anion concentrations of both salts are equal.
b) the addition of these salt concentrations will have a total
   Ca concentration of 65 ppm.

For the first equation, we know that the gram weight of calcium sulfate (X) multiplied by its anion contribution is equal to the gram weight of calcium chloride (Y) multiplied by its anion contribution, i.e., the sulfate concentration equals the chloride concentration.

$$147.4X = 127.4Y$$

Solving for Y, this equation simplifies to:
$$Y = 147.4X \div 127.4 = 1.16X$$

For the second equation, we know that the calcium contributions from these same gram weights must equal a total of 65 ppm Ca. The calcium contribution of calcium sulfate is 61.5 ppm and the calcium contribution of calcium chloride is 72 ppm, therefore:

$61.5X + 72Y = 65$

substituting for Y gives us, $61.5X + 72(1.16X) = 65$

$61.5X + 83.5X = 145X = 65$

$X = 0.448$ grams per gallon of calcium sulfate

plugging X back into our equation for $Y = 1.16X$

$Y = 0.520$ grams per gallon of calcium chloride

Multiplying these weights by the 300 gallons of water to be treated gives the composition:

65 ppm Ca
66 ppm SO_4
66 ppm Cl^-

The calculation is exactly the same when using grams per liter and liters.

Dilution of Strong Acids

Problem
How do you calculate the amount of acid that is equal to X number of milliequivalents?

Solution
There are really two problems here: 1. (the basic question above), and 2. How do you make a lower-concentration solution that is easier to measure and safer to handle?

The partial answer to the first question is to create a 1 Normal (N) solution of the acid. The definition of a 1 N solution is that 1 liter contains 1 equivalent of the solute (the acid), and thus 1 milliliter contains 1 milliequivalent. So if you needed, for example, 1.8 mEq per liter to acidify 1,135.5 liters (300 gal) of hot liquor, 1.8 x 1135.5 = 2,044 milliliters of this 1 N acid solution.

The next problem is, how do you create a 1 N solution from a higher concentration of commercial acid?

Creating a 1 N Solution of Hydrochloric Acid

Let's start with hydrochloric acid, which is typically sold at a concentration of 37%. The first thing to understand is that this is a weight percentage, not a volume percentage. Acids are always sold by weight percent.

To solve these problems, you need to know the molecular weight, the density, and the concentration of the acid (w/w %). These values are listed in Table 27.

Table 27—Acid Parameters

Acid	Mole Weight (g/mole)	Density (g/mL)	Concentration (w/w %)	Equivalents per Mole
Hydrochloric	36.45	1.18	37%	1
Sulfuric	98.08	1.84	98%	2
Lactic	90.08	1.209	88%	1
Phosphoric	98.0	1.69	85%	~1*

The equivalents per mole for phosphoric acid vary; see Figure 47 in Appendix B.

The first step is to solve for the molar concentrations of these standard solutions, and then convert those moles/liter concentrations to equivalents/liter using the number of equivalents per mole.

Multiplying the density by 1,000 gives us the weight in grams of a 1 liter solution.

Multiplying that solution weight by the concentration weight percentage gives us the solute weight (grams of acid) in the 1 liter of solution. Dividing the solute weight by the mole weight of the acid gives us the moles per liter, which is called the molarity (M).

Density x 1,000 x % ÷ Mole wt. = M (moles per liter)

For 37% hydrochloric acid, this works out to:

1.18 x 1,000 x 0.37 ÷ 36.45 = 11.978 or 12.0 M

Hydrochloric acid has 1 equivalent per mole, so 12 M = 12 N. In the case of sulfuric acid, a 12 M solution would be a 24 N solution because it has 2 equivalents per mole. To calculate the volume in milliliters of this 12 N solution to use to create a 1 N solution, divide 1 liter (i.e., 1,000 mL) by the number of equivalents in the concentrated solution.

1,000 mL ÷ 12 N = 83.3 mL of 37% hydrochloric acid are needed to create a 1 N solution.

But what if you bought a 10% solution instead of the 37%? The same calculation applies—you just need to know the density. If it is not listed on the label, it can be estimated by ratios, but remember to subtract the 1 from the density like you would when working with specific gravity (which is the same thing),

e.g., 10%/37% = x/0.18

X = 0.0486 and therefore the density of a 10% solution of hydrochloric acid is about 1.0486. According to Internet sources, the actual value is closer 1.0474, so the estimated value is close.

These same calculations work for any strong acid that fully protonates. For weak acids like phosphoric, an additional calculation is necessary to determine the number of equivalents per mole as a function of pH, and that is where Figure 47 from Appendix B comes in.

CAUTION!

Always "Do what you oughta, add acids to water."

Do not attempt to pour water into a strong acid, it will react violently and splash! Dilutions of concentrated acids should be done slowly and carefully by trained personnel. The dilution of acids typically releases heat and the solution may get hot while pouring. The preferred method is to pour the concentrated acid into a beaker full of water sitting in an ice bath.

Neutralizing Alkalinity with Strong Acids

Problem
The brewing water contains 150 ppm of alkalinity as $CaCO_3$. How much acid do we add to reduce this alkalinity to 50 ppm as $CaCO_3$?

Solution
The first step is to convert the alkalinity from ppm as $CaCO_3$ to mEq/L, by dividing by the equivalent weight of $CaCO_3$ (50). The problem then becomes, how much acid is needed to reduce 3 mEq of alkalinity to 1 mEq of alkalinity? The answer is simply 3–1=2 mEq of acid. If we have a 1 N solution of acid prepared as in the previous problem, then only 2 milliliters of the 1 N solution would be needed (per liter).

Note: This is an entirely different kind of problem than the acidification examples presented in Appendix B. There the question was, how much alkalinity is left by acidification from pH_1 to pH_2? Here the starting and ending pH are not known, and we are only estimating the amount of acid to neutralize a particular amount of alkalinity. We are also assuming that all of the acid will react with the alkalinity, i.e., that no other reactions are taking place and no other substances are present that could react with the acid. This is a different set of assumptions.

Problem
Assuming the reaction is $Ca(HCO_3)_2 + 2HCl \rightarrow Ca + 2Cl + 2CO_2 + 2H_2O$, how much acid is needed to reduce the alkalinity by 50%, assuming that the water test report states the initial alkalinity is 100 ppm HCO_3^{-1}?

Solution

The stoichiometric equation:

$$Ca(HCO_3)_2 + 2HCl \rightarrow Ca^{+2} + 2Cl^{-1} + 2CO_2 + 2H_2O$$

is balanced, meaning that the same number of elements exists on both sides.

However, the equation can also be written like this:

$$Ca^{+2} + 2(HCO_3^{-1}) + 2HCl \rightarrow Ca^{+2} + 2Cl^{-1} + 2CO_2 + 2H_2O$$

which gives us a better view of one essential bit: that it doesn't take 2 moles of hydrochloric acid to reduce 1 mole of calcium bicarbonate; rather, it takes 2 moles of hydrochloric acid to reduce 2 moles of bicarbonate, or essentially 1 for 1.

Note: Two moles of hydrochloric acid for 1 mole of calcium bicarbonate is technically correct, but when calcium bicarbonate is dissolved in the water as temporary hardness, the calcium leaves the equation, leaving us just the bicarbonate ion reduction reaction.

To reduce the bicarbonate concentration by 50 ppm, convert it to mEq/L by dividing by the equivalent weight of bicarbonate (61), 50/61 = 0.82 mEq/L

Therefore, 0.82 milliequivalents of acid are needed per liter, and the volume of acid can be calculated as shown previously.

D

Water Charge Balance and Carbonate Species Distribution

It can be difficult to understand the differences between water reports. What makes one more reliable than another, or more representative? To some extent, it depends on your objectives—do you want to see the average concentrations from several areas around the region, or from different times through out the year, or do you want a snapshot of a specific source and time? If you want to base your decision on averages, then a difference of 3 milliequivalents in the cation-to-anion electrical charge balance may not be a problem. If you want to replicate a specific water for a specific beer, then verifying that the water report balances is a good quality check.

What do we mean by balance? We are talking about the electrical charges of the ions in the water. Water is electrically neutral, meaning that it doesn't normally contain an electrical charge. The sum of the negative electrical charges for the anions should equal the sum of positive electrical charges for the cations. But some ions have different values of charge: such as +2 for calcium ions (Ca^{+2}), +1 for sodium ions (Na^{+1}), or $^-3$ for phosphate ions (PO_4^{-3}). The difference in charge between various ions is found by dividing the molecular weight of each compound by the number of charges. This value is called the equivalent weight. Dividing the concentration (in mg/L or ppm) of an ion by its equivalent weight gives us the milliequivalents per liter (mEq/L) of the substance. Summing the mEq/L totals for both the positive and negative ions in the solution is how we determine if the water is electrically balanced or not.

Let's revisit the example from Chapter 7. In that example, the cation and anion milliequivalents for the water profiles in Table 15 (p. 141) were summed and compared to see it they were equal. In the first case for the Dortmund water, they were not.

Summing the cation mEq/L gave 11.25 + 3.3 + 2.6 = 17.2

Summing the anion mEq/L gave 2.95 + 1.7 + 2.5 = 7.1

The ion balance is quite far apart and therefore the given ion concentrations are probably not representative of the real water, although they may be close. The second profile, from Table 16, is very similar but differs markedly in charge balance. The primary difference between the two profiles is the anion levels. The Dortmund profile from Chapter 7, Table 15, converted to milliequivalents per liter:

Dortmund Water Profile
Table 15

	Ca^{+2}	Mg^{+2}	HCO_3^{-1}	Na^{+1}	Cl^{-1}	SO_4^{-2}	Sum (+)	Sum (−)
mg/L	225	40	180	60	60	120		
mEq/L	11.25	3.3	2.95	2.6	1.7	2.5	17.2	7.1

The following is another profile for Dortmund, from Chapter 7, Table 16.

Dortmund Water Profile
Table 16

	Ca^{+2}	Mg^{+2}	HCO_3^{-1}	Na^{+1}	Cl^{-1}	SO_4^{-2}	Sum (+)	Sum (−)
mg/L	230	15	235	40	130	330		
mEq/L	11.5	1.2	3.8	1.7	3.7	6.9	14.5	14.4

Let's suppose for the sake of argument that the profile from Table 15 has a water pH of 9. Looking at Table 28 (p. 277), the carbonate distribution at pH 7 shows that bicarbonate (HCO_3^{-1}) represents roughly 96% of the total alkalinity and carbonate, $CO_3^{(-2)}$ makes up the other 4%. Therefore if we were handed this unbalanced profile with the current 180 ppm (2.95 mEq/L) of bicarbonate, we can calculate that the total alkalinity is actually 2.95/96% = 3.07 mEq/L. Of course, 3.07 mEq does not bridge the imbalance gap in this particular case. Nevertheless, the point is that the effect of water pH on the carbonate species distribution can result in undercounting the total anion milliequivalents if just the bicarbonate concentration is given instead of the total alkalinity.

Another possible source for the discrepancy in the Table 15 profile may be if the calcium and magnesium hardness where actually reported "as $CaCO_3$." They may have been transcribed incorrectly as simply Ca ppm, instead of calcium hardness as $CaCO_3$. If that were the case, then dividing by the equivalent weight of calcium carbonate, instead of those of calcium and magnesium, gives us 4.5 and 0.8 mEq/L, respectively and the milliequivalent sums become 7.9 and 7.1, which improves the balance.

Dortmund Water Profile
Table 15

	Ca^{+2}*	Mg^{+2}*	HCO_3^{-1}	Na^{+1}	Cl^{-1}	SO_4^{-2}	Sum (+)	Sum (−)
mg/L	225	40	180	60	60	120		
mEq/L	4.5	0.8	2.95	2.6	1.7	2.5	7.9	7.1

Hardness as $CaCO_3$

If we were to speculate that the water pH was 7.4 at the time of measurement, then per Table 28, the total alkalinity would actually be 3.24 mEq/L, and the anion sum would be 7.4, which is closer yet. This exercise was pure speculation, but it serves to illustrate where potential errors in water reports can stem from.

Dortmund Water Profile
Table 15

	Ca^{+2}*	Mg^{+2}*	HCO$_3^-$ 1	Na^{+1}	Cl^{-1}	SO$_4^-$ 2	Sum (+)	Sum (−)	Sum (−)
mg/L	225	40	180	60	60	120	7.4		
mEq/L	4.5	0.8	2.95	2.6	1.7	2.5		7.9	7.4

* Hardness as CaCO$_3$

Errors during laboratory testing or reporting can be a source of water report imbalance. However, an unbalanced water report doesn't necessarily mean that any or all of the reported ion totals are incorrect. One source of error can be that the water contains other ions that were not tested or reported. Significant concentrations of normally minor ions such as iron, potassium, nitrate, nitrite, or silicate can easily skew the balance if not included in the testing protocol. A water report that includes these minor ions is more likely to balance. At a minimum, a water report should include the major ions noted in the tables above. A water report that has a cation-to-anion balance within 1 mEq/L is considered adequate. Balancing within 0.1 mEq/L is considered quite acceptable. It does not take much of a change in concentration between the ions to create a 0.5 mEq/L difference—a change of 5–10 ppm in a couple of the ions will do it.

Table 28—Percentage of Carbonate Species as a Function of pH (from Figure 13; p. 66)

pH	Carbonate %	Bicarbonate %	Carbonic Acid %
4	0	0.42	99.58
4.2	0	0.66	99.34
4.4	0	1.04	98.96
4.6	0	1.63	98.37
4.8	0	2.56	97.44
5.0	0	4.00	96.00
5.2	0	6.20	93.80
5.4	0	9.48	90.52
5.6	0	14.23	85.77
5.8	0	20.83	79.17
6.0	0	29.42	70.58
6.2	0	39.78	60.21
6.4	0	51.15	48.85
6.6	0	62.39	37.6
6.8	0	72.44	27.54
7.0	0	80.63	19.34
7.2	0	86.80	13.14
7.4	0.1	91.20	8.71
7.6	0.16	94.17	5.67
7.8	0.25	96.09	3.65
8.0	0.41	97.26	2.33
8.2	0.65	97.87	1.48
8.4	1.03	98.04	0.94
8.6	1.62	97.79	0.59
8.8	2.55	97.08	0.37
9.0	3.99	95.78	0.23

Index

Fines, 222; filtration of, 224-225

Flavor, xx, 70, 75, 103, 120, 139;
hop, 148; malt, 140; off, 5, 6,
179; qualities of, 6-7, 71; sodium
and, 154

Flavor ion effects, 147-149

Flocculation, 25, 109, 129, 224

Fluoride, standards for, 37

Foreign extra stout, 126, 160;
brewing, 168-176

Free amino nitrogen (FAN), 59

Free chlorine, 26, 192, 199

Fulvic acid, 186

GAC. *See* Granular activated carbon

Gas chromatograph, 199

Gases, 9, 10, 212; removing, 210;
solubility of, 64

Generally Recognized as Safe List
(FDA), 209

Glycol, 206, 208

Gram molecule, 52, 105

Granular activated carbon (GAC),
181, 196, 197, 198, 214, 240;
filtration, 199, 202, 203, 213

Gravity, 156, 214; lautering time
and, 123 (fig.)

Greensand, 25, 182

Grist, 71, 76, 101

Grist ratios, 70, 71, 240; pH shift
with, 70 (table)

Groundwater, 16, 17, 21-24; acidic,
23; alkaline, 128; dissolved
minerals and, 23

Gypsum, 22, 23, 24, 122, 143, 148;
calcium chloride and, 265-267

HAA5. *See* Total haloacetic acids

Hard water, 8, 24, 58, 60, 205;
softening, 9

Hardness, 2, 3, 5, 9, 16, 67, 75,
160, 201, 205, 208, 210, 212,
256; adding, 162-163, 164;
boiling and, 146; carbonate, 146;
chalk and, 109; increasing, 175;
magnesium and, 109; reducing,
103, 105, 108 (table), 190;
temporary, 103, 107, 111, 145,
146; total, 49, 52, 53-54, 55, 107

Heat exchangers, 9, 201, 206, 207,
208, 209; photo of, 207

Heating: decarbonation and, 145;
reduction in hardness/alkalinity
by, 108 (table)

Helium, 18, 19

Helles beer, xviii, 145, 148

Henry's Law, 62, 65, 199, 240

Herbicides, 15, 35

Heretic Brewing Company, photo
of, 210

Home Brewers Conference, xvi

Hooper, Egbert, 2

Hop oils, thoughts on, 227

Hops, xv, xvii, xviii, 30, 146,
147, 150, 167, 179, 224;
character of, 69, 156, 175;
chemistry and, xix; varieties of,
4, 140

Hops (Neve), xv

Hot-column deaerators, 201, 215

How To Brew (Palmer), 69, 70

Humic matter, 186, 218

Hydration, 30, 71

Hydrochloric acid, 109, 113,